# THE PSYCHOGEOGRAPHY OF URBAN ARCHITECTURE

# THE PSYCHOGEOGRAPHY OF URBAN ARCHITECTURE

## DAVID PRESCOTT-STEED

BrownWalker Press
Boca Raton

*The Psychogeography of Urban Architecture*

BrownWalker Press
Boca Raton, Florida • USA
2013

ISBN-10: 1-61233-695-7
ISBN-13: 978-1-61233-695-4


www.brownwalker.com

Cover photo by Julie Borninkhof

Library of Congress Cataloging-in-Publication Data

Prescott-Steed, David, 1975-
  The psychogeography of urban architecture / David Prescott-Steed.
     pages cm
  Includes bibliographical references and index.
  ISBN 978-1-61233-695-4 (pbk. : alk. paper) -- ISBN 1-61233-695-7 (pbk. : alk. paper)
  1. Architecture--Psychological aspects. 2. Geographical perception.  I. Title.
  NA2540.P74 2013
  720.1'9--dc23

                                                        2013010201

# CONTENTS

# ACKNOWLEDGEMENTS

This book explores the relationship between thinking and walking, its theory and its practice, in the context of everyday life. I am fortunate enough to be able to share mine with two very special people—my partner, Julie who has always encouraged me to go out and get some fresh air, and my daughter, Olive, a curious little alien, in the presence of whom so much seems strange again.

I would also like to thank my friends and peers in Melbourne and Perth and hope that you enjoy this experiment in creative cultural praxis.

To question the habitual. But that's just it, we're habituated to it. We don't question it, it doesn't question us, it doesn't seem to pose a problem, we live it without thinking, as if it carried within it neither questions nor answers, as if it weren't the bearer of any information. This is no longer even conditioning, it's anaesthesia. We sleep through our lives in a dreamless sleep. But where is our life? Where is our body? Where is our space?

....

To question what seems so much a matter of course that we've forgotten its origins. To rediscover something of the astonishment that Jules Verne or his readers may have felt faced with an apparatus capable of reproducing and transporting sounds. For that astonishment existed along with thousands of others, and it's they which have moulded us.

What we need to question is bricks, concrete, glass, our table manners, our utensils, our tools, the way we spend our time, our rhythms. To question that which seems to have ceased forever to astonish us. We live, true, we breathe, true; we walk, we open doors, we go down staircases, we sit at a table in order to eat, we lie down on a bed in order to sleep. How? Where? When? Why?

—Georges Perec
('Approaches to What?' from "L'Infra-ordinaire,"
in *Species of Space and Other Pieces*, 210.)

# CHAPTER 1
# INTRODUCTION

## Wandering in the City: A Non-linear Narrative

A close-up image of an ornate bed post which has what looks to be a thick red cord tied around the top, the length of which trails off towards the floor, out of view. In the unfocused background, a woman can be seen straightening the white top sheet of a large bed. We don't know her name and we don't know what her voice sounds like. All we know about her is what we can see on the surface; she is wearing a white shirt and a knee length black skirt. Her hair is tied back so as not to get in the way during work. Perhaps she is wearing her work uniform; the clothes that signify her laborious, routinised identity.

She can still be seen in a long shot taken from down the hallway, stroking the bed to take out any residual creases. She seems to take pride in the task; executing it with care and consideration. Nobody else is around at this time; just her, involved in her labour, and me, an anonymous voyeur. The length of the red cord is now in better view as it shifts curiously on the parquetry; tightening as if it were suddenly being pulled from afar.

Outside the entrance to the hotel, just beyond the wrought iron railing, a doorman walks ahead of a giant red ball of wool that is on its way down the stone steps. He extends both his arms to stop the wool from tumbling into the street. He edges it gently onto the grey pathway. At first, the top of a woman's head is all that can be seen of her behind the ball. Though, soon she can be seen in full view once again, as she walks behind her red ball of wool. She is no longer wearing her uniform. Instead, she wears a casual outfit. Dressed in a pastel sleeveless summer dress with her hair down, she casually rolls the ball along the pathway; the giant red mass reaching almost to her shoulders in height.

The woman continues walking towards the tall columns that mark the entrance to the city's Old Post Office; giant stone trees that frame the dark iron gates. On the walkway, the various colours of the flowers displays stand out against the greyness of the concrete jungle and yet they, themselves, are nothing compared to the vibrant red of the wool ball that the woman pushes along—while a single strand leaves a growing trail behind her.

It provides a record of where she has been, much like the trail of white pebbles, and later breadcrumbs, which was left by Hansel and Gretel while the woodcutter's wife led them deeper and deeper into the forest. Florists tend to their stock, a business man walks past with a cup of coffee held in his hand, and pedestrians walk by in the opposite direction. People are going about their business as usual and paying little attention to her as she continues to push the big red ball slowly by. They are all carrying out their roles; performing various tasks, each one with its own aims, goals, destinations, and measures of productivity. They each possess a direction that sits within the expectations of the central business district. While all these things are happening around the woman, there is no suggestion that she knows where she is going. There is no hint of direction, of intention or of a suggested destination.

As I ponder the woman's apparent incongruence with those people around her, an apparent lack of economic motivations, I see her and turn to face the iron gates. Having decided to push the ball in this direction, I watch as the woman pushes the wool up the stone steps, through the open dark gates and into the building whose shadiness contrasts highly against the brightness of the clear day's sky. She looks up with interest as she enters the building, noticing its wrought iron ornamentation before going all the way inside. A close up of the ever growing line of wool shows that it now extends around the corner of one of the gate, turning sharply around the corner of the form to provide evidence of a sudden change in direction.

The woman can be seen walking alone, still, down a busy city lane way. A man, who brushes up against the ball as he hastily passes, offers a friendly apology, to which she responds with a calm acknowledging nod as if to say "No harm done. Good day to you, too." Having reached the end of the laneway, she turns left along a path. A birds-eye view from the top of the tall stone buildings makes her appear dwarfed below by the sheer scale of the built environment. Either end of the elbowed lane along which she walks, would take us to some unknown place—just another point in the labyrinth of the city she is wandering through. A close-up of the woman finds her looking up to the buildings. Still, she doesn't seem to know where she is going but, rather, it is as if she were being led by the buildings, by the city landscape, by the buildings themselves. Though the woman looks to a narrow stretch of sky shining its light down between the rooftops, she does so from a cultural space that seems to exist beyond the reach of the natural environment. A path of light stretches the length of their enormous silhouettes has the illusion of moving about as her body traverses the space, as her eyes move sporadically, without predetermination, varying their focus amid the capitalist architecture.

The woman looks around under a glass roofed mall, indulging her curiosity. This is what guides her. For a moment, she stands on a street path and turns her head to look in different directions, gauging her location. The low camera angled close-up of her body draws attention to this act of looking in a way that creates a sense of disconnection from her surroundings, despite her continuing navigation through the guts of the city. This absence of ambient details suggests her physical or even personal disorientation, like a little girl lost in the city. In the foreground of another laneway, enclosed and buffered by the height of the factories and warehouse that line it. The slowly shrinking red ball of wool emphasises, by contrast, the dull and mostly empty surroundings. Two men in the background, wearing grey suits, seem to be in the process of moving an old couch.

The woman is now asking an elderly gentleman in a grey suit for directions. His old age and pleasant demeanour imply that his knowledge of the city has grown over time. He gestures for her to continue down this way and she listens with intent while the woollen ball rests behind them both, in a rare moment of inactivity. Once again, the buildings in the background seem to capture the daylight while blocking out all view of the sky in a way that shows the city to be very much an enclosed space.

It is as if the city is also being framed as one in which mystery dwells—in which you might not only lose your way but, to take it a logical extreme, in which you might never find your way again. You might even get lost and end up somewhere entirely unexpected, that is, if you had any expectations to begin with. Maybe this thought will be distressing. Perhaps this unpredictability is what feeds into the excitement. An awareness of the risks that come with exploring a strange place are often enough to sharpen the senses and widen the eyes; enough to see it start, enough to keep it going. Perhaps this is also an important part of exploring familiar places in unfamiliar ways by leaving oneself open to the possibility of something or nothing happening. By noticing what does. By not dwelling on what doesn't. Only time will tell how the woman's walk will unfold, or where it will end. For, now, the focus has been placed squarely on the journey; on the seemingly aimless and winding path to which she is committed; the path that she creates one step, one solitary moment, after another; marked and measured by a red ball of wool, by the blood line of her journey.

A view of the woman as she strolls between ornate glass chandeliers and past a model spiral staircase and Victorian furniture, gives the adventure an atmosphere that is, perhaps, akin to *Alice in Wonderland*. The woollen ball is now slightly smaller than before. Because of its gradual unravelling, the ball is much easier to manage, though the woman still needs the assistance of strangers to help her lift it up and onto an old wooden tram. Some passengers alight as she prepares to board. A moment of glare caused by the sunlight disrupts the image. The 'flicker' is just enough to dazzle the eyes and add to the surreal, half sleep ambience. The red wool is pulled rapidly as the tram moves off and gathers speed along the tracks. This causes the woollen ball to spin in situ on the carriage floor near to the open doors. This seems to amuse the woman, who smiles while looking down on the action.

Another bird's-eye view finds the woman rolling the red wool down one flight of a triangular staircase. Suddenly, she loses her grip on it and, extending her arms sidewards in an attempt to secure her footing in the stairwell, the woollen ball takes off down the remainder of the flight. It bounces down another flight; rolling faster and faster towards the bottom. The chances that she will be able to catch up with it at this stage are remote, to say the least.

Nevertheless, she is visible in the background, running after her trail maker. Watching from the inside of a cafe, in which a man with a white paper bib sits eating his meal at the window, the woollen ball can be seen rolling past outside. The woman is running close behind. A red dress, visible in the shop window across the way, and the line of wine bottles placed neatly along the cafe window sill, signify two things that are abundant in this place of leisure and pleasure.

The ball rolls into the circular cathedral gardens. Water ripples on the curved roof around the perimeter. The central square echoes the shapes that are formed by the numerous pillars around the outside. The sites of decadence are only a short distance away from those places of sanctity. Here, finally, the red ball slows to a stop and she catches up. In retrieving her ball of wool, the woman notices a length of blue wool that is hooked around a wrought iron bench. She looks around as if to seek out the owner but no-one else is in the round garden. The blue wool is a trace of somehow else's meandering and who, going by the colour, is probably a man. Looking at the unfamiliar wool, she tilts her head in an expression of curiosity and, now picking up her ball, begins to follow the strange thread through the stone arches and along a graffitied laneway. The path of the blue wool ends abruptly where it reaches a decorated building wall; appearing as if to disappear straight into it. The mysterious Kings Cross wall at platform 9 and ¾ in the Harry Potter movies provides a suitable frame of reference. The blue wall has actually disappeared under the base of a doorway that is difficult to see, having been almost completely camouflaged by the wobbly-lined design that has been painted on the exterior. The woman continues to indulge her curiosity by reaching out her hand, taking hold of the door handle, and opening it. Then she steps inside.

The woman has entered a long and empty corridor, comprising entirely of stone arches. Along this hallway, and extending far into the distance, is the blue woollen thread. She continues to follow it in order to find out where its owner is going, where he has gone, who he is. Along the way, the blue wool can be seen resting along the top edge of a leather sofa. She runs her fingers beneath it as she passes, without stopping, before walking up a narrow spiral staircase at the end of the corridor. Once more, we are being led closer and closer to an indeterminable destination, if such a thing exists at all.

Having climbed to the top of the staircase the woman reaches another doorway. This one leads her outdoors and onto a clearing on what appears to be the roof of the building, if not and patio adjacent to one of the upper floors. A number of lush green plants line the patio's stone border. From here, a person is able to look out and over to the town clock that, although it once dominated the skyline, is now just another building amid an ever growing forest of sky scraping apartments and ant's nest office blocks; each one complete with its very own human colony, its idiosyncratic social organisation and associated hierarchy. Yet, here she is, apart from all of that; standing at the edge of the rooftop, right next to a large blue ball of wool.

Only two or three metres away, a man in a brown jacket is leaning against the wall. Having been peering down onto the city street, at first he has his back to the woman but soon stands up straight as he turns around to see who is there. He appears to be a little unsure of what to do next but is not visibly perturbed by her presence. She looks at him with a friendly expression, without a word, and still holding the ball of red wool in her left arm. Although it once almost equalled her in height, its constant unravelling that meant that the woollen ball is now the size of a round party balloon. The man continues to stand there as well, watching her watching him, returning the unthreatening gaze before gesturing a gentle and understanding nod with a gentle bite of his lip. It seems not so much that they know each other but, rather, that soon they will.

An orange length of wool extends from left to right, as does a pink length beneath it. The furry fibres catch the sunlight to illuminate the outside of the cord. Reaching between the foreground and the distance are four thick woollen threads—green, blue, orange, and yellow. Lying still along the cobble stones, their origin is as much of a mystery as their destination. One limit is indistinguishable from the other. An old white Roll Royce drives across the background.

Two tall plain walls create a narrow walkway. Almost a dozen threads of thick wool are strung along it. They are all of different colours and overlap each other in various places. In the same way that the red strand of wool has traced the path of the woman and in the same way that the blue strand of wool has traced the path of the man, these other strands of wool are meant to represent the paths of other people who have walked around the city space. Each strand is a record of human movement through an environment made from concrete, steal, and glass; the passage of the organic through the inorganic. They are the randomly crossing trails of strangers whose origins and destinations, to the viewer, are also invisible; indeterminable. The journey takes place in the midst of things; it takes us along the course of a nonlinear narrative.

A bug's eye view of a tree lined park also contains the various strands of coloured wool. Some litter the leafy lawn while others have been woven between and around the trees ahead. People's paths can cross each day without them ever knowing who has gone before them or who is yet to arrive. The city is alive with the experiences of its inhabitants. They make it what it is. As individual lives come and go, new threads add to the multitude of desires, interests, adventures, and interactions that are woven into an ever evolving cultural fabric. This fabric is represented as creative, relaxed and welcoming, suggesting that it's easy to weave yourself into the city. "It's easy to lose yourself in Melbourne."[1]

---

[1] Tourism Victoria Video Room, "Lose Yourself in Melbourne," Accessed July 10, 2010, http://www.visitvictoria.com/videostub/4F2E7E78-A361-4753-AE5E130F5 15F1201.cfm

## Lose Yourself in Melbourne

When I first saw the *Lose Yourself in Melbourne* advertisement, I was living in Western Australia, sitting in front of the television and being lazy in the afternoon. Not really paying attention to which program was being shown, instead, I was indulging in speculation as to what I was doing with my life, where I thought it was going, wishing that there was something exciting to do that might adequately distract me from the banalities of everyday that prompted me to lump myself on the couch in the first place. By all accounts, life was fine, but the sudden flicker of the television screen to an advertisement about Melbourne, a city that I had been to a couple of times on holiday, caught my eye. Little did I know then that something so seemingly simple and unassuming as a tourism promotion would lead me and my wife to take a turn at the fork in the road, packing up all our belongings, selling what we no longer needed in a monster of a garage sale, and moving to the other side of the country. Little did we know that the woman and her ball of wall would be like the seed of doubt that makes you wonder whether you're on the right path, getting the best opportunities, living life to the full. On each subsequent time that I noticed the advertisement, I gave an increasing amount of attention to the representations, assumptions, and meanings it contained.

Offering the viewer a nonlinear city-based narrative, the advertisement invites the viewer along on a seemingly aimless walk—a carefree and creative experience, which entails using the city not as a place of work or product consumption, but rather as a space of creativity. The advertisement invites the viewer into a space of potential, of adventure, and play.

This prospect might seem peculiar for those of us who are used to thinking about the city as a focal point of industrialised labour. Notions of the city have often conjured up imaginings of utilitarian hovels—the countless same-same apartments that compartmentalise the lives of the people who inhabit them (names including Walter Gropius and Le Corbusier might spring to mind). Maybe we will think of the CBD—the central business district and understand that the city is where money is made, lost, exchanged; that this built environment represents the height of productivity in the late modern age—the age in which industrialisation is no longer a brave new venture but an established part of everyday thinking and action.

The city is filled with cafes and shops. Even during a rare 2am city walk, on a Thursday morning, I have been surprised to see literally hundreds of people going about their business; chatting with friends, waiting for taxis, wandering in and out of all-night establishments. In this day and age, in which the notion of a city that never sleeps is not alien to us, the city still has the capacity to surprise us with its energy; its neon eyes blinking and watching the bodies littering the streets, like the industrialised cells of a creature writhing 24/7.

Certainly from day to day, the city is that place where you might go when you want to meet friends for lunch or enjoy a social drink. The city is where you might go to work during the day or night, or both. The city is where you might see a movie, or buy a new book, an exhibition or performance, a busker in the mall, where your path might cross that of a talkative stranger. Cities harbour the spectacle, the novel and enjoyable—the countless possible activities; at least, that is the promise of the city. What these activities are, from person to person, is anyone's guess. Nevertheless, they all embody our motivations to pursue our interests, to meet deadlines, to pick up a last-minute bargain; they are the everyday tasks that find us acting in certain pre-established ways; they occupy the familiar paths that we take via public or private transport, or on foot. They comprise our habits and routines, our claims to a common cultural sensibility.

While the endless movement of the city shows it to be a place of many motivations and meanings, the *Lose Yourself in Melbourne* advertisement asks the viewer forget about all of these familiar patterns with which they might experience the city, such as where they involve our engagement in shopping or working. It invites the viewer, you and me, to let down our guard; to loosen up by letting go of preconceived, city-based goals. It wants us to sweep aside all of these conceivably routine or boring things. It invites us, instead, to simply 'make it all up' as we go along. When I first saw this advertisement, it was as if it was asking: "Why get so consumed in all of the routine? The city is your build environment, of course. But why not use it also for playing in? Why not embrace your opportunity to improvise everyday life? Quite literally, this is a chance to think on your feet. Take the shops, offices and street, and turn them into your playground."

Because of the high value that I place on creativity, the reminder that city-life itself could be our most vital work of art led me to consider my own routines, my preconceptions, my experience of this built environment or, to put it in another way, all those things that help make up my cultural subjectivity. It led me to consider how I might challenge these things that I so easily, it would seem, take for granted as being normal, natural, or inevitable. I got the impression that the viewer was being invited to explore a built environment, one that I understood as epitomising the daily grind (a commuter-congested sinus, sneezing globs of office politics, gossiped around water fountains that offers some ludicrous reference to gardens throughout the ages, or the minutia of management meetings being masticated by the minutes). Yet, in the *Lose Yourself in Melbourne* advertisement, the world of such dull things seems far, far-away. In this particular case, Melbourne provides the viewer with a focal point—a metonym, that 'part' which stands in for the 'whole.' This city is represented as being much more than the sum of its parts. Not only the home of the central business district and the centre of consumerism, it is also being depicted as a site for singular adventures—the kinds of escapism that can be enjoyed during a lunch break. You can work in the city, but also, as might a child who has been let out for recess, you are free to play a solitary game of mystery and intrigue—a game that takes place in the labyrinth of the built environment; in the body of a sophisticated modern machine.

Approaching it, now, not from the perspective of what is seen, but rather from the perspective of what is heard, the advertisement's soundtrack features Joanna Newsom. We can hear Joanna playing her harp while she, with her distinctly childlike voice, sings a song about the "sprout and the bean," about sleeping "all day," about "a golden ring," "a twisted string," about going "outside," about "the hollow chatter of the talking of the tadpoles."[2] Each lyrical fragment conjures a precarious avant-garde fantasy world that is conducive to the modernist backdrop; an ambience of playfulness and non-seriousness, of attention being made to the small observations that take place within the bigger picture of the game. These lyrics feed back into the overall message of the advertisement by giving voice to the ideas to which the advertisement's imagery also alludes.

Because the advertisement promotes a particular notion of the city space, we can also say that it privileges a particular ideology—a coherent system of ideas, values and beliefs that shapes our interpretations of the world. In general, ideology gives us a framework for how we interpret what takes place around us. Here, and to the extent that the *Lose Yourself in Melbourne* advertisement was commissioned by Tourism Victoria, the viewer bears witness to an ideology that has been given government approval.

It is commonplace to experience ideology being transmitted into our lounge rooms at the easy flick of a button. This is precisely what happens each time we turn on the television set, listen to the radio, a song or DVD. Current affairs programs, comedies, cartoons, animated films for children, nature documentaries; they all contain words and pictures that are packed full of meaning. Sometimes these meanings, value, and ideas reflect our own; sometimes they do not. I can't remember when the Christian Television Association stopped broadcasting "Hello my God" ads[3]; perhaps around the same time that the mass media became more invested in promoting its commitment to a multi-cultural Australia, or at least more invested in creating this impression. But seeing this ad after arriving home from primary school, following a weekly afternoon of religious instruction, was a prime example of my own exposure to ideological messages being disseminated by the mass media. It marked the first time that I became curious about the messages that I was, often unwittingly, inviting into my private space.

Advertising is well invested in the business of ideology. It relies whole heartedly on the mass media's capacity for reaching the ears, eyes, and minds of diverse populations and geographical locations. Advertising is able to capi-

---

[2] J. Newsom, "Sprout and the Bean," [song] from *The Milk-Eyed Mender* (Chicago: Drag City Records, 2004).
[3] The CTA advertisements can be viewed on Youtube.

talise on the sophisticated virtual and telecommunications networks that our modern world affords us with apparent ease, in order to circulate beliefs, values and assumptions with increasing efficiency and financial viability. One advertisement may try to convince us that its central focus, a cleaning product, will solve all of our problems when it comes to making those shower screens as clear as clear can be. It might claim to have the answer to our problem—one that we didn't know we even had prior to switching on the television. Another advertisement will try to temp us with the steaming hot and spicy aroma of a barbecued chicken, complete with extra oily fries and a sugary drink.

Advertising tries to convince the viewer that it has what he or she needs—that its solutions are ideal as his or her solutions. It presumes that what it has to tell the viewer is what he or she needs or wants to know, to hear, and to think about while each of us go about our everyday life. We don't have to agree with what we are being told, but there is always scope to do so. It all depends on what we desire in the world, what we aspire to, as well as what we wish for ourselves to be. It depends upon how committed we are to these promoted assumptions 'made personal.' In the instance of watching an advertisement that depicts a lady wandering around the city with a massive ball of red wool, once again we are still being offered a package containing certain carefully chosen ideas, beliefs and observations. Once again, we are being guided around an 'imagining' of the world, just as we might, elsewhere, find ourselves being guided around a shopping catalogue or a dine-in menu at a fancy restaurant of our choice. Just like the catalogue or menu, we are still being offered a product except that, here, the product is an ideal the producer of ideals is not a restaurant, a clothing outlet, or a fast food joint; it is a government funded agency. Driving the *Lose Yourself in Melbourne* campaign, Tourism Victoria also shows itself to be in the business of establishing and disseminating ideological ideas—ways of thinking about, making sense of, the built environment. The advertisement is proof of Tourism Victoria's push to implant these ideas into the lounge rooms of an Australian viewing audience. In this sense, Tourism Australia is also a socialising agency because it encourages viewers to adopt, maintain, and even communicate to each other, certain notions and meanings pertaining to the city space.

A socialising agency can be a church or a school, it can comprise of mentors, friends and family. What these elements have in common is their capacity to learn cultural ideas and ideals, as well as to teach them. The notion of a socialising agency is relevant to, using Peter Brooker's words, any "assembly of individuals held together by an AESTHETIC and political IDEOLOGY, CLASS position and…, quite markedly, by personal friendship, marriage or partnership and a shared 'social conscience'."[4] Such social formations are socialising agencies to the extent that they encourage certain be-

---

[4] P. Brooker, *Glossary of Cultural Theory*, 2nd ed. (London: Hodder Arnold, 2003), 105.

haviours that are deemed acceptable in view of that shared conscience, and discouraging of those behaviours that are conceived to be in 'opposition to' or 'at odds with' it. No doubt holding its own kind of social conscience, one that upholds a tourist aesthetic of planetary exploration, the exotic 'other,' romantic travel narratives at the centre of which the potential tourist is encouraged to imagine his or her self, while rendering all incongruent aspects of the host environment invisible. The primary goal of Tourism Victoria, in its role as a socialising agency, is to play this game of allure and retreat in a way that encourages the public to think about the city—Melbourne—in a particular, pre-designed way. We can take it as a given that the ideals on in the offer, in *Lose Yourself in Melbourne* campaign, further justify this agency's position in the broader cultural environment.

As Nietzsche so eloquently put it, "what convinces is not necessarily true—it is merely convincing."[5] Thus, we may take all that we see in the mass media with a pinch of salt. As the public becomes more and more media savvy, the viewer is much less likely to accept whatever messages they are exposed to at face value. If digging beneath the surface of an advertisement is the easiest way to interrogate it, the extent to which an advertisement's ideology is accepted, digested, even pursued, is dependent upon the extent to which its content is seen as being logically coherent. In other words, for the advertisement to have any success at all it must place preferred features and characteristics of the city in the foreground, whilst omitting or obscuring our view of those which might otherwise prove to undermine its claims, those preferences. In short, the advertisement shows a woman wandering around by herself, in strange and uninhabited alleyways, minus whatever conceivably physical and/or moral dirt a viewer might expect them to harbour on a day to day basis.

This is the game of allure and retreat of which I have made mention. The advertisement shows the lone and self-losing woman very safely exploring the lesser seen corners of the city, turning this way and that without as much as a care for her direction or for her safety. Is she about to step into a makeshift brothel or X-rated peep show venue, stumble over a homeless person who's simply trying to stay warm beside a cathedral stairwell? Is the woman with the red wool mere moments away from treading on a used intravenous needle? Will she soon get her purse stolen by a drug addict who's trying desperately to raise enough money for another fix? Will the female wanderer be unfortunate enough to witness a desperate individual jump in front of a moving tram or train, or to smell the acrid stench of horse urine along a southern section of Swanston Street? Will she join other tourists, perhaps even some locals, in gaining pleasure from a ride in a city-based horse and cart, like some kind of pseudo-royalty on parade with their equine slaves? Will she bear witness to an old lady who, after an afternoon spent limping

---

[5] F. Nietzsche, *The Will To Power*, Preface (Nov. 1887-March 1888).

along uneven pathways, now faces a fine of $165 for travelling without a valid ticket?

We may rest assured that the answer to all of these hypothetical questions is "no." It is highly unlikely that the woman in the advertisement is going to encounter images of homelessness, crime, pollution, looks of frustration that follow news of late or cancelled trams and trains, or car accidents. It is unlikely that the advertisement will make any mention of redundancies or any other symptoms of economic crisis. We can say this with confidence because such things would only expose the limits of the ideal, test it, challenge it, undermined its claims to logical coherence. Such anomalies are sequestered from the advertisement. They are the aspects of city life that remains beyond the limits of the expectations and experiences that are dominant in this society. They are displaced by the ideal; they are pushed into silence and obscurity, beyond the frame of the televised picture.

Tourism is big business; there is no funding allocation for the accidental and the unintentional; there is no scope for unmanaged risks, for disruptive 'unknowns', which is quite ironic given the style of stroll in which the woman with the red wool is engrossed. We can put money on the fact that what we are shown will have been re-approved and sanitised long before it was ever going to reach our eyeballs, our eardrums, and our meaning making minds. Because we can feel confident that the woman will not accidentally and unintentionally bump into adversity during the advertisement's 90 second presence, we remain focussed in the frame of her mysterious adventure. What we experience, then, is the product of careful filtering—pure idealism.

In summary, the general trend for advertising tells us about the conditions behind the *Lose Yourself in Melbourne* campaign. Advertisements take up valuable broadcasting time. The success of its ideological message is dependent upon that message maintaining logical coherence at all times—its ability to privilege one point of view over other possibilities by leaving out or silencing those aspects considered contrary to the ideal. Thus, while an advertisement might hope to 'wow' us with what is present, with that which appears in front of the viewer, this is no reason to keep from thinking about what might lie beyond it, behind it. It is valuable to consider what is being silenced, omitted, of simply taken for granted so that a richer understanding of what is present may be appreciated—to make further sense for what is being communicated to an audience.

In order to put an advertisement to task we need to dig deeper than the depth provided. It is useful for the viewer to reach beyond the 2-dimensionality of the television screen and into the 3-dimensionality of the social circumstances from which it has emerged and which continue to provide it with a vital frame of reference. But this cannot be done from the comfort of the lounge room sofa. It cannot be done with the air of passivity with which tele-visual content can be so conveniently consumed. At its very core, putting the *Lose Yourself in Melbourne* advertisement to task requires the movement of arms and legs; it requires the viewer to physically, intellectually, as well as emotionally reach beyond the frame of the televised picture—to pursue an active and critical engagement in that broader cultural context. Making sense of what is given means stepping outside and accessing relevant and tangible points of reference—those occupying not a virtual but a material reality—and trying to finding out where they have come from.

## Self and Society

If a key to enriching our understanding of what is present is peering behind it, into it, then it stands to reason that each moment of cultural experience can be enriched through an understanding of its historical context, that past from which the present moment always extends. That is why we can read the *Lose Yourself in Melbourne* in two ways. First, we can say that it depicts a person's experience of the city, in the moment, perhaps in a lunchbreak or during a holiday period; here, we can say that the advertisement privileges the dynamic relationship between the self and a very modern society. Consequently, we may also say that, by concentrating on a person's walk around the streets and buildings that comprise the city, around this particular kind of build environment, it always depicts that person's relationship to history. Even though the advertisement prioritises a fixed focussed on the immediate present, it cannot escape the fact the past that has led to whatever is taking place 'now.' Making further sense of the *Lose Yourself in Melbourne* advertisement means looking into the setting of its non-linear narrative—taking the time to consider the historical circumstances and the cultural conditions of a modern society.

A modern society is a peculiar state of affairs, driven by myriad technological advancements in relation to which it organises and reorganises itself in increasingly sophisticated and efficient ways. This society is also a privileged minority world in which people talk quietly, passionately, and aggressively into small plastic boxes on the trams, the trains, or even when a cashier is trying to tell them their fee but can't get a word in edgeways because a more important conversation is taking place between the customer and his or her plastic box. These people tend to consume too much sugar, caffeine, and fizzy drinks. They sit in front of glowing, flashing rectangles, push their fingers against small plastic squares, and alternate between watching their fingers and watching the shapes that keep appearing on the rectangle. Sometimes, their fingers will stop and they'll just sit there and stare at the glowing rectangle, perhaps muttering to their self in the process. Perhaps they will sit inside their built environments all day and, at five o'clock in the afternoon, will walk down to the front door and say to another person, standing down there, "What has the weather been like today."

If we think that these people are quite peculiar, it might be surprising to consider that we are these people. Most of the global population doesn't live like we do—in the modern West. And despite how unusual we are, we might still walk around each day without mindfulness of this observation—as if our activities were not simply second nature, but rather nature itself. But ours are not natural, normal, or inevitable sets of circumstances. Rather, they might seem to be so after a while, once we become accustomed to them, once they become our customs, our culture, our routines and habits—once they become our common-sense.

In this sense, the social world can be investigated in terms of its constructedness—in terms of the way that ideas, values, memories, desires, institutions, relationships, to mention just a few considerations, comprise our lives—then the process of delving into history is valuable. We can look search history in the hope of seeing this idea in practice, and as a strategy for enriching cultural experience today. Because, in order to get to the stage where things seem like second nature, we have to do them a lot; the more we do them, the less we need to think about them; making and coffee or getting to work, or conducting our manual labours, these practices and processes become our routines and habits. The more habitual our behaviour, the less critical we are of it.

But, you might ask, isn't this what makes modernity great, that we can evolve our efficiencies and economies, making what we have better and better? The answer is yes, if the aim is to improve the efficacy of our habits—when we conceive of sustainability as a form of growth. But this kind of growth sees scope for improvement only in the way things are, rather than in the interrogation and revision of those very behavioural foundations. The foundation of everyday life is taken for granted. Perhaps it is an accident of birth that has led us to invest ourselves intellectually and emotional, materially, in a modern society. Maybe there was something about it that attract us from elsewhere, like a mosquito lured into the realm of a luminous zapper, or a tiny fish that has become transfixed by the glowing lure that hangs in front of an angler fish's gaping, toothed void.

Just like the city environment, our customs are also constructed. By recognising this, and by taking stock of the constructedness of our cultural circumstances, of our modern life, it becomes possible for us to reach beyond what is given and into its motivations—achieving alternative levels of meaning. Perhaps by wandering around the city, by having a creative look around, the woman in the *Lose Yourself in Melbourne* advertisement is partaking in a seemingly aimless stroll that offers an analogy for how a person might also 'make strange' his or her own cultural circumstances. To stroll aimlessly around the city might well be the same thing as strolling aimlessly around the cultivated self.

Thus, when I make mention of a cultural strategy, I am always thinking that this is best when it is also a critical strategy, because accessing new kinds of cultural meaning means the opportunity to apply them to our lives, today. By reaching into the guts of our cultural assumptions about what is normal, natural, or inevitable, we can proceed to make them seem strange again; the preciousness of our culture disintegrates and we begin to develop new ways of seeing and, essentially, this is what this book is about. The modern mind-set is one in which society is accustomed to believing in the promise of the machine; since the enlightenment period there has been a tremendous redirection of faith in the power of the human mind to reason and rationalise—to improve life through humankind's own efforts.

The process of actively shaking up the habits of everyday life, of challenging the spaces in which they take place, becomes a means to enriching cultural experience. When things become habitual, taken for granted, the shock of the new grows dull; seems increasingly ordinary, even passé. To make culture strange is to appreciate it in a new way, in a critical way, but also in a personal way, a culturally subjective way. Not only may we view the *Lose Yourself in Melbourne* advertisement and dig deep into its historical context, we may do so for the express purpose of applying the spoils of this task to our own lives. This appeal to a material reality becomes a challenge to the ideological content that the advertisement communicates, which further helps us to sort through its meanings (so as to better formulate our own), it implications, and its expectations (reasonable or otherwise).

This is why it is of the upmost importance to make clear that this project of engaging critically with culture is unique. It stems from a body in the world that can be no other body than me. This tells us two things about the narrative to come: 1. it is auto-ethnographic in nature, meaning that I shall being using personal experience as primary data, as a process as well as a product; 2. it includes historical and theoretical 'anchors' that ground my cultural subjectivity. This enables me to address the relationship between self and society in a very practical and communicable way. Recognising the self as a cultural being, recognising myself as my most immediately accessible cultural being, is very convenient. However, auto-ethnography always runs the risk of descending into narcissism when it overemphasises the self and starts to forget about society. My dedication to avoiding this risk is precisely why this book is divided into two halves, the first laying out the cultural and historical anchors, and the second documenting my response to these as I put them into practice.

By keeping historical and theoretical anchors clearly in sight, those which inform my own negotiation of this theoretical and practical cultural exploration, I aim to capitalise on the value of personal experience. This is especially so due to the notion of the 'self' that I have in mind; any self (or, to play on Rand's terms, any *ego*[6]) that would like to engage more critically with his or her day to day experience. The fact that I possess a late modern sense of self is accidental; my more general understanding is that the self to be a

---

[6] A. Rand, "The Soul of an Individualist," *For the New Intellectual: The Philosophy of Ayn Rand* (New York: Signet; First Thus edition, 1963), 81.

thinking entity that negotiates intellectual, material, and emotional realities, often in complex ways. So, of course, this book can only be about a trajectory of making something out of this circumstances; this cultural dimension of everyday life. On that level, it is less my own cultural circumstances that it is my method of engagement—one that can be applied elsewhere, by other people.

It's needless to be put off by my mention of a 'cultural' self. It's fair to say that our lives are entirely cultural, that culture is not just about elite practices like theatre and gallery going, cheap recordings of Baroque classics, violin sonatas and partitas, cello suites. We take part in culture each time we get out of bed and get our breakfast out of the cereal box, or brush our teeth with coloured plastic devices that taste so much better when they're minty. Culture is there when we interact with one another, in the hopes and dreams and the memories held by each of us. We all have something to gain from learning about it. My conceptualisation of the self is directed towards inclusion and not exclusion. We are in culture together for, as Nicholas Mirzoeff confirms, "there is no outside to culture."[7]

If 'going on' in the world is always contextualised by a condition of 'interiority'—of always being 'inside' culture—it's no wonder that cultural mindfulness is also a kind of self-consciousness; developing an understanding of our build environments always takes place through personal eyes. This is fine, for in our reflection upon the ideals of modernism, we know that once such dream was the dream of objectivism and several decades have gone by since we realised that this was unreasonable. How can we claim that god is dead and then attempt to take a godlike stance, for surely this becomes a deathlike stance, peering into the crevasse of our own creative potential?

In addressing the dynamism between the self and one's society, it is necessary to take some clues from the pasts from which we extend, which through our pictures, literatures, and other forms of representation, have managed to draw out a few moments more. This means discussing a strategy that has been used to engage critically in everyday life in the built environment, namely the city. The city is an ideal setting for this discussion in that so far as it is a paradigm of modernity. To reflect upon the material and ideological consequences of modernity (this being a feature of the late modernist mindset) is to engage critically with the past and to do so in a way that can enrich day to day life today.

A major conceptual thread running through this book is the idea that the routines, the rituals, the traditions, and the habits that we *follow* often foster feelings of safety, security, well-being, contentment, even happiness in us. But my response to this idea is to state my belief that these 'knowns' come at a great cost by comprising a significance hindrance to self-growth. Having

[7] N. Mirzoeff, *An Introduction to Visual Culture* (London and New York: Routledge, 1999), 23.

been brought up to respect the opportunity to 'make something' of myself, to 'make something' of my life, the creative practice has held a key place in what I consider to be a life worth living.

But might we explore this further? What abstract structure can I use to communicate what is at stake in the matter? The most appropriate metaphor that I can think of is the metaphor of the abyss—that which is taken to be unfathomable, indeterminable, the great unknown. In terms of creative cultural engagement, therefore, exploring the dynamism between the self and society, if it is a process of learning in order to enrich (of investing thinking in practice), then it is also a process of challenging your limits and stepping out into the unknown, to see what happens. Also for theorist Sharon Wegscheider-Cruse:

> The risks of self-growth involve going into the unknown, into an unfamiliar land where the language is different and customs are different and you have to learn your way around … the paradox is that until we give up all that feels secure, we can never really trust the friend, mate, or job that offers us something. …. If we reject deliberate risk taking for self-growth we will inevitably remain trapped in our situation.[8]

Understanding that the self is social, that we are all cultural beings, on a broader scale, I take this to imply that the comforting embrace of familiarity is a hindrance to the advancement of human creativity. In this sense, there seems to be a strong synchronicity between self-growth, as a creative cultural trajectory, and the critique of everyday cultural practices. It means stepping into the unknown by challenging the 'known'—especially those things that appear to be so obvious that they barely even need to appear at all anymore.

If words such as 'routine', 'ritual', 'tradition', and 'habit' are some of the umbrella terms that we use to denote the myriad practices and gestures whose patterns we *follow* for feelings of safety, security, well-being, contentment, even happiness in us, then stepping into the unknown puts these feelings at stake—not only these feelings but also a person's practical relationship to the material world that contains their expression. The risks of the 'unknown' are the risks to our safety, our comfort; the unknown risks the pleasure of our contentment. But I would rather slip off of the edge than retreat and never know. I'd much rather embrace the abyss than resent it. It seems clear to me that we have much to learn from the unknown that we may enter each time we step beyond our comfort zones, outside of our customary fields of reference.

How can I make this assumption so early on in the piece? My claim is based upon my own experience of the world and upon the information that I

---

[8] Cited in A. Giddens, *Modernity and Self-Identity: Self and Society in the Late Modern Age* (Stanford, California: Stanford University Press, 1991), 78.

have gained by observing society around me. I go to work and my friends go to work, and my family goes to work, I see strangers going to work. I go to the shops, my friends go to the shops, my family goes to the shops, and I see strangers going to the shops. Perhaps we pride ourselves on our manual dexterity when it comes to how quickly we can now type an email, build a web page, fold a napkin, or even make the bed. The 'familiar' is often taken to be a valuable path to the virtues of speed, efficiency, economy. We are rewarded by our habituation, our repetition. Maybe we even start to identify ourselves in terms of it; for example, the quickest cyclist, the quickest runner, the fastest person to solve the Rubik's cube, the first person to balance a record number of coins end to end on top of each other, the most hot dogs eaten in one sitting. Such feats of human skill lead to trophies, titles, and other symbols of prestige and notoriety.

Seeing beyond ourselves, sustaining a mindfulness of our impact on, and influence by, a material reality, means trying not to take what we have around us for granted. We can easily become so familiarised with our routines and our circles of friends, with our jobs, our favourite sports, our hobbies, that it's as if they were never anything other. When I started to drive to work and back—the same old route every day—when I could do it just about without even thinking (so that I may as well have been a half asleep citizen, driving at speed along the ever busy freeway), I knew it was time to shake things up a bit. I knew it was time to actively challenge the banality and the habituation of my everyday life. But this was not enough. It was important that I try to make this experience useful for other people as well. After all, it would be hypocritical to claim an interest in cultural engagement and then keep it all to myself.

The woman with the red wool seems intimately engaged in this process of pushing past the familiar, on her own terms and at her own pace. As an ideal, the aimless stroller taps into the theoretical concerns relevant to negotiating the dynamism between personal dispositions and cultural forces. If we take the *Lose Yourself in Melbourne* advertisement as a starting point, we can use it to map a trajectory from the past to the present, from the ideal to the material, from theory to practice, all the while challenging what we see along the way.

## The Structure of the Book

As mentioned, this book is organised into two intimately related parts. I use this word 'intimate' without reservation, for we may appropriately call these complimentary parts 'theory' and 'practice.' Like yin and yang, the theory will include elements of practice and, in turn, the practice will include elements of theory. In agreement that the absence of one is the poverty of the other, we may understand that they are like two halves of a coin of cultural capital that intimately co-exist—that theory and practice are best when they are warm to each other, when they go-on with each other in mind, when they remember, respond, to work as a team—that best practice is theoretically informed and that the best theories are those with a practical application.

For all intents and purposes, this is a *praxis* based book in that it examines both of those sides. Of course, we shall look further into this term in due course, as we transition from the theoretical to the practical—as we proceed to put the former to the test or, as we may also put it, as we go on to 'walk' the 'talk'. For now, it is pertinent to say that the kinds of theory and the kinds of practice that this book addresses denote a marriage made in cultural history, and one that can be taken to have ongoing relevance today, each day. In the book's historically grounded first half, I introduce a range of key conditions that characterised the emerging modern world. Of particular interest are the 17th century Enlightenment principles that provided hope for a more prosperous and rationally organised future—much needed after almost a thousand years of Europe being ravaged by religious upheavals. Enlightenment principles underpin modern thinking and, as an example of this thinking in practice, the transition from rural, traditional ways of living to a privileging of urban, dynamic, and mechanised means of social organisation. In this section, we gain an understanding of the historical conditions upon which our contemporary cultural circumstances have been founded.

Such a historical overview cannot begin and end with accounts of material changes impacting upon people's early modern lifestyles. In order to go beyond an 'us/them' approach to the past, it is necessary to acknowledge a range of responses that were made to these changes on an intellectual *and* an emotional level. For this purpose, I shall be making explicit reference to Charles Baudelaire's notion of the flâneur—the rather poetic and pseudo-aristocratic figure whom leisurely strolls the city streets simply to experience them. Baudelaire's strolls took place around Paris. He wandered the busy streets in a style that might have been thought of as quite idle, because his public meanderings were not conducted with the aim of getting to an office or to a shop or to this or that destination. Baudelaire's practice was to walk without motivation, without a destination—an end or finitude—in mind.

The Situationist International also picked up on the idea that walking without an outcomes-based motivation opens the doors to new ways of seeing one's environment. By actively breaking out of the routine paths and causeways that governed the everyday lives of the middle-class, they sought to engage with what they considered 'unfamiliar' by their neighbours standards. For this book is very much about getting up and walking around the built environment, around the countless artefacts of people, their existential evidences. It's very much about how to negotiate these in a way that enrich everyday experience by fostering a space of theory and play in which a constructive and creative criticism of these same 'knowns' may be gathered. The first, theoretical half of this book draws our attention to the role of the long and winding walk through the city place—an unmotivated meandering in a space design for directed productivity. The name of this practice is 'dérive'—an aimless stroll which is indulged in by the pseudo-aristocratic flâneur in the context of a modern city. Paying attention to the historical meanings of the dérive makes it possible to explain why and how it finds the flâneur not in opposition to their built cultural environment, but rather at odds with it—at the critical crossroads of how culture acts upon the individual and how an individual chooses to act in light of their cultural circumstances. By discarding all familiar motivations, by ceasing to treat the city as a place of work or consumerism in favour of using it as a space of play, the flâneur seeks to cut through the monotony of things, to inhabit a space beyond convention and habituation. Is the flâneur like a child in the machine, a spanner in the works? Is this what it takes to be an adventurer in the early modern age and to be one today? I shall be addressing such questions in this book, all the while giving names to the key figures and places within which their adventurous activities have taken place.

By clarifying the cultural conditions of an early modern world, and by locating the flâneur's dérive as a response to those conditions, it is possible to conceptualise the dérive as an alternative solution to the demands of industry upon the human body. In close relation to this clarification, we find the dérive serving as a context of resistance because it stands 'at odds' with broader cultural expectations; Baudelaire's pseudo-aristocratic idleness has very little to do with appealing to the virtues of efficiency, machinery, and capitalism. Thus, by examining this 17th century notion, we can get a sense of its importance for giving further depth to our reading of the *Lose Yourself in Melbourne* advertisement, our growing mindfulness of its implications for everyday life in the twenty-first century.

Chapter 3 contextualises the twenty-first century relevance of the dérive by showing how early modern cultural circumstances have become institutionalised. It is sceptical of the privileging of convenience that pervades a late capitalised society and, with it, a sense of entitled for such comfort. Rather than idealising novelty, standardisation, commodity culture, and commodity driven notions of self, this chapter adopts a scepticism that is partially informed by the Frankfurt School of critical theory—the school's interrogation of mass culture and mass communication. It explores late modern culture in terms of the cost of stability—the 'cost of' a stable life-world that can manifest as a 'cost to' self-growth, cultural creativity, and critical thinking. At the very least, the dérive provides an opportunity for a person living today to intentionally place his or her self at odds with the numbing effects of routinisation and habituation in a built environment.

Having reached this point at which common-sense assumptions about the virtues of contemporary culture have been challenged, Chapter 4 demonstrates how the dérive, in view of the preceding cultural criticisms, presents as something much more than a leisurely preoccupation. Rather, by building upon its capacity to resistance to industrially disciplined human behaviour, we come to see how the dérive might be useful out of a purely historical context. It joins other European reference points to broaden the story of thinking and action—the role of walking in the process of thinking about culture and about our relationship to nature. Nietzsche was a keen stroller and his aphoristic writing style has a lot to do with this beloved activity. As he moved along, his heart rate increasing and causing him to breathe harder on the crisp *Schwartzwald* air, his mind would have become more alert as the *endorphins* stimulated his mind, body, and pen. With the physical activity making his mind more active, he'd have to stop briefly, every now and then, to write his thoughts down before recommencing his journey.

To be clear, I am not proposing that the reader accept walking as a methodology. If this were the case, then walking to the library could be logged as research. Of course, to suggest this would be misleading, if not entirely irresponsible. Instead, we can appreciate the way that bodily movement invigorates mental activity, and simply capitalise on this physiological circumstance in the process of applying a critical cultural mindset. Walking is not the methodology, unless we are to work the matter of walking techniques into this investigation. Rather, it is more useful to conceive of walking as that which carries the senses, the reasons for engaging with the built environment in a particular way; walking carries the method around. With this information, we become ready to focus in on the notion of praxis. Thus, Chapter 4 provides a bridge between the theoretical emphasis of the first half of this book and the emphasis on practice (specifically in terms of the application of theory) that pervades the second.

Chapter 5 grounds the second half of this book in the practice of defamiliarisation. The purpose of this chapter is to illuminate the notion of defamiliarisation as a process of confronting the 'take for granted'—of making the routine and monotonous seems strange again. Defamiliarisation is the process of estranging everyday life in order to see it in a new a revitalised way. It marks an attempt to enrich cultural experience and exposes another dimension of Baudelaire's notion of the dérive. In order to elaborate on this thematic connection, I shall provide examples of creative practitioners whose activities have been geared around intentional cultural estrangement—not so much a distancing from the norm in the sense of giving life into anomy or criminality, though the notion of deviation is not entirely escapable. Rather, Craig Raine, George Perec, and Jim Henson's character Uncle 'Traveling Matt', from the Fraggle Rock series, each demonstrate how much there is to be gained from forcibly disrupting cultural complacency, from being duly responsible for actively discontinuing the smug self-satisfaction, the self-righteousness that pervades our false sense of security in an inherently unpredictable world—a bovine contentment that de-motivates active resistance and, thus personal empowerment. This chapter takes the position that the more we believe that things are 'as they should be' the less likely we are to believe that our own actions can make a difference in the bigger picture. The task, then, is to question why we put such a huge expectation on ourselves in the first place.

With this thought, Chapter 6 begins an extensive demonstration of my claim that the absence of practice is the poverty of theory, and vice versa (crossing over into Chapter 7). With so much attention given to the defamiliarising dimension of the dérive, its capacity for enriching cultural experience, along with the privileging of praxis, the need to 'walk the talk' is extremely important. My interest in the dérive was burgeoning at the same time that I moved from one side of Australia to the other, at the end of 2008. There is much to indicate that my personal interest in the dérive reflected an ambition to make a fresh start and to be as critically engaged in this new beginning as possible—in order to make the most of whatever opportunities it would proffer. I shall clarify my own context of engagement with the theory—my reasons for a move to make theory actionable in my own everyday life. Thus, this chapter details the first dérive that I conducted after relocating from Perth; it comprises a walk around an IKEA department store, providing considerable opportunity to engage with notions of commodity culture, standardisation, novelty culture, and pseudo-individuality that are included in the theoretical backdrop of the book's first half. In the midst of these dérives I made extensive notes about my surroundings and the thoughts that they evoked.

If, with the help of a 'pilot dérive,' Chapter 6 serves to introduce the practice based second half of the book, then Chapter 7 takes this opportunity and runs with it. This chapter comprises of an extensive dérive conducted in five phases and on five different occasions (the end-point of the first phase providing the starting point of the second phase, and so on through all five phases). This chapter shows me to be making theory actionable by conducting my own dérive and performing the role of the flâneur. To adopt this self-imposed estrangement is to place myself at odds, if only temporarily, with the white noise of everyday life. Like the flâneur, I aim to see things afresh and to use these insights as food for further cultural consideration. With my first outing, I began to understand what it means to walk without direction in a place that's also a machine, as Le Corbusier described the city. After hours of walking, I began to feel like I was gravitating closer and closer towards the consumer centre. Thus, what takes place on an intellectual *and* emotional level when, after an extended length of time spent in the city, I still have come across anything that I might want to buy? If the motivation to buy is acute, this alone is enough to make a person feels at odds with his or her culture. This is one thing that I considered during these dérives and served to promote further engagement with the expectations and conditions a built environment.

If practice goes back into providing some fuel for further thinking, for more theory, what role might dérive-induced exhaustion have on a participant's reflection on that practice? I shall try to find answers for this and all of the other questions as I attempt to do justice to ideals, being as honest as I can when negotiating my own expectations in the process; I shall try to find them in the streets near where I live, down the road, behind public benches, within the confines of the city and the central business district, in the marks that an artist makes for a portrait in the mall. I shall look high and low in my memories and ideas that any one present evokes. I shall look everywhere I can to find a way of achieving my goal. I shall make the theory actionable, and no doubt wear myself out in the process.

These dérives go a long way to framing the second half of this book as auto-ethnographic—something to which I have previously alluded. They are a prime opportunity for theories of the dérive and its support for defamiliarisation to be seen, now, in practice. As the negotiator of theory in this book, it is entirely appropriate, perhaps even necessary, that I also put it into practice—to test the theory so as to further its critical investigation for the benefit of the reader. To neglect such an opportunity may, with fairness, be deemed irresponsible for, without practice, the theory remains incomplete—its relevance to everyday life unsubstantiated. Practicing the theory, first hand, means putting it to the test; it means maintaining an unwillingness to allow the allure of an ideal to obscure potential anomalies and impracticalities. Of course, certain impracticalities shall become evident as we move through the five phases of the dérive—the personal case studies that will explore my own intellectual *and* emotional response to the built environment in an attempt to intellectually *and* emotionally relocate myself within it. Thus, the conclusion reflects upon the historical contexts of the theory and the ways that these can drive theory-driven practice for people living today. Such reflection requires a mindfulness of the day to day implications, benefits, challenges, rewards and impracticalities of the dérive and of defamiliarisation.

Having said this, in no way do I claim that the theory I have provided in any way exhausts the subject matter. This is not intended to be a definitive text. Nor do I conceive of any reason why my own defamiliarising dérives should be given any priority over other people's dérives. The intention is to express support for a more critical negotiation of the built environment. In practice, this is not always possible; life gets in the way, not to mention physical exhaustion resulting from extensive walking. More than anything, it is intended as food for thought for contributing to a fascinating field of discourse—fascinating enough, I hope, for other people to put themselves in the picture, to practice the theory on their own terms and at their own pace.

While the examples given have been conducted in Melbourne, it stands to reason that there are countless other countries that I could visit and feel varying degrees of estrangement or vulnerability; I certainly look forward to extending this project to places like Paris (to wander around that very place from which most of this theory has emerged), Berlin (not least of all because it provides very little public seating), busy London town, or the Turkish bazaars. What would it be like to dérive in Romania, in Nietzsche's Schwarzwald, in the floating city of Venice, or in a market place in Bangalore? The world is rich with contexts that would challenge our own notions of what is natural, normal, or inevitable; that confront our expectations and habituations. But what better place is there to start than right outside our front door? In any case, it sure looks like a nice day for a walk.

The street becomes a dwelling for the flâneur; he is as much at home among the facades of the houses as a citizen is in his four walls. To him the shiny, enamelled signs of businesses are at least as good a wall ornament as an oil painting is to the bourgeois in his salon. The walls are the desk against which he presses his notebooks; news-stands are his libraries and the terraces of cafés are the balconies from which he looks down on his household after his work is done.[9]

## Conceptualising Early Modernity

There is an excitement that comes with not knowing quite where we are going (as if, like too many chefs, too many pre-determinations and expectations were also enough to spoil the broth). For some, the unknown is frightening but, for others, the unknown can motivate a person to reach out into the world. Perhaps this is the kind of joy experienced by the *Lose Yourself in Melbourne* advertisement's woman with the red wool. To ascertain the validity of this insight, it would be useful to explore how she is reaching out into the world—the pre-conditions for her pre-occupation. It would help to have access to a precedent, to learn from distant mentors, from other such experiments. How might we commence our intentional estrangement, get the ball rolling? The image of someone wandering aimlessly around Melbourne might seem peculiar, or incredibly easy in its carefree façade; it might seem literally and figuratively out of step with city based customs and expectations, or with advertised allusion to a modernist fantasy world. Yet this solitary practice has a significant cultural history; there are richly layered precedents for the practice of 'drifting through' the city space. What is more, exploring some of these demonstrates that appearances are most certainly deceiving. For, far from the practice of absent minded social disengagement, we find that they are invested in a vital commentary on the modern world. The dérive shines through as an opportunity to communicate, to articulate, the relationship between self and society going against the grain in order to better understand it. Information plus action equals change. This chapter discusses the historical foundations of the contemporaneous application of this sentiment.

One of the most striking things about the way that the woman in the *Lose Yourself in Melbourne* advertisement experiences the city is the extent to which she bears the character of the *flâneur* (the individual who wanders without purpose). This French word, denoting "stroller", "lounger", "saunterer",

---

[9] C. Baudelaire, quoted in S. Giles, *Theorizing Modernism: Essays in Critical Theory* (London and New York: Routledge, 1993), 54.

"loafer," was "employed by the Marxist critic and theorist, Walter Benjamin (1892-1940) in his reading of the nineteenth-century French poet, Charles Baudelaire."[10] It denotes the person who strolls around the city in order to be a part of the crowd but who remains alienated from it by way of his or her watchful and critical eye. Providing us with a more detailed starting point, Andrew Hussey explains that the word *flâneur*:

> arrived in Paris from Normandy and was a perfect description of the elegant idleness that so many young men feigned as their primary purpose in the city...The *flâneur* would become a stock figure of the nineteenth and twentieth centuries. The cult of idleness in this period was a pseudo-aristocratic response to the utilitarian demands of work and industry. The *flâneur* would thus, ironically enough, become a key element in the defining of modernity.[11]

Hussey informs us that the *flâneur*, particularly in Baudelaire's sense, can be understood as an early modern response to an emerging industrial society—a response that members of a rapidly growing lower class expressed. "Walking the streets of the city, experiencing the distinctive anonymity of the urban crowd, and drinking in appearances....The flâneur did not just revel in the city; he also sought to understand it."[12] These members' lives had become increasingly disconnected from the natural world, all the while becoming more and more disciplined by the demands of the modern world. This, being a central cultural condition, shall be our foremost point of departure.

Before the industrial turn of the 18th century, individuals, families and communities had been organised around traditional values and practices. The pre-modern world is relatively stable. You will most certainly know who your neighbours are. Perhaps a boy or girl will be taught their parent's skills and have some part of their self-identity predetermined in this way. A pre-modern world is concerned with the known, the tried and true of old cultural practices like the way that people dress of the gods they worship.

In the 18th century, the processes of industrialisation were disrupting the traditional world beyond recognition by attracting people to the city, by shifting the focus to the unknown, to novelty and consumerist practices. Traditional values were gradually being replaced by values and practices that functioned for the health of a booming economy, and which were justified by the promise of mass production.

A clear example of this disruption is the Luddites movement, initially comprising of skilled textiles craftsmen. These workers were most politically active in Nottingham in the years around 1811 in response to the impact that

---

[10] P. Brooker, *Glossary of Cultural Theory*, 2nd ed. (London: Hodder Arnold, 2003), 102.

[11] A. Hussey, *Paris* (London: Penguin Books, 2007), 162.

[12] C. Jones, *Paris: Biography of a City* (London: Penguin Books, 2004), 319-20.

mechanisation would have on their livelihoods, their standards of living, their sense of self-identity, their feelings of security and safety in view of the familiar. The time came when the arrival of machines meant a new skill had to be acquired—the task of the unknown, the unfamiliar, insecurity, the question of the self.

The introduction of textiles machines led to their fear of what seemed to be inevitable redundancy and unemployment. The craftsmen experienced wage reductions and the added indignity of having to compete with unnapprenticed workers. Their leader, Ned Ludd, was known for having destroyed two stocking frames used to manufacture inexpensive stockings. Because mechanisation meant an increase in the efficiency and accuracy of production, in the reduced need for human help, these mass produced items could be sold for less than the ones that people like Ludd made and sold. This was incredibly bad news for textiles craftsmen across Britain and from 1811-12, as news of Ludd's desperate actions traveled to them (perhaps by way of one of the new-fangled railway routes), likeminded Luddites followed suit, destroying wool and cotton mills in response to the growing industrialisation.

People were willing to go to some lengths to preserve their ways of life, their stability. In fact, some people were prepared to commit murder. A Luddite attack on William Horsfall's Ottiwells Mill in 1803 gives us a glimpse into Yorkshire's local history:

> Horsfall and his father were among the most recalcitrant of mill owners in the vicinity of Huddersfield and were aggressive in their introduction of dressing machines to the region's woolen manufacture. Horsfall is perhaps the most famous in his connection to one of the Huddersfield Luddites, George Mellor. In one confrontation prior to the attack on Rawfolds Mill, Horsfall struck Mellor across the face with a riding whip as Mellor comforted a poor woman whose infant had starved. Weeks later, Horsfall was shot dead on Marsden Road after leaving the Warren House Inn. Mellor and two Luddites were found guilty and hanged for the crime.[13]

As the divide between the producers of goods and the owners of the means of producing those goods widened, everyday living conditions remained poor. It wasn't until 1880 that factory owners to members of the public. The luxury of enjoying the spoils of industrialisation was a luxury reserved for a wealthy minority whose pleasure and leisure was being generated by the majority who were finding themselves with little choice but to work long hours in the overcrowded and disease ridden proto-cities.

---

[13] K. Binfield, *Writings of the Luddites* (Baltimore; Maryland: The John Hopkins University Press, 2004), 200.

Culture was clearly being divided in two main groups: those who were in control of the emerging industrial environment and those who were being controlled by it. An example of this is many instances of many mill owners in industrial towns donating a town clock to the community. If time was money, the visibility of a town clock ensured that the watch-less workers would know when it was time to return to the factories. Life was no longer simply governed by the seasons but by the demands of industry, thus the matter of social organization was crucial in ensuring the viability of a burgeoning industrial society.

People are still governed by machinery, by clocks. If you watch morning television, you might also be accustomed to seeing a digital clock counting the minutes in the bottom left or right hand corners of your screen. But then, when the advertisement break arrives, the clock disappears. We are reminded to get a move on by the morning program, but drawn back into forgetting by the latest cook book or exercise machine.

The idea that industrial culture brought had its benefits *and* disadvantages was part of everyday cultural discussion by the twentieth century. With Colin Jones' description of Paris' "incomparable museums and galleries which have acted since the nineteenth century as a repository of western artistic culture," we can look to this part of the world when considering how this modern conundrum has been creatively negotiated.[14]

From the beginning of the French revolution (1789) up to and including the Paris renovations brought about by Haussmann in the 1860s, there was a change in the cultural ideals of the French people. Haussmann undertook what, for many decades, would remain the largest transformation of a city in the world. The Paris of the mid nineteenth century was an unsanitary, dangerous and congested city. The years between 1800 and 1850 had seen the population double to more than 1 million inhabitants, with two thirds of those individuals living below the poverty line.

Within the space of only 25 years, Paris had suffered 9 uprisings, giving Napoleon III enough time to see firsthand just how easy it was for the French people to erect barricades that kept him and his soldiers away from their narrow, undercover streets. On June 22, 1855, Napoleon appointed and urban planner by the name of Baron Haussmann to modernise Paris. It was Napoleon's aim to achieve better control over the flow of traffic, to encourage economic growth, and to make the city more resistant to revolution. Haussmann's project entailed stream rolling over the old Paris in order to make room for the creation of a new Paris. He tore up many of the old twisting buildings, removed apartment houses, and replaced them with wide, tree lined boulevards and expansive gardens. One of his first priorities was the purification and decontamination of the water used for washing, drinking, and cooking. Haussmann also created large avenues and grandiose monu-

---

[14] C. Jones, *Paris: Biography of a City* (London: Penguin Books, 2004), XVIII.

ments. New cafes were constructed with terraces spilling out onto the pavements along which 'anyone who was anyone' in Paris could casually wander by.

Another part of this modernisation of Paris was the construction of new apartments which were far too expensive for the working class and, this, led to the heart of Paris becoming mostly bourgeois and, in turn, unaffordable for the working class population—residents who were slowly being pushed out into the belt of districts surrounding the city limits.

Haussmann played a key role in transforming Paris into a home and playground for the newly empowered bourgeoisie. Its theatres, restaurants, monuments, streets, and apartments characterised the new urban spectacle. Modern technologies were novel conveniences with the rising bourgeoisie could enjoy and which a majority of the population could not. These new spaces would be much easier to control by military forces if, and when, a disgruntled public challenged leadership power. Not only this, despite an imbalance in economic privileges, or maybe even in light of it, the layout of Haussmann's city renovation encouraged the bourgeoisie to flaunt their new wealth. It truly had become a city of the spectacle.

This new social space, complete with *flâneur aesthetic,* was depicted in many artworks from the time. A prime example is Gustave Caillebotte's painting *Paris Street; Rainy Day* (1877). The painting is of an intersection near the Gare Saint-Lazare, which is a railroad station in the north of Paris, and is one of the most recognisable depiction of late 19th century urban life. Caillebotte was born into an upper-class family, made wealthy at least in part by the military textiles business that his father had inherited. The young and curious Gustav began to draw and paint around the age of 12, at about the same time that his father purchased a large property alongside the Yerres River, nearly 20 kilometers south east of Paris.

The utilisation of the countryside by Parisians is discussed in detail by historian T. J. Clark. Examining the 19th century origins of the practice of painting modern life, Clark argues that "the environs of Paris from the 1860s on were recognized to be a special territory in which some aspects of modernity might be detected, at least by those who could stomach the company of the petite bourgeoisie."[15] He notes that the imagery of landscape painting came to be intimately shaped by bourgeois fancies. Artists filled their canvasses with Parisians sitting on the lawn, boating, nevertheless still sitting amongst the signs of emerging industry; consider Claude Monet's *Le Train dans la campagne* (c. 1870), Berthe Morisot's *Les Blanchisseuses, plaine de Gennevilliers* (1875), Claude Monet's *Une Baignade á Asnières* (1883-84), or Eduoard Manet's *Argenteuil - Les Canotiers* (1874).

---

[15] T. J. Clark, *The Painting of Modern Life: Paris in the Art of Manet and His Followers* (Princeton: Princeton University Press, 1984), 147.

In each, modernity provides a dominant backdrop to everyday life, to work as well as to leisure. "The lines laid down since 1850 ... had quite abruptly made the countryside available to Paris, as part of a weekend or even a work day."[16] The rise of the petit-bourgeosie changed the landscape with its leisurely collective presence. The impressionistic manner suited this era of rapid growth well; traditional paradigms for composition were being dispensed with and the light seeking quickness of the brush stroke, in its rapid execution, meant for the documentation of passing moments. The subject matter moved also; "the transition from the old imaginative artist and dreamer to the energetic modern worker" was to be found in Impressionism."[17]

The summers spent along the Yerres River gave Gustav the opportunity to develop his observation skills; the carefree pastime activities of a bourgeoisie enjoying the spoils of a privileged modern life who had left the city centre in droves by rail to lose themselves, if only for a short time, in the idyllic country atmosphere. The city centre, the height of mechanical production and reproduction, the source of many fine and shiny new incomes, was also the context of an exploding population, poor working conditions, and the very real but little understood threat of environmental pollution from factories.

Born and raised in Paris, Gustav Caillebotte would have been well aware of the changes taking place in his historical and cultured city (as well as an accomplished artist, he was also a qualified lawyer and an engineer. His painting only became a serious pursuit after his return from the Franco-Prussian war, which ended in 1871). Losing both his parents before 1880 (his father died in 1874 and his mother in 1878) Caillebotte was in possession of significant financial wealth that gave him the means by which to work on his painterly impressions.

When not entertaining himself with hobbies such as stamp collecting, yacht building, orchid horticulture, or other of his interests, Caillebotte painted many scenes of everyday life. Looking at *Paris Street; Rainy Day*, Caillebotte's modern aesthetic is evident. As art historian Richard Brettel says:

> In *Paris Street; Rainy Day*, life-sized figures walk toward us on the sidewalk of the rue de Turin just before it crosses the rue de Moscou. This complex intersection, part of the new city plan of Paris designed by Baron Georges Haussmann, was located just minutes from the Saint-Lazare train station and the cast-iron Place de l'Europe, from which one could view the trains rushing back and forth from the countryside. Caillebotte

---

[16] T. J. Clark, *The Painting of Modern Life: Paris in the Art of Manet and His Followers* (Princeton: Princeton University Press, 1984), 149.

[17] S. Mallarmé, cited in M. Teich and R. Porter, *Fin de Siècle and its Legacy* (Cambridge: Cambridge University Press, 1991), 147.

himself owned property in this neighborhood, and Edouard Manet's studio was less than a five-minute walk from this intersection.[18]

The war, the invention of steel allowing travel across long distances that had never been experienced by the public before, Hausmann's resigning of the Parisian streets, the industrialisation of civilised life that was becoming ever increasingly manifest as a society of the spectacle, made way for new forms of social engagement, but by doing so they also made room for new cultural critiques. These changes in the map of Paris, combined with the social and economic changes that industrialisation also caused, led a certain kind of individual to immerse him or herself in the metropolis—in Walter Benjamin's words, "botanizing on the asphalt."[19]

Thus, we may now revisit the early modern comment known as the *flâneur*. In view of feeling increasingly disconnected from the natural world, in view of becoming increasingly disciplined by the demands of the modern world, the Baudelaire's botanist could challenge, even show contempt for, these cultural circumstances. This ideological gesture could be turned into a practice, if only for a single afternoon, by the *flâneur* doing perhaps precisely what they were not supposed to be doing; they could take what was constructed as a context of mechanisation and machine-like productivity, and use this city as a means to achieving an alternative outcome.

Industrial culture tends to be suspicious of activities that do not directly lead to, or relate to, financial reward. It's an attitude embedded in our abstract thinking—in our metaphorical language. When the notion that 'time is money' forms a framework for how we think about the world, blatantly flying in the face of this 'common-sense' offered a way for the *flâneur* to enjoy a moment or two of resistance to a society. Such idleness was a response to the conceivably dehumanising currents of industrialisation that has also been adopted with relative enthusiasm in the not too distant past. During the second half of the twentieth century, the notion of the *flâneur* was given considerable attention by the various members of the Lettrist International (LI) and, later, the Situationist International (SI). These groups of revolutionary artists and theorists, which operated in Paris during the 1950s and 1960s (with SI reaching its peak with the riots of May '68), adopted the style and attitude of the *flâneur*, using it as a stance with which to re-enter the urban setting and, in this sense, navigate the architecture of capitalism. With the Situationist International evolving out of the Lettrist International, both groups were interested in examining how the built environment impacts on how individuals think, act, and feel. Perhaps the repetitive shapes of the skyscrapers or their domi-

[18] R. Brettell, *French Impressionists* (Chicago; The Art Institute of Chicago and New York: Harry N. Abrams, 1987), 45.
[19] W. Benjamin, cited in R. Koshar, *Histories of Leisure* (Oxford: Berg Publishers, 2002), 65.

nation of the horizon line were enough to lead people to feel increasingly separated from nature and, therefore, alienated in their own built environment. Perhaps the fast pace of modern life caused a perpetual sense of urgency that undermined individual attempts to take time out to appreciate the wonder of the moment. Motivated by the next big sale or the fear of losing some income, it can often be difficult to find the time to stop and have a look around. In this sense, going on a seemingly aimless stroll can be understood as a peaceful protest against all aspects of modern culture that has an aptitude for reducing human interaction to a monetary value.

Of course, there are many possibilities for interaction with a city space; the examples offered here are merely drops in a much deeper ocean. Nevertheless, what remained important for figures such as Guy Debord (a key member of LI and SI) was the task of studying, wherever possible, the various impacts that the modern world had upon them in terms of how they though, how they felt about themselves and about others, how they behaved in the course of everyday life. The name given to this area of study was psychogeography and, in their attempt to conduct psychogeographic research, members of these groups would assume the character of the flâneur and wander aimlessly around Paris.

They would indulge the freedom to follow whatever random events or objects happened to catch their eye so that, as a flâneur, a walk could begin or end anywhere at all. Their aim was to create situations that invariably challenged or offended bourgeois sensibilities, expectations, values, assumptions. What would unfold along the way was forever a mystery until the very moment that it happened. It was by each individual allowing him or herself to become lost in the built environment and by treating it as a space of play that the Lettrists and the Situationists paid attention to, and reflected critically upon, their experiences of modernity. There is some indication of this in a short piece called "Next Planet" that was published in a Lettrist magazine (Potlatch) and written by A. F. Conord; it offers insight into the kind of thinking that was being developed.

> Although their buildings are gone, a few disturbing pyramids resist the efforts of travel agencies to render them banal. The Postman Chaval, working every night of his life, built his inexplicable "Ideal Palace" in his garden in Hauterive, the first example of an architecture of disorientation. In this baroque palace, which *detourns* the forms of certain exotic monuments and stone vegetation, one can only lose oneself. Its influences will soon be immense. The life-work of a single, incredibly obstinate man cannot, of course, be appreciated in itself, as most visitors think, but instead reveals a strange and unarticulated passion. Struck by the same desire, Louis II of Bavaria built, at great expense in the mountain forests of his kingdom, hallucinatory artificial castles, before disappearing in shallow waters. The underground river that was his theatre

and the plaster statues in his gardens intimate a project as *absolute* as it was tragic. There are plenty of reasons for riffraff psychiatrists to intervene and for paternalistic intellectuals to launch a new-found "naïf" with page upon page of nonsense. But the naïvety is theirs. Ferdinand Cheval and Louis of Bavaria built the castles that they wanted to build, in accordance with a new human condition.[20]

Two curious individuals are featured in Conord's writing; Ferdinand Cheval and Louis II of Bavaria. Ferdinand Cheval was a French postman who began building Le Palais Idéal (the "Ideal Palace") in 1879 at the age of 43. Apparently motivated by the shape of stone that he had tripped over, he began collecting stones during his mail run, carrying them in his pockets before upgrading to a basket and then a wheel barrow. Cheval would return home and, over a period of 33 years, used the stones he had found to build a castle which incorporated a range of architectural styles. He had spent the last 8 years building a mausoleum for himself in the Hauterive cemetery and was buried there after his death in 1924. Since 1969, Cheval's Ideal Palace has been protected as an official cultural landmark. The other person who Conord refers to is Louis II of Bavaria. Duke Louis II (Ludwig Friedrich Wilhelm II) lived from the 25th of August, 1845, to the 13th of June, 1886, and is famous for commissioning the remarkably ornate Neuschwanstein Castle in Bavaria's south west. Recognisable as the inspiration for the castle in the Walt Disney Pictures logo, it would serve as his retreat, the source of tremendous debt, and the site of his mysterious death (declared a suicide by drowning).

Among other things, Conord's reference to these two men signifies his appreciation of the affinity between human imagination and the built environment. Both figures create their own castles; private domains that stand as an attempt to say something unique about the individual. Walking around their creations, Cheval and Louis could become lost in their own fantasy worlds; each providing a form of escape from external influences and potential interferences.

## Theory of the Dérive

Conord's writing draws our attention to capacity for architecture to reflect how a person thinks and feels; this information helps us to further build our understanding of the historical context of woman's strolling pre-occupation in the *Lose Yourself in Melbourne* advertisement. We can also detect that Cheval and Louis had certain ideas that they wanted to see translated into a material existence and they made steps to ensure that that happened. The process of constructing these unusual spaces had the capacity to both confirm or chal-

---

[20] A. F. Conord, "Next Planet", in *Potlatch*, Paris, July 19, 1954, translated into English by Gerardo Denís, Situationist International Online.

lenge those preliminary expectations and notions; architecture plays an extensive role in human behaviour. As Chtcheglov's observed, "Architecture is the simplest means of articulating time and space, of modulating reality, of engendering dreams."[21]

Haussmann's renovation of Paris was perhaps a more inhuman way of disciplining how and where people moved around the city space. The new architectural forms lining the grand boulevards symbolised personal wealth and high social status. The long street fronts were prime real estate for businesses that desired to capitalise on the allure that could be generated by extravagant window displays (by way of subsequent retail sales). This is a phenomena that the French novelist Émile Zola demonstrated in great detail in his book entitled *Au Bonheur des Dames* which is based on the inner and outer workings of what is arguably the first department store; Le Bon Marché.[22]

Fast forward to the post WW2 era, and Paris is a buzzing consumerist centre; a highly organised society of the spectacle within which everyday life can quite easily be reduced to the level of one long shopping spree. Thus, as a way of breaking out of this capitalist/consumerist framework, to the budding *flâneur*, the prospect of pointless meander must have seemed like quite the medicine. It meant an opportunity to deny the now seemingly 'natural' function of the city space as the seriously motivated provider and distributor of mass produced goods by way of a relatively playful and random reencounter.

This kind of activity was precisely what interested the members of both the Lettrist International and the Situationist International as they sought to invigorate the historical proven revolutionary spirit of a people that was seemingly being swallowed up by the general entrenchment of day to day life in the abundant digestive juices of commodity fetishism. Each aimless walk was referred to as a *dérive*; a French verb that means 'to drift.' Guy Debord's explanation of the *dérive* addresses how it entails the abandonment of goal orientated movements through the modern built environment.

> One of the basic situationist practices is the *dérive*, a technique of rapid passage through varied ambiences. Dérives involve playful-constructive behavior and awareness of psychogeographical effects, and are thus quite different from the classic notions of journey or stroll. In a dérive one or more persons during a certain period drop their relations, their work and leisure activities, and all their other usual motives for movement and action, and let themselves be drawn by the attractions of the terrain and the encounters they find there. Chance is a less important factor in this activity than one might think: from a dérive point of view cities have psycho-

---

[21] I. Chtcheglov, "Formulary for a New Urbanism" (1953), cited in Ken Knabb, ed. *Situationist International Anthology* (Berkley: Bureau of Public Secrets, 2002), 50.

[22] E. Zola, *The Lady's Paradise* (1883), Oxford World Classics (Oxford: Oxford University Press, 2008).

geographical contours, with constant currents, fixed points and vortexes that strongly discourage entry into or exit from certain zones.[23]

What is being suggested is that, when we enter a built environment such as a city we tend to navigate it with an idea about where we want to go, and whom we want to meet, firmly in mind. Perhaps we will visit the city with the intention of shopping at a preferred fashion outlet, or because we need to get to our place of work at a particular time. Maybe we would like to see a movie that is screening at a city cinema, before which we might go somewhere in order to meet a friend or loved one. It doesn't matter what the motivation is. What matters is that in each instance a kind of motivation nevertheless exists. It is that expectation in mind that informs which route we will take and, in this way, what we will see along the way to achieving it. To add to this idea, the built environment is always signposted in a way that impacts directly upon the route that we will choose. Looking around the city, it is not long before we notice signs such as "No Entry", "No Exit", "Detour", and "Keep Out". As well as contributing to the visual pollution that countless advertisements create, these signs encourage us to move around in a prescribed fashion.

The Situationists were wary of the way that peopled tended to follow particular routes in, around, and out of the built environments. Their attitude was not so much a response to the acts themselves, as if they were overtly malicious or harmful, but to their underlying conditions. The increasing familiarity of day to day activities led people to become desensitised to them and, in this way, meant that these activities were often taken for granted. For the Situationists, what people were overlooking, through the relative invisibility of habitual experience, was the way that capitalist power centres steered us around the place for their own benefit (such as their perseverance and gradual expansion) rather than for the mental health and well-being of their inhabitants; these being the mass population upon whom capitalism ultimately relied. While this familiarity afforded day to day life a certain sense of predictability and stability, its anaesthetic function worried the Lettrists and the Situationists. Thus, much like the nineteenth century pseudo-aristocratic flâneurs, the *dérive* was one strategy of urban interaction that both organisations used in an attempt to counteract the clockwork monotony of everyday experience in an industrial society.

In Debord's definition of the dérive we find a strategy of defamiliarisation, made manifest through urban wandering, in which the individual is mobilised to see the city space in a different way and, in so doing, invigorates their capacity to examine how the built environment, as one of a variety of

---

[23] G. Debord, "Theory of the Dérive" (1958), reprinted in Ken Knabb, ed. *Situationist International Anthology* (Berkley: Bureau of Public Secrets, 1995), 50.

late modern cultural circumstances, can "influence, shape and structure [their] everyday activities."[24]

The notion of the dérive is central to psychogeography. SI understood psychogeography as an opportunity to examine how a built environment influenced how people felt, thought, and behaved. This, in itself, constitutes an appeal to defamiliarisation by identifying attempts to elevate human activity beyond the monotony of everyday routines and meanings, towards the realisation of novel experience. To the extent that psychogeography, as a term, encompasses a wide range of inventive approaches to the exploration of the built environment, psychogeography motivates creative critical thinking.

In an industrial culture it is the built environment, rather than nature, that becomes the habitat of individuals, and which play a role in our identities. The built environment becomes a stage on, and throughout, which our identities are played out, as it were. They contribute a material context to the broader set of cultural circumstances that impacts upon personal dispositions.

Where dissected (constructed, divided, compartmentalised) space becomes the site of creative negotiation, I am reminded of D. W. Winnicott's notion of 'potential space'—a theory explaining the play space of the infant. Winnicott postulates 'potential space' as the place in which the imagination commences development. It is a space in which, by means of transitional object use, the infant breaks down an illusion of oneness with the mother and gains irreversible entry into the symbolic order. Thus, for Winnicott, potential space becomes "the source of all subsequent creative and cultural activity and experience."[25] This insight leads to his argument that, in the absence of an opportunity to generate potential space, the opportunity for the infant to have "cultural experience", in particular cultural creativity, is at stake.[26] "[N]o link with the cultural inheritance" means that there will be "no contribution to the cultural pool."[27]

Perhaps the child plays by using a stick as a sword and by pretending that an old hollow tree stump is an impenetrable fortress. While play space elevates human activity from the monotony of everyday meanings, the playfulness of potential space is nevertheless impacted upon by the composition of a material reality, where things exist in their spatial relationship to each other. The instability of play space, similar to that of the dérive, lies in Debord's acknowledgement that at "any moment, 'ordinary life' may prevail

---

[24] D. Inglis, *Culture and Everyday Life*, The New Sociology, series (London and New York: Routledge, 2005), 11.

[25] D. Pigrum, *Transitional Practices and Place: "Potential Space," the place of the classroom and the "semiotic chora" in secondary arts education.* Paper presented at the Philosophy of Education Society of Great Britain, Oxford University New College, (2004b, April), 1.

[26] D. W. Winnicott, *Playing and Reality* (London and New York: Routledge, 2005), 101.

[27] Ibid.

once again. The geographical limitation of play is even more striking than its temporal limitation. Every game takes place within the boundaries of its own spatial domain."[28] Here, psychogeography appeals to a nomadic aesthetic, via the instability of space and the unmeasured oscillation between urban mobility and urban monotony. However, as we can plainly see, nomadicism is much more than what is conceived, in the gypsy stereotype, of the aimless loner, dislodged from civilised society. Romany migration has had its fair share of political motivation.

Braidotti supports the model of the nomad as a "style of thinking", "a creative sort of becoming" and "critical consciousness."[29] Where this style of thinking feeds creative praxis, through its translation into everyday activity, the dérive presents as a playful, and critical, negotiation of the interfaces of personal dispositions and the broader set of cultural circumstances that frame them, ideologically and materially. Taken in this way, the dérive offers a historical frame of reference for the enrichment of an interdisciplinary creative praxis.

**Alternative Solutions**

We may now relate this historical information to *Lose Yourself in Melbourne*'s woman with the red wool with more detail. The first step to this is accepting that, while her activity has a distinct air of indulgence, it also has a practical and sustainable dimension that deserves attention. We can use this historical information to help us see the depth of what is immediately given—the contents of the television screen—in order to develop another perspective of that content. In as much as history helps us make sense of what we are experiencing now, the activity of applying (to) history sets us at odds, not necessarily in opposition to, that experience.

Rather than be disconnected from everything outside of the television set, the *Lose Yourself in Melbourne* advertisement reflects on a rich historical landscape. By reflecting on it also, a viewer can review the advertisement in a more informed way, with more tools at hand. In order for me to make use of this reflection, I asked myself, "How does this cultural meaning, this ideal and modern mythology, relate to me. How does this historical information, these past examples, relate to my live now, living in Perth, Western Australia. It meant considering the campaign in more than just ideological terms. I started to think about the flâneur, and the dérive in terms of how I could put them to work; in terms of how I could make those ideas actionable in my own life, as a way of enriching my material and practical reality. I was looking for something new, something exciting, unpredictable, perhaps a social setting of

---

[28] G. Debord, "On the Passage of a Few Persons Through a Rather Brief Unity of Time" (1959), in *Complete Cinematic Works* (California: AK Press, 2003).
[29] R. Braidotti, *Nomadic Subjects: Embodiment and Sexual Difference in Contemporary Feminist Theory* (New York: Columbia University Press, 1994), 1; 6; 5.

which I was not familiar, which was not consumed by institutional monotony. I desired a life in which I didn't just drive the same old roads to and from work and the shops and the few other places that I frequented; a life that hadn't sunken slowly into banality. Reflecting on the historical contexts of this advertisement, of the flâneur and the dérive, played a central role in my decision to leave Perth for a new life in Melbourne.

What might an activity such as the dérive have to offer the individual today? Whatever the answer may be, the anonymous woman's advertisement-dérive doesn't seem to entail quite the critical register via which the Lettrists or Situationists challenged a bourgeois status quo. While her modern Melbourne manifestation cannot avoid playing into a western European tradition (one that interrogates capitalist culture in search of a conceivably more authentic existence), her 'quest' is represented more as a form of passive recreation than as a political comment made manifest in human action.

The *Lose Yourself in Melbourne* advertisement seems to have domesticated flâneur, and the dérive for the viewing pleasure of a potential tourist or proud Victorian; both plausible options given that it remains unclear as to whether the woman is learning her way around Melbourne for the very first time or whether she is enjoying a rare opportunity (a day off work, perhaps) to simply stroll after having lived in the area for some time. The fact that I first saw the advertisement not in Melbourne but on the opposite side of Australia suggests that it was Victoria's official appeal to outsiders to spend their holiday(s) in Melbourne (hence the observation that nearly everyone else is still working). In any case, its use value is not limited to a strictly external audience.

Reminiscent of the Situationists and the nineteenth century pseudo-aristocratic time wasters, the woman with the red wool also walks randomly around a built and capitalistic environment. However passively, she is also acting in a way that is contrary to the customary demands of the central business district; mainly by quietly and creatively exploring the space and allowing herself to be led by whatever comes her way. Whether it is the interesting façade of some Victorian architecture, the friendly face of a passing stranger, or a trace of someone else meandering which has crossed her path along the way, Melbourne is posited as having a lot to offer. Inner city laneways, arcades, boutiques, secret alleys are all there waiting to be found—some by accident, others on purpose.

This outline of early modernity has drawn attention to just what Hussey had in mind when he spoke of modernity's "utilitarian demands of work and industry"—demands that he posited as the preconditions for the 19th century Parisian *flâneur* and his elegantly idle practice, the dérive. By taking the historical nuances of the *flâneur* and the *dérive* into account, we can notice how the *Lose Yourself in Melbourne* advertisement presents us with a user friendly version of what can essentially be a kind of critical cultural statement or, as some might phrase it, a context of resistance to the power hierarchies that govern the inner workings of late modern life. In a culture where productivity is a virtue, the *flâneur* (as a notion) and the *dérive* (as its practice) make for a statement of active cultural engagement and, in that sense, of some degree of personal empowerment. If self-empowerment is to be taken as mere indulgence, then so be it. But I would strongly disagree. Even in a highly organised, technologically and financially driven society, it is perhaps more important than ever for individuals to find their own way in, to engage actively within, the built environment. In a compartmentalised culture, one that distances us from certain vital skills, our ability to be active can be demonstrated as we create the space to tread beyond the pathways and ideological maps that are prescribed and provided for. I am referring to such institutions as governments, churches, and retail markets—socialising agencies that have a lot to do with how we act, what we do, and who we want to be.

Exploring the importance of the dériving flâneur for today's culture starts by understanding that we are still living in an industrial society, that the questionable modern conditions have not disappeared, simply become like second nature so that we forget how odd they really are. In this forgetting, we might feel less of an urge to challenge them, and now that we are very much emotionally, intellectually, and practically invested in them.

In order to support this claim, we need only look at how everyday life is filled with events that were once peculiar practices but which, over time, have gradually transformed into habitual behaviours. Peering into the context of what is often the necessary and life-saving habituation of daily life, this process will give colour to the way that the dérive stands at odds with the mechanics of modern life (despite, and because of, it being intimately motivated by these). If the *Lose Yourself in Melbourne* advertisement gives us is a 90 second rendition of a modernist fantasy world, then moving on to consider how the theory of the 'dérive' relates to 21st century daily life does two things: it reminds us that the dérive has a vital and constructive cultural function; and offers evidence as to why the dérive seems so fantastical in the first place.

# CHAPTER 3
# A CONTEMPORARY CONTEXT

## Experiencing Late Modernity

To this point we have seen that, though it occupies a mere 90 seconds of tele-visual broadcast time, the *Lose Yourself in Melbourne* advertisement relates to a long history of thinking, feeling, and behaving in the city—the built environment. We have found that this history is one in which people such as Charles Baudelaire, Guy Debord and his Situationist associates, painters such as Gustave Caillebotte and Berthe Morisot—creative people who have sought to capitalise on their sensitivity to the world around them and who have, in this sense, have tried to make sense of the modernist context. These figures are among many other who have actively observed, and made critical comment on, their experiences of an industrialising culture.

The fact that the *Lose Yourself in Melbourne* advertisement makes sense to a television viewer in the 21st century, the fact that the historical details to which I have made reference can be used to enrich an interpretation of what the woman with the red wool is doing, is unsurprising. For the minority West is still intimately engaged in an industrialised culture. Our present cultural experience can be described as the institutionalised version of the disruptions to tradition, families, skills, and modes of human communication that were that characterised early modernity.

This claim can be demonstrated with ease. For, while routine practices, such as trading money for clothing, food, and medicines, brushing our teeth or putting out the rubbish bin, might not seem like the topics of exciting conversation, nevertheless they are integral to our understanding of who we are and of the cultural circumstances in which we operate on a daily basis. We do not live isolated lives, simply evolving personal narratives of which we are placed forever at the centre. Rather, we are also members of one or more social formations, living in relation to particular material, ideological, political, geographical, and technological contexts. Thus, our routine practices communicate something about our personal dispositions as well as these greater cultural factors. As Georg Simmel states, "'even the most banal externalities of life' are expressions of the wider social and cultural order."[30] It makes sense that many of the routines practices experienced by someone living in an industrial Western culture, will be shared by others who live under similar circumstances. It is in this sense that an increased awareness of these circumstances, therefore, translates into an increased awareness of who we are as individuals.

---

[30] George Simmel, cited in D. Inglis, *Culture and Everyday Life*, The New Sociology, series (London and New York: Routledge, 2005), 3.

What is this wider social and culture order of which Simmel speaks? What are some of the features that set it apart from other social and cultural orders? In short, in what ways can our culture be identified as such? First of all, we are living in a set of social and cultural circumstances known as late modernity. Unlike throughout the early stages of modernity, the historical period and cultural condition that began with the industrial revolution in 18th century Britain, late modernity is, what British Sociologist Anthony Giddens refers to as, a "radicalized" modernity, a "post-traditional order, in which the question, 'How shall I live?' has to be answered in day-to-day decisions about how to behave, what to wear and what to eat—and many more things—as well as interpreted within the temporal unfolding of self-identity."[31] This multiplication of the numbers of choices that a person must make, choices that were not available in the rural societies prior to the industrial revolution, means that late modernity is the point at which traditional culture has been entirely displaced by the processes of industrialization—in which the latter have become normative.

The displacement of culture from nature can be detected in the annoyance that we feel when we find that the local shop has run out of our favourite chocolate biscuits, or cut of meat. This annoyance exposes something far more fundamental than the emotionally charged disdain of the shop keeper's incompetence. It shows that we have become critically unskilled. We are quite well versed in choosing between rib-eye, sirloin, t-bone or pot roast. We are up to date on per kilogram prices and may feel like a winner when we get a good deal. But most of us will never have a clue as to what it might be like to work on a cattle station from which it may have come, such as the South Australian Anna Creek Cattle Station, running between 20,000 and 60,000 head of cattle? The processes of industrialisation have facilitated a dramatic intrusion of Western life into the global sphere. Yet, reaching into the refrigerated meat section at our local super market, it would probably never have occurred to us to consider how, covering an area of over 34,000 square kilometres (26,000,000 acres) Anna Creek Cattle Station is bigger than Israel. Many of us choose to consume meat but neglect any idea of what our products have been through prior to us taking their packages out of the general store.

## Commodity Culture

A commodity is any object or service that can be bought or sold and industrialised cultures are commodity cultures. Our culture is organised through the buying and selling of commodity forms and these impact directly on how we communicate with each other. For example, in order to communicate to someone that we love them, we might see fit to buy him or her a valentine's

---

[31] A. Giddens, *Modernity and Self-Identity: Self and Society in the Late Modern Age* (Stanford, California: Stanford University Press, 1991), 14.

card or flowers or chocolates. An expression of great love might entail the generous individual buying all of these things for a loved one. Beyond the limits of Valentine's Day, it is possible that we experience the desire to impress or pander someone that we care about and decide to demonstrate this desire by treating the lucky individual out to for a meal at a fancy restaurant, perhaps following a viewing of a popular film. These expressions of affection are less a matter of necessity than they are a matter of convention as it exists in a particular culture and in view of a particular set of material circumstances. Not everybody wants or needs the same things. Not everybody will enjoy being taken out to see a movie on the big screen. This is a desire that has developed over time and which is still not practiced by everybody. For example, how might a poor couple in remote Indian villages such as Peharsar, Garah or Khuri celebrate love for one another?

Does not having access to the above mentioned commodities mean that their love, at least the expressions of love and affection, are somehow not as strong; or lacking? Of course not. Clearly, it would be preposterous for such a claim to be made. It is not difficult to demonstrate that the buying of dinners, flowers, chocolates, and movie tickets are not necessary for expressing love. Therefore, what is it that drives the desire for these kinds of things? Why do people, in full view of the arbitrary nature of these, continue to invest in them? The answer to one of these questions goes a long way to setting up the conditions for an answer to the other. What drives these false needs is advertising and the cogs of consumer culture that promote such means as important. Their meaning is constructed and circulated via the mass media. As the disposers of income, individuals needn't agree with the meanings that they are faced with but, like any cleverly structured education, the repetition of this meaning leads to its familiarity and, in turn, its institutionalisation as a common-sense aspect of day to day thinking. This point of view helps to answer the second question because what it suggests is that, by creating a wall of meaning, through the convenience of a sophisticated mass media and through the ongoing affirmation of that meaning, alternative possibilities are taken away from the spotlight. The more that a person's attention is directed to one option, the less time and effort he or she has left to consider the meanings of other possibilities.

One result of this is conflict between those who accept the dominant view and those who do not, particularly when the contrasting positions constitute both sides of an intimate relationship. So that, one person in the couple who does not value the use of commodities for the expression of affection runs the risk of disappointing the partner who does believe in this value. Will the other person remain disappointed or will the initial individual be driven by guilt and emotional conflict to go against his or her beliefs and buy some goodies anyway? Whatever the circumstance, whatever the result, it is up to the couple to communicate what they need and expect. The point that I am trying to make here is that examples exist that expose the extent to which commodity culture, as a material reality, penetrates our emotions, our values, ideas, and beliefs and, as a direct result of this, play a central role in how we form and develop our interpersonal relationships.

As an alternative example, consider how we might enjoy a good chat with our local mechanic, even if that person is someone who we would never socialize with normally. We might tell the hairdresser our life's story and, perhaps if we keep going back to this same hairdresser, we might find ourselves developing a deeper rapport with him or her. These interactions, while bringing a sense of contentment and the comfort of familiarity to our days, they are human relationships based solely on the provision and consumption of services. They are acts of interpersonal communication embedded in financial transactions. In a late modern age, day to day social behaviour is rife with such interaction. They constitute the foundations of a late modern cultural coherence and what is being articulated here are the trappings of this as a form of social cement.

Not only material objects and skills, but ideas and concepts can be treated as commodities. Consider the cost of a good education and how much money we might be prepared to pay in order to access knowledge. On this point, every day ideas and concepts are bought and sold in the mass media, delivered to a mass consumer audience in the form of magazines and newspapers, television, the radio, the internet. The mass media buy and sell ideas to the extent that we give them our money in exchange for access to their content, acknowledging that it is entirely possible for us to purchase several different media products and receive much the same snippets of information in each. Looking through a paper such as the West Australian, we will notice many of the articles containing the word Reuters at the end. Reuters is a current affairs information company with a broad scope, supplying text, graphics, still and moving imagery to media outlets around the world. A newspaper will often purchase world news from Reuters, repackage that information in the house format, usually employing tabloid techniques, and then sell the resulting products on to us.

Inhabitants of a late Modern age get to live, what I call, 'the illusion of little effort taken', having by-passed all of the work, the labour, that goes into preparing a whole range of commodities and, at the drop of a hat, enjoy the freedom of being able to proceed straight to the cash register to confirm their full possession. Take, for example, the way that hunting and gathering or growing a crop in a field has been replaced by five minutes car rides to the local supermarket for the buying of pre-grown, pre-processed, pre-packaged and priced goods off of their designated shelf. This kind of short-cutting has become so common place that it is taken as a right, that is, our entitlement. But, not only is consumption disconnected from production, the rule of 'cause and effect' is upheld in the way that a, not exclusively but extensively, de-traditionalised West has created an industrial culture that demands instant gratification and instant novelty.

In order to address the first of these two demands, consider how easy it is to take part in 'retail therapy'. If we are feeling sad or down on ourselves or if the day has not gone quite how we would have liked, perhaps we will take time out to visit a nearby shopping mall. Upon arrival, and now visually stimulated by the bright lights and shiny new products, we can find ourselves distracted enough to forget all of our worries and go on, if only for a limited time, as though everything is okay. It might only be once we get back to our home or place of work, and once excitement has worn off, that we come face to face with the reality of having spent far too much money on things that we might not have even needed or, at the very least, had not been a part of our reason for going.

Perhaps the items and interactions that I have drawn attention to are among those purchased by an unsatisfied consumer, in search for mental calm or emotional reassurance. In a study entitled "Misery is not Miserly", published in the June 2008 edition of *Psychological Science* by a team of researchers from Carnegie Mellon, Harvard University, Stanford University, and the University of Pittsburgh, it has been shown that heightened self-focus leads to an increased and direct correlation between spending and mood. The researchers recruited 33 people (13 females and 20 males) and showed them either a short film clip about "the death of a boy's mentor (from *The Champ*)" while the others watched "a video clip about the Great Barrier Reef (from a National Geographic television special)."[32] The participants were then given the opportunity to buy a common consumer item—a sporty insulated water bottle. The resulted indicated that those who had watched the sad film clip offered around 377% more for the bottle than those who watched the 'neutral' clip ($2.11 vs. 56c, respectively).[33]

With their theoretical roots planted in William James's (1890) Principles of Psychology, the team concluded that, because "the study used real commodities and real money, the results hold implications for everyday decisions" (Abstract). Add to this a report released by the Australia Institute, a public policy research centre, in March of 2005, which estimated the total wastage through careless and impulse buying, on food alone, to be a massive $5.3 billion each year, "comprising $2.9 billion in fresh food, $630 million of uneaten take-away food, $876 million of leftovers, $596 million of unfinished drinks and $241 million in frozen foods."[34] But how good do these buying

---

[32] C. Cryder et al., "Misery is Not Miserly: Sad and Self-Focussed Individuals Spend More", (Research Report) *Psychological Science: A Journal of the Association for Psychological Science*, Vol. 9 No. 6, Sage Journals Online, 2007 Accessed July 8, 2010, 526. http://www.psychologicalscience.org/journals/ps/19_6_inpress/Cryder .pdf
[33] Ibid., 527.
[34] Donald, Dasey, "How our Greed Costs Millions Every Year," May 8, 2005, Accessed Feb 11, 2010, *The Sydney Morning Herald*, http://www.smh.com.au/news/National/How-our-greed-costs-millions-every-year/2005/05/07/1115422849473.html

trends make us feel if we take into account that the combined figure equals the gross domestic product (GDP) of East Timor, Micronesia, the Marshall Islands, Greenland, Vanuatu, Samoa, and Tonga put together?[35] It begs the question of how much more 'disposable income' goes into impulse buying across the whole spectrum of commodity forms. But when around half of the world's population (approx 6.7 billion) are living in poverty, that is, for less than AUD$2, what is the true cost of our demand for happiness?

## Novelty Culture

Another demand that has been created by the processes of industrialisation, one which plays directly into the issue of consumerism, is the demand for novelty. When we are dazzled in the shopping mall, it is rarely by dishevelled front window displays of dusty books and broken furniture. Rather, it is what is new and exciting and fresh that always seem to succeed in catching our attention. While a resin model sporting the name plate "Jesus is my Coach", depicting a white clothed Jesus helping a small boy prepare to hit a baseball while another boy looks on, might be conceived to carry some religious significance, it is appealing primarily for its peculiarity. While a beer hat might keep you hydrated on a sunny day, its most immediate value is its novelty value, the fact that it is essentially impractical or, at least, is amusing enough for its impracticality to be accepted. What practical function is served by an inflatable green alien, a giant pencil, or a glow in the dark condom, other than to be used as a plaything or the focal point for polite conversation? Yet, Inglis gives a certain "cultural *exhaustion*" as the reason why what is new is not always most admired:

> What I mean here is that in the nineteenth century, and for most of the twentieth century, there was a shared sense among most sectors of society that new ways of doing things were always emerging and that there were always novel things to discover, if only one made the effort to find them (Lyotard, 1984). But in the last couple of decades of the twentieth century, a certain sense of fatigue had set in, especially among people working in 'creative' sectors of the economy, such as those working in the media, advertising and the arts.[36]

Inglis goes on to explain that this led to a shift in cultural perspective whereby the forms and styles, that filled the past, were now like pieces of a puzzle that could be played with for the purposes of simple reproduction or parody, for example. A culture that privileges a superabundance of novelty is not sustainable because, after a while, the very notion of the 'new' becomes

---

[35] *CIA World Fact Book*, 2008 figures.
[36] D. Inglis, *Culture and Everyday Life*, The New Sociology, series (London and New York: Routledge, 2005), 71.

'old.' Once it has become a normal, inevitable, natural part of day to day experience, it begins to lose its lustre.

This loss of value is what Inglis means when he says 'exhaustion.' Under such a circumstance, the future-directedness of modernity experiences a rupture and the past—history—enjoys a renewed cultural function. The dérive is an example of this much broader contemporary pertinence of historical notions and practices. The 'Lose Yourself' advertisement borrows from the past, reconceptualising it in the present to communicate a cultural message about the human condition as it is played out in a built environment. It shows the past at play in the present; the aimless stroll subverts the dominant modernist ideology of the progress fixated, and economically driven, central business district. It is postmodern in its reflection upon this space, in its playfulness, in the flâneur's idle, pseudo-aristocracy. The dérive is modern in its incredulity towards the modern machine—in its parody of the foundations of our privileged society.

## Standardisation

I am merely scratching the surface of the implications of the practices that we take for granted in a late Modern age. We could still go on to discuss how industrialisation has led to a globalised economy, the ideological implications of its highly developed mass media. But by making these critical comparisons, by working toward a conceivably more balanced perspective, it becomes possible for us to shunt ourselves out from a kind of sleep walking that we all slip into at one time or another. It helps to remind us that, while we may hold the ideological assumption that the devices of our everyday life are natural, normal, inevitable, perhaps even fair, quite clearly they are not. Nevertheless, the fact that such things may not occur to us means that, as individuals living in a late Modern age, we are directly affected by commodity culture? It is a point of view held famously by, the critical theorist Theodore Adorno.

Adorno was a member of the Frankfurt School that emerged at the University of Frankfurt am Main's Institute for Social Research in the early 1930s. The Frankfurt School was not a school in the most recognised sense of the word, but a group of social researchers, critical theorists and philosophers that also including such names as Jürgen Habermas, Max Horkheimer and Walter Benjamin. The Frankfurt School criticized Western industrialised society for bringing about alienation and domination, and so worked to establish the conditions for the individuals' liberation from the constraints of consumer culture and, in this way, from the spectres of false experience. The Frankfurt School has continued to have a significant impact on Social Science, despite the fact that it has been, at times, accused by critics of developing an elite critique of mass culture.[37]

Adorno theorised how the culture industries, these being the manufacturers of cultural artefacts and meanings, impacted upon everyday life and put forward the argument that all contemporary cultural life is dominated by the commodity form. Adorno was not hostile to "mass culture" or "popular culture" as such, but to the specific repressive form it assumed under the impact of the "culture industry." Adorno saw the culture industry using two approaches drawn from mainstream industrial production; 'standardisation' and 'pseudo-individuality'.

An industry that seeks financial viability at any level, must maintain operational, procedural and technical compatibility. In other words, establish organisational confidence that products can be made and distributed efficiently. If compact disc were available in ten different shapes and sizes, the number of people able to play music in their home sound systems would radically diminish. The profit margins of music distribution companies would go into rapid decline and an entire industry, as we know it today, would face almost certain extinction. There is a necessary logic behind the standardisation of goods but, it is a logic that must exist in the world directly alongside the demand for novelty. The apparent newness and uniqueness of an item is tarnished by the realisation that it is just one of countless identical items. In order to mask the over-riding 'sameness' of commodity culture, to hide the irony embedded in the fact that so many people use mass produced clothing and gadgetry to express their so-called individuality, the illusion of uniqueness and difference must be professed. Adorno and Horkheimer are united on this front.

> The sociological theory that the loss of the support of objectively established religion, the dissolution of the last remnants of pre-capitalism, together with the technological and social differentiation or specialisation, have led to cultural chaos is disproved every day; for culture now impresses the same stamp on everything. Films, radio and magazines make up a system which is uniform as a whole and in every part."[38]

---

[37] In his preface to Bottomore's revised edition of *The Frankfurt School and its Critics*, Hamilton explains describes the Frankfurt School critics as having been "led by their pessimism." Hamilton, himself, suggests how Horkheimer, Marcuse, and Adorno are "[p]erhaps best seen as 'radicals in despair.'" Tom, Bottomore, *The Frankfurt School and its Critics*, Key Sociologists Series, (UK: Routledge, 2002), 8.

[38] T. Adorno, & M. Horkheimer, *Dialectic of Enlightenment* (London: Verso, 1979), 120.

## Pseudo-individuality

Standardisation plays an important part in commodity culture, not least of all by keeping prices competitive in the marketplace. It works well for technical equipment and an array of objects, but we have already found that a commodity can be more than these. That is to say, is standardisation appropriate for ideas or concepts? Adorno and Horkheimer thought not, arguing that popular entertainment had been standardised to the point that cultural product was predictable and uncritical. Standardisation in the culture industries, he observed, leads to stereotyping and the categorisation of the individual.

> In the culture industry the individual is an illusion not merely because of the standardisation of the means of production. He is tolerated only so long as his complete identification with the generality is unquestioned. Pseudo-individuality is rife: from the standardized jazz improvisation to the exceptional film star whose hair curls over her eye to demonstrate her originality. What is individual is no more than the generality's power to stamp the accidental detail so firmly that it is accepted as such. The defiant reserve or elegant appearance of the individual on show is mass produced like Yale locks, whose only difference can be measured in fractions of millimeters. The peculiarity of the self is a monopoly commodity determined by society; it is the…finger prints on identity cards which are otherwise the same, and into which the lives and faces of every single person are transformed by the power of the generality.[39]

The idea that the culture industry generates, and thrives off of, standardisation, can be seen quite clearly when we turn our attentions to such examples from genres ranging from popular music, television sitcoms and home renovations shows, games shows, and so on. "Once the makers of cultural products think they have hit onto a winning formula, they stick with that formula, because they know that repeating it will be lucrative."[40] If we consider this in terms of sit-coms, boy bands, and even current affairs programmes, we may understand how the culture industry recycles what will sell and steers away from the rest. While this is profitable, convenient, and generally entertaining, it doesn't say much for creative cultural progress.

In the recent documentary film *Scott Walker: 30 Century Man*, an animated Brian Eno enthused about Nite Flights' sonic experimentation, while

---

[39] T. Adorno and M. Horkheimer, *The Culture Industry: Enlightenment as Mass Deception*, in S. During, The Cultural Studies Reader, 2nd ed. (Oxford: Routledge, 2007), 40.
[40] D. Inglis, *Culture and Everyday Life*, The New Sociology, series (London and New York: Routledge, 2005), 81.

castigating the conservatism of most contemporary pop music. "We haven't got any further than this," he sighed. "It's a disgrace."[41]

## The Cost of Stability

To say that "routine lives require routine pleasures"[42] is perhaps to frame the mass media among other modern institutions, as a *pharmakon*. 'Pharmakon' is a term famously used by Derrida to describe that which can be both a poison and a cure. While the standardisation of mass media products can be thought to satiate "[t]he desire for and pleasures of the familiar in doing so, it also runs the risk of actively dumbing down and stagnation of popular culture."[43]

Is modernity enslaving or a liberating? Perhaps the answer to this question would much depend on the disposition of the individual, the extent to which he or she chooses to engage in everyday life. If our everyday practices reflect "the wider social and cultural order", as Simmel has said, and it is precisely the routinisation of these practices that leads to their uncritical reproduction, there might well be a swing to the former.[44] But there are always two sides to an argument. An anti-consumer and anti-advertising stance is not always appropriate. As Inglis points out, "we could say that the coming of the new media allowed an expansion of people's horizons, opening up to a large number of people ideas and things they had never had exposure to before."[45]

There is no doubt that people who live under late Modern conditions are part of a privileged minority. Most of the people living in the world do not live in the industrialized West, so that what makes up the everyday experiences of you or I will in many ways be, perhaps profoundly, different from that which shapes the everyday experiences of those living in the majority world. What might seem normal and ordinary to you or me will probably seem quite strange and peculiar to a member of the Piraha tribe living in the Amazon jungle, for example. This is not to say that one culture is better or worse than another. Simply, it means that what we do each day, even those activities which might seem insignificant and mundane, all contribute to who we are and, in turn, influence the meaning that we continue to make of our lives, and of the lives of those around us.

But whatever we chose to do, to the extent that they constitute the 'normal' and 'ordinary' aspects of our everyday lives, routine practices tend to go relatively unnoticed. They are often excluded from the focus of mental

---

[41] S. O'Hagan, "Interview: Scott Walker," The Observer, http://www.guardian .co.uk/music/2008/nov/09/scott-walker-interview

[42] J. Fiske, *Understanding Popular Culture*, (London and New York: Routledge, 1989), 62.

[43] K. Negus, *Creativity and Culture* (London: Sage Publications Ltd, 2004), 74.

[44] D. Inglis, *Culture and Everyday Life*, The New Sociology, series (London and New York: Routledge, 2005), 3.

[45] Ibid., 85.

attention--passing by again and again as if part of an invisible backdrop to conceivably more important concerns. What is more, routine activities often take place with such regularity that they tend to demand little or no thought at all. After all, why take the time to think about how we are brushing our teeth when there are far more pressing matters of work commitments, mortgage repayments, and interpersonal relationships to consider? While these are the practices that occur on a regular basis as pervasive features of our behaviour, both in private and in public. Thus, the 'everyday' often denotes a recurring realm of thoughtlessness or, more to the point, of uncritical thinking. As Giddens points out:

> We live day-to-day lives in which for most of what we do we can't give any reason. We dress as we do, we walk around as we do … these things are part of a tissue of day-to-day social activity which really isn't explained. It's hard to say why we do these things except that they're there and we do them.[46]

Where everyday life is repetitive, the individual is able to carry on with the presumption of its predictability and, by direct association, their own safety. As if to say, if one has been successful in surviving what has happened before, so long as it can be ascertained that an equivalent practice is forthcoming and that the routinisation, the ritualisation of this practice will continue much further into the future, then the individual can assume a degree of ongoing comfort and the relative certainty of a continuing personal and social life. Perhaps it is this sense of physical security that helps to maintain a mental buffer between the individual and possible threat that ensures cognitive stability—the deferral of the feeling that one's life is crashing down around oneself, that might arise from a degree of sensitivity to the experience, the risk, of unpredictability. Of course, it can be justifiably said that life, at its very core, is unpredictable. Each moment that we are alive, we step into the unknown, into an uncharted future of which we are inherently ignorant. Our inability to see one second in front of us is a part of our human condition. Surely if we possessed such an ability, society would witness a marked reduction in traffic and domestic accidents, a reduction in gambling, a heightened sense of self-awareness, a greater knowledge of death. Perhaps it is precisely the unpredictability of life that sets the motivation for repetitive practices, for they allow the individual to continue each day with the presumption that they are wholly in control of their own life.

While the predictable aspects of life help to support the comforting sense of stability, it is these very aspects that reduce the need to assess what is ahead, even what is happening at any one moment. The assumption that one

---

[46] Anthony Giddens, cited in J. Tomlinson, *Cultural Imperialism: A Critical Introduction* (London: Pinter, 1997), 174.

knows what is ahead, weather forecasts, economic forecasts, interest rate locks for mortgages, form a life plan. I shall buy this home at this price with the help of a mortgage that is set at this rate of interest, and in 40 years I shall own it outright. The task of preparing for the future becomes a commodified task that is carried out in consultation with the products of institutions.

Life-insurance, health insurance, income insurance are just a few of many steps that people take in an attempt to steer lives in a desired direction. For the long term, in a particular way, we understand that circumstances may arise that disrupt our plans, impact upon our desires for what form the unknown shall become manifest. By way of these examples, life's unpredictability is represented and communicated as a negative trait; the profit margins of insurance companies rely heavily on a perceived negativity, a negativity of the unknown, the wayward, the unscripted. The individual who expresses no direction is regarded as a loser because surely the aimlessness that they articulate contrasts the general consensus regarding the advancement and productivity of late modern culture. Predictability is encouraged as a positive cultural aspect because it is by repeating actions, by habituating cultural activity that cultural activity can be successfully regulated and potential hurdles can be pre-empted. A general consensus in favour of the routinisation of everyday life finds individuals in a state of self-censor, through which they appeal, as if spontaneously, to the homogenizing forces of capitalism and the self-perpetuating demands of urban society.

It seems odd to me that much of everyday experience goes by without so much as a nod. The Western industrialised society is very much a privileged minority, the result, so far, of less than two centuries of technological advancement, and yet there is a tendency for us to slip into the monotony and familiarity of a 9 to 5 urban existence. Maybe we will wake up, get ready for work, go to work, work, go home, feed the fish, have dinner, and then 'reward' ourselves by spending two of three hours, 'switched off' in front of the television. In what way is the passive state rewarding? In what way is the homogenisation of everyday life liberating or enslaving; does its familiarity and predictability promote or dissolve a critical engagement with the cultural circumstances in which we life? The question of familiarity has attained significant publicity, for example in the opening dialogue to the film *Trainspotting* (1996) where, through the words of main character Mark Renton (played by Ewan McGregor), the quandary is summed up with aplomb:

> Choose life. Choose a job. Choose a career. Choose a family. Choose a fucking big television. Choose washing machines, cars, compact disc players and electrical tin openers. Choose good health, low cholesterol and dental insurance. Choose fixed-interest mortgage payments. Choose a starter home. Choose your friends. Choose leisure wear and matching luggage. Choose a three-piece suite on hire purchase in a range of fucking fabrics. Chose D.I.Y. and wondering who the fuck you are on a Sun-

day morning. Choose sitting on that couch watching mind-numbing, spirit-crushing game shows stuffing fucking junk food into your mouth. Choose rotting away at the end of it all. Pissing your last in a miserable home; nothing more than an embarrassment to the selfish, fucked-up brats that you've spawned to replace yourself. Choose your future. Choose life. But why would I want to do a thing like that? I chose not to choose life. I chose something else.[47]

Those who are familiar with the *Trainspotting* narrative will know that Renton's choice was heroin, though this would have to be one of the least productive and least sustainable options available. Yet Renton taps into a mindset that experiences anxiety at the thought of a life which may just as well be re-phrased as a 'prescription', complete with unsettling irony. Contrary to first impressions, *Trainspotting* can be taken as a call for help in terms of a feeling of urgency to save the future from habitual behaviour. Marx described religion as the opiate for the masses. In a commodity culture it is the allure of entertainment and novelty, instant gratification and communication, the indulged narcissistic impulse that contextualise the advanced capitalist injection. In this privileged minority world, consumers get high on material satisfaction, shopping mall bargains, profitable deals, and other arbitrary notions. In this sense, the heroin addiction running rampant through the film's key characters more than slightly parodies the habituation of life to which the rest of the 'clean' community clings. Not only does *Trainspotting* offer sound insight as to the costs of drug addition, it does not fail to provide critical comment on the perils of boredom, complacency in day-to-day behaviour.

In court, having narrowly escaped a custodial sentence for his misdeeds, Renton reassures the stern judge, "With God's help I'll conquer this terrible affliction." Renton's verbal delivery is so dead-pan that a sardonic inflection is unmistakable. But what we can take from this is further suggestion that, despite the fact that familiarity can facilitate feelings of safety and security, it is perhaps erroneous to presume that such feelings are a direct measure of our personal success in this world (as if the confirmation of our practices, by way of their repetition, seems somehow to be an affirmation of our importance and, perhaps, righteousness). Yet, for Renton's character, these very conventions for attaining a so-called meaningful life are precisely what is ruining it for him—a contemporary resonance with Jean Baudrillard's observation with regard the working class's seduction by needless material comforts: "Everywhere one seeks to produce meaning, to make the world signify, to render it visible. We are not, however, in danger of lacking meaning; quite the

---

[47] *Trainspotting*, directed by Danny Boyle, screenplay by John Hodge (adapted from the book by Irvin Welsh), 1996.

contrary, we are gorged with meaning and it is killing us."[48] On the one hand, this is what Renton felt was killing him too; on the other hand, it is what led him to use heroin to slowly kill his connection to the routinised culture surrounding him.

Thus, before jumping to the conclusion that safety is equivalent to success, it is fair to consider what it is that contentment puts at stake. In order to gain some insight in to this matter, it is useful to reflect upon Sharon Wegscheider-Cruse's point that:

> The risks of self-growth involve going into the unknown, into an unfamiliar land where the language is different and customs are different and you have to learn your way around … the paradox is that until we give up all that feels secure, we can never really trust the friend, mate, or job that offers us something. …. If we reject deliberate risk taking for self-growth we will inevitably remain trapped in our situation."[49]

Self-growth involves risk, and both these things stand in relation to the unknown. We can think of this 'unknown' in purely literal terms as that which we experience to evolve as individuals. New experiences, perhaps new cultural environments. Maybe we will learn a lot about people and about ourselves when we travel to other countries and have to negotiate different customs, language barriers, and so on. Or maybe we can think about the unknown in terms of the unknown future that we continue to face in front of us with each and every second that passes. The unknown up against which our self unravels, up against which the responsibility of the self is realised. If we are to stick to this future orientated interpretation of the unknown then we can say that self-identity, as something that we build from moment of moment, is the construction that we make on the edge of the unknown.

Challenging the familiarity of day to day life does not end with a critical engagement of culture; the inseparability of self and society means that this is as much of an opportunity to learn something about oneself. For Yalom, the self-aware moment "is the time when one stands before the abyss and decides how to face the pitiless existential facts of life: death, isolation, groundlessness, and meaninglessness. Of course there are no solutions. One has a choice only of certain stances."[50]

Here is an issue to explore that leads us back to Baudelaire's seemingly aimless wandering around the streets of 19th century Paris. By considering the

---

[48] J. Baudrillard, "Seduction of the Superficial Abyss," in *The Ecstasy of Communication* (New York: Semiotext(e), 1987), 63.
[49] S. Wegscheider-Cruse, *Learning to Love Yourself: Finding Your Self-Worth* (Florida: Health Communications Inc., 1987), 82.
[50] I. D. Yalom, *Love's Executioner and Other Tales of Psychotherapy* (New York: Penguin, 1991), 260.

implications of the habituation of human activity in an industrial society, by taking into account the benefits and disadvantages of a stable life world and, then, we may move into a process, a stance no less, called defamiliarisation that brings us back to the promise of the dérive. Furthermore, it lays the final stone before I walk the talk, before I put this theory into practice.

Let's start with the example of someone who travels into the city in order to get to work, that person is likely to travel along a particular route several times every week. They travel along it with such frequency that it might seem that they could so it in their sleep; with their eyes closed. It is one aspect of what we can call a 'stable life-world.' A person's life-world has a lot to do with an ability to 'go on' each day in a certain way. While it is closely related to a person's 'comfort zone' there are differing views on whether such stability is beneficial or detrimental.

For some, a stable life-world has the benefit of reducing the need for us to go on in the face of unthinkable anxiety. If everything was in a constant state of flux, we would not be able to rely on the infrastructure of our society to provide us with convenient access to food, clothing and medicine. Without predictability, we would find it hard to trust our friends and neighbours. Predictability in everyday life means that we can drive on the roads with a reasonable degree of organisation and safety. It means that the prices of products will remain relatively stable and that public transport will, for the most part, run according to an agreed schedule.

A stable life-world can be described as one in which we have the luxury of not needing to worry about where our next meal is coming from; it means not having to worry about who to turn to if we find ourselves hurt or in some other kind of trouble. We live in the relative luxury of being able to access electricity at the mere flick of a button, hot and cold running water that we can drink without fear of getting sick. So that, when we believe ourselves to be faced with the downfall of this stability, it might seem that a great deal of what we value is suddenly in jeopardy. Maybe the prospect of the end of a stable life-world will mean the increased activity of our survival instincts. One example of this stems back from the Y2K scare at the beginning of this century in which the precautionary actions of the Eckhart show us what is at stake when predictability threatens to go AWOL.

Having a Terabyte hard drive in the back pocket might not seem like such a big deal anymore and there are powerful computer processors that will fit neatly on the head of a matchstick. But when computers started being used, they were large and cumbersome and, unlike today, memory space was quite scarce. One of the ways that this precious memory space could be preserved was by leaving out unnecessary information such as, for example, abbreviating the numbers that indicate the year. Instead of using four digits for the date, systems used two—meaning that a year such as 1970 would simply become 70 and meant that the amount of space required for that piece of data was cut in half. We all know how rapidly computer technology has moved forward in the past few decades but, even though the need to save memory space decreased over time, many systems were still using this convention of abbreviating the year-date. As the year 2000 got closer and closer, the public became increasing concerned about the potential legacy of this convention after computer nerds around the world started to speculate about what would happen when the clocks rolled over into the new millennium. With the year about to change from 99 to 00, there was a concern that the numerous systems still using the two-digit abbreviation would not recognize that it was 2000 and, instead, think that it was 1900 again. IT specialists anticipated what they called something called the 'Millennium Bug', otherwise known as 'Y2K', a computer glitch that would bring with it a whole range of unforeseeable and undesirable consequences.

Speculation about the repercussions of Y2K resulted in all manner of apocalyptic visions as people wondered whether or not banking systems would break down, perhaps resulting in the loss, or loss of access to, vital finds. The questions began to snowball. What would be the broader implications of this disruption for the national and global financial exchanges that we rely on? What would happen to welfare, medical equipment, air conditioners, elevators, electricity grids and traffic control systems, or any other system that used digital technology? Some experts even suggested the possibility that missile systems could be confused by the bug and subsequently launch themselves into whatever country they just so happened to be pointing at. While this particular outcome seemed unlikely, it was enough of a threat for the Pentagon to get a little worried. For everyone else, the potential for general social disorder seemed very real indeed.

There were even those sectors of the community who entertained other kinds of apocalyptic beliefs such as the belief that the Millenium Bug marked the arrival of Armageddon—as some kind of melodramatic extension of it signalling the end of the world 'as we know it'; the end of the familiarity to which we had grown accustomed and, in that way, deeply reliant. This general wave of paranoia and vulnerability created prime conditions for greedy capitalists to make a few extra dollars, into the millions of course. While the industrial world braced itself for the end of certainty, what remained predictable was the typically sensationalist fashion with which Y2K products were cashing in on the confusion. Michael S. Hyatt's book entitled *The Millennium Bug* which told the reader *How to Survive the Coming Chaos* made its way onto the New York Times' Best Sellers list. At this time, the prospect of social disorder wasn't being treated more like a destiny than a possibility because it created a market for the products. Another example was the Y2K Personal Survival Kit which promised to provide with information on *How to Quickly Prepare for any Man-made or Natural Disaster*.

Everyone knew that, whatever the outcome, this new market had a limited lifespan with an immovable used by date and so manufacturers were pushed to capitalise on the situation as completely as possible before it arrived. With hype as profound as this, it is little wonder that, anti-bug software was selling by the truckload in the years leading up to the end of the millennium. It is equally as understandable that, faced with the increased demand to protect themselves and each other, families such as the Eckhart's from Ohio took significant measures to stave off, to ensure some resiliency against, the negative impact of whatever systematic and social fallout might eventuate.

By around 1997, the Eckhart family were regularly stockpiling food in their basement. They had collected a whole year's supply of canned chicken chow-mien. They had bought a gas powered home generator in case of power cuts, they regularly practiced emergency drills and learnt how to use firearms, they familiarised themselves with basic medical and dentistry skills. Furthermore, the Eckhart's converted all of their savings into gold just in case the banks went down. They even bought a waterbed just in case, as Lacayo et al point out, they needed to drink the water.[51]

As it turned out, all these efforts were to prove wasted because when the year 2000 came around nothing happened. There was no financial breakdown. There was no civil unrest or rioting on the streets. There were no electricity grid mishaps or missile disasters. There was no sudden greater need for do-it-yourself dentistry. And the Eckhart family didn't have to drink their bed. But, while we might now look back and have a bit of a laugh at people's responses to Y2K panic, no-one really seemed to know what was going to happen. Yet, even before the year 2000 arrived, this very panic was demonstrating something quite profound about who we are as a culture and about how we operate as an industrial and technologically advanced society; about the material and institutional circumstances under which we operate. The pre-millennium 'freak out' showed that we truly had become a digital culture.

A stable life-world has its advantages but, as the old saying goes, "you don't know what you've got until it's gone." Sometimes we need to be faced with a loss of familiarity in order to realise the cost of having it. The disadvantages of living in a stable life-world are as numerous as the advantages, but some of these include the dependency which sometimes gets forgotten as we increasingly take these things for granted. It reminds me of the idea of the supplement that adds something more to the whole but which, as time passes, starts to become a part of that whole. Whereas at one time, removing the supplement would have been uneventful, now doing so leaves a void where it once was. It removal discloses a lack or insufficiency that hadn't existed before. How many times have we felt lost without or mobile phone or our personal organiser. It is not so much that these things are inherently necessary for the adequate function of our everyday lives. More to the point, we have created the conditions in which this would appear to be the case. By way of

---

[51] R. Lacayo, et al. "The End of the World as We Know it?" (*TIME Magazine*, Jan 18, 1999), Accessed February 11, 2010, http://www.time.com/time/magazine/arti cle/0,9171,990020-1,00.html.

the rapid progress of communications technologies and other digital systems, we have become the creators of our own dependencies upon them. Our expectations and desires have changed because of them and they have changed in line with our expectations and desires. It is not always a vicious cycle, but a cycle all the same, and one in which it pays to stay critically minded.

A part of being constructively critical about our material and cultural circumstances is taking into account the pros as well as the cons. Having broadband internet access with unlimited download is a wonderful luxury, with which we can talk to friends and family via web cams, to keep in touch over diverse time and space differences. While we retain our physical limitations, we are no longer bound to the local in the way that past generations have been. Search engines are as much the necessary tools for diligent researchers who require access to academic articles that are located in databases around the world, as they are for lazy learners for whom a walk to the library seems like far too much of an effort.

A tool such as the internet might be just one feature of the multifarious ideas, environments and activities that make up a person's life-world. While these continue to run along smoothly, that person can continue to partake in their routines and rituals without interruption. A person can carry on 'as normal' in the course of day to day social behaviour, taking their mind off of basic needs like food, shelter and clothing, and redirect it to more personal pursuits such as participating in sports, taking time out to read a novel or to practice an art form, meeting with friends and engaging in meaningful conversation—in short, to pursue happiness and pleasure.

One problem of having a stable life-world is that sustained familiarity is fertile soil for complacency. When everything remains pretty much the same, it seems safer and less threatening but, over time, as we become accustomed to having certain people, objects, activities around us, we run the risk of taking them for granted. They start to lose the shine that they might have once held when they were still new, still novelties; when they still had the power to attract our attention. Once the lustre has begun to wear off, our attention moves towards other things. If we expect them to remain where they are, as they are, then it seems to matter very little if we take our eyes off of them for a few moments, think about something else. Perhaps we become bored of the same old thing. The problem is that, when we are not looking, when we are not paying attention to our surroundings, we also run the risk of overlooking small changes that are made or of failing to notice why such changes have been made in the first place. Little by little, things can change with such apparent insignificance that the evolution also becomes familiar.

If a person living in 1930 was somehow transported into the present moment and went looking for a house to buy, with a mere few thousand pounds in their pocket, there would be absolutely no chance of them signing the contract for a new home in the suburbs. Likewise, if a person alive today went back to 1930, with the 500,000 dollars received from their sold house, entire towns would be up for grabs. As time plods along, changes occur which we can reasonably digest and make allowances for. We can quite easily adapt to gradual change. While familiarity can be comforting, a problem arises when things become monotonous and mundane. Rather than follow Mark Renton's course of action and spend one's days *non compos mentis*, the estrangement that is promoted by the dérive doesn't cost a fortune, if anything at all (it puts the person 'at odds' with his or her surroundings, in part, by fostering a non-monetary experience of the capitalist context). The dérive combats boredom and complacency not by dulling the senses even further but by shifting them out of the framework to which they have become accustomed. What is more, there is a lot to be said for fresh air and exercise.

# CHAPTER 4
# ENGAGING IN LATE MODERNITY

## Critical Thinking

To this point, we have addressed to key considerations. In the second chapter, we outlined the historical circumstances that led to the figure of the flâneur and to the dérive as a strategy for critical cultural response. This was a response to an emerging industrial culture with all its hopes for a new world and its concurrent disruptions to traditional ways of thinking and behaving, as well as to traditional methods of social organisation. The modernist ideal entailed liberating human beings from the demands of physical labour, thus taking them into a new age of superior luxury and personal fulfilment. Yet, modernisation created a material reality that existed in stark contrast to this ideal; it comprised the poor conditions of the factory workplace, the crowded and unsanitary proto-city environment, and the question of who to be in this strange polluted world. Building upon this historical foundation, the previous chapter went one step further in this cultural trajectory by showing how the circumstances of early modernity have now become embedded in our lives today.

So common-place are the demands of industrialised labour, so second nature, that perhaps we will be forgiven for treating them as if they were sacrosanct—beyond the reach of critical consideration on the level of everyday thinking. Nevertheless, over the past 50 years, we can locate contexts in which the dérive, as a city-based strategy, is as relevant, if not more so, than ever before. In light of modernity's institutionalisation, it is perhaps more important than ever before to embrace the dérive as a tool for breaking out of the daily routines in the context of which we find ourselves industrially disciplined. We can now see that, in the *Lose Yourself in Melbourne* advertisement, the woman with the red wool veritably re-contextualises this historical practice by conducting it in a late modern city without question. However, in doing so, the critical component is missing; it has been omitted from the televisual frame of this non-linear narrative to produce 90 seconds of ideological coherence. Anyone who is not aware of the dérive's historical context might well also remain unaware of this particular lack. However, in tracing back this historical trajectory, it has been possible to draw attention to the value of re-investing this dimension into the practice.

This is the investment to which I hope to do justice as I put myself to the task of making the defamiliarising theory of the dérive actionable—as I put it into practice for the purpose of breaking my own culturally convenient behaviours, relocating and confronting my own defamiliarised place within the built environment. While I may communicate this hope, it stands to reason that I can but come to the table with my own sets of beliefs, experiences, ideas, and educational opportunities. Thus, it is all I can do to attempt maximum clarity and honesty when negotiating the theory in a material reality.

The fact that some of my cultural capital will impact directly upon how I make sense of the dérive as a tangible cultural experience, is what has determined the character of this part of the book. Between the theory and my own forthcoming practice of the dérive, it is important to build this bridge, comprising the key features of my own cognitive terrain that I hope will make the communication of my person al experience much more useful for the reader; that he or she may retain the opportunity to make any necessary adjustments along the way, as he or she considers how it relates to his or her own life. In this chapter, we shall consider the significance of the dérive by approaching it from alternative directions. These help to flesh out the critical context of a dérive as it may take place in a city today. Central to this 'bridge' will be our attention to a physiological connection between thinking and walking. This will lead us to the notion of 'praxis'—one that, so long as the dérive is reinvested with its critical cultural dimension, can be demonstrated through the dérive.

To begin, the prospect of making theory actionable is motivated by what I have referred to as the cost of stability—its capacity to massage the critical faculties into a relaxed and passive state. A reminder of the function of critical thinking is an appropriate one. Although the views expressed by Adorno and Horkheimer arose from their own particular socio-cultural setting, their rather bleak view of commodification of culture are nevertheless useful when thinking about culture today. Their critical accounts communicate the idea of pseudo-individualisation as an ideological process, with individuality being an ideal circulated by the mass media. Media is taken as that which, in itself, functions to hide the process of standardisation. "The power of the culture industry's ideology is such that conformity has replaced consciousness."[52] Popular music and film are seen to act as a form of social cement, which encourages people to reconcile themselves to mediocrity. "It is catharsis for the masses, but catharsis which keeps them all the more firmly in line. One who weeps does not resist any more than one who marches."[53] In other words, it is a fabrication, a desirable façade, and one that provides the apparent novelty or uniqueness of the product for the consumer. According to Adorno, the effect of the culture industry is "mass deception," impeding the development of critical thinking by perpetuating false needs.[54] For Adorno, critical thinking

---

[52] T. Adorno, *The Culture Industry: Selected Essays on Mass Culture* (London: Routledge, 1991), 90.

[53] T. Adorno, *Essays on Music* (California: University of California Press, Ed. Richard Leppert, 2002), 462.

[54] T. Adorno, and M. Horkheimer, *The Culture Industry: Enlightenment as Mass Deception* (London: Continuum International Publishing Group, 1976).

was the tool for working towards the kinds of social solutions that lay beyond the limits of this kind of façade, baring the devices of the false needs he claimed were generated in a mass culture by the culture industries.

When I see the Aussie Home Loans advertisement broadcast on the television and, in it, I hear the company director urging the viewer, "Don't think about it, just call us,"[55] I begin to wonder whether a critical audience is an inherently unprofitable one. When I read a magazine interview in which the Latin-American singer Shakira is quoted as saying of cultural creativity "There's no rational factor involved and the miracle of art or music just happens and you're just a witness to it" I continue to wonder why thoughtlessness is still deemed so appealing.[56] Perhaps encouraging a mass audience to do no more than passively witness what is taking place before him it, like some pseudo-spiritual force affecting viewer disempowerment. There is a good reason why the mass media is often faced with cynicism.

Part of the 'virtue of un-critical thinking', I believe, stems from the way that the very notion of 'critical' is afforded almost exclusively negative connotations in the broader community. With the request to "not be so critical" often made as strategy for avoiding that which is conceivably challenging or confronting to another. But this association is problematic when we consider that, without critical thinking, the individual remains in a vulnerable position, certainly more susceptible to coercion than he or she would be if they were to exercise the ability to look beyond what is presented and immediately apparent.

So long as everyday life is reduced to a series of familiar actions, everyday life will remain stagnant. It takes a leap into the unknown for growth to take place, on both a personal and on a cultural level, thus the absence of thought translates as hindrance to individual and collective progress. So that, while the familiarity of routine might retain the appeal of comfort, safety, and security, it is precisely these 'entitlements' that reduce the opportunity: 1) For the individual to capitalize on their critical faculties in a way that finds them taking an active and central role in the meaning making processes that frame their life; and 2) For the individual to make steps to affect any adjustments might be deemed to impinge on their basis human rights and/or creative potential. Thus, it is precisely at the level of everyday life that there remains a vital need for the mechanics of critical thinking. In order to explain what is meant by the term 'critical thinking,' I shall break it down into three component parts;

First of all, critical thinking refers to the sets of skills that are necessary to generate and process information. This might include analytical skills such as an understanding of ideology, metaphor, metonym, and so on, that can be

---

[55] Aussie Home Loans advertisement broadcast on Australian television in 2008.
[56] The West Magazine, "The Curiosity that Shakes Shakira," *The West Australian*, 2007, 25.

used to both generate and uncover a range of meanings in which the individual might come into contact on a regular or an irregular basis. In other words, such skills constitute methods of demonstrating cultural sensitivity. Secondly, critical thinking entails the habit, based on intellectual commitment, to use those skills to guide behaviour. That is to say, it is necessary to apply analytical skills on the level of everyday thinking as a way of transforming how everyday life is 'played out' by the individual. This can also be understood as the application of theory to everyday activities, which also involves the ability to make ethical decisions.

Of all the historical figures that have recognised the importance of critical thinking, Socrates has been the most influential, using his critical reasoning to set the stage for future Western philosophy. Athenian Socrates lived in the fourth century BC and he is famous for laying the groundwork of western philosophy. He believed that the best way to live was to concentrate on self-growth as opposed to material wealth. By subjecting beliefs and ideas to questioning, and then by subjecting a person's reasoning for their beliefs and ideas, and so on, he found that he was able to uncover confused meanings, inadequate evidence, of self-contradictory beliefs that existed below the surface. The Socratic method of inquiry, as it is now known, is a method in which commonly held beliefs and explanations are deeply reflected upon. It is this method of critical thinking that led Socrates to establish the idea that we could not simply rely upon people in positions of authority to have sound knowledge and insight, and to his bold conclusion that a life devoid of critical thinking is barely a life at all. In his translated words, "An unexamined life is a life not worth living."[57]

By exploring how people in authority often held confused and irrational views, Socrates paved the way for the tradition of critical thinking as it continues today. He knew that how people thought impacted directly on how they acted, and on the kinds of activities and experiences in which they took part. As Alain de Botton points out, Socrates believed that if you went through life not thinking about things, you would inevitably, and unwittingly take on board errors about what a good life entailed.

Critical thinking is less about conducting oneself in a way that can be taken as unfair or disparaging than it is about remaining actively aware of what is happening around us. It is this understanding of 'critical' thinking as indispensable for active cultural participation that leads me to be suspicious of those who see this term only in a negative light; where an aversion to critical thinking can seem too much like an invitation to passive living. This might sound a little harsh, but that is perhaps what happens in a culture that privileges immediate gratification and pleasure over other experiences. We have become so accustomed to convenience that we run the risk of mistakenly believing that something needs to be easy just to get done. We have what is

---

[57] Socrates, *Apology*, 38a.

known as a 'too hard basket' in which we can put things and, thereby, perhaps relieve ourselves of the responsibility of dealing with them. The fact that critical thinking is not easy is what can make it so rewarding and, to this end, more sustainable. It enables the individual to take an active and central role in the meaning making processes that frame their life, and gives the individual a basis of support from which to affect any adjustments in view of things that might be deemed to impinge on their basic human rights and/or creative potential.

Sometimes engaging in critical thinking will mean stopping to ask yourself, "what am I doing and, furthermore, what are the implications of my actions?" "What is happening around me, and what are the implications of these occurrences?" More often than not, developing our cultural awareness will mean adjusting our behaviour to become more ethically sound. This might mean restricting the amount of water that we use, or making smarter choices when it comes to the products that we buy. Over the past few decades, the public have become more sensitive to the problems associated with e-waste and the use of plastic, leading to a move to more environmentally friendly goods and services. Thinking critically about how our needs are impacting on the environment has seen public awareness forcing a marked shift in consumer practices. On other occasions, thinking critically will mean having to stick to your guns; digging your heals in despite adversity.

## Thinking and Walking

Critical thinking promotes good health, especially when you're thinking on your feet; healthy body, healthy mind. Descartes gave us "Cogito ergo sum" (French: *Je pense donc je suis*; English: "I think, therefore I am").[58] But is it enough? Surely I can't simply think myself into existence, like some passive ever-hopeful student of life. I recognise that there must be something more than thinking—more than theorising. It is important for me to test these ideas out in everyday life as well, to see whether or not I am deluding myself in my thoughts, by what I've been shown and by what I've learned—by addressing whatever void there might be between my ideology and a material reality. I think therefore I am....but then what? What comes next?

Thus, a theoretical backdrop forms just one side of the coin. For it to be considered part of a critical and creative praxis, it remains to be asked, "Where might we find defamiliarisation at work, at play; playing at work, working at play?" Well, it is in the context of the dérive that we can conceive to exist in all of these variations. It is in the context of the dérive that defamiliarisation not only fosters critical thinking but, furthermore, finds it manifest in the form of a creative negotiation.

---

[58] L. Brown, ed., *The New Shorter Oxford English Dictionary*, Vol. 1 (Oxford: Oxford University Press, 1993), "Cogito," 434.

The curious stroll was popular as a way of resisting the 9 to 5 and capitalist monotony of the central business district by treating the city as a space of play and uneconomic creativity. The dérive becomes an opportunity to engage with the city from a renewed perspective, a chance to explore the structured spaces that make it up in a decidedly unstructured way—the old gothic arcades, empty alleys, hidden inner city streets that tend to be overlooked by locals and visitors once they have digested their surroundings, perhaps because they exist outside of the boundaries of the shopping precincts or because they do not exist on the well-worn pathways between home, car, and work. Out of sight, out of mind. They might fall outside of the fields of vision of the thousands of people who negotiate the city each day, tooled up with their methods and motivations—their minds eye on the destinations marked by shops, offices, places of education, the state library or art galleries, the comfort and familiarity of homes reached via a tram stop or car park space. Each one of these destinations result in motivated pathways through the city—each one a means to an end that, in turn, might be found to detract from the sites of surprise and impromptu interactions that are also, otherwise, possible. It would seem that the campaign draws on, and therefore disseminates, the ideological notion of the creative potential of the individual who seeks the fun, mystery and adventure, even romantic love, that exists tucked away in the little alleys and bistro's of the labyrinth.

At the same time, the city can be a serious space for some and a space of play for others. Of course, the extent to which one possibility is experienced over the other will depend largely on the inclinations of the individual and on the amount of time available. Food and housing cost money even in a fun city. There are always going to be material conditions that impact upon how we experience an ideal. But, in the same way that a child interacts with transitional objects for the development of their sense of self, their basic trust in the primary care giver, so too can an adult re-discover the city when open to being placed beyond the mothering embrace of that which the routines and habitual pathways that are so widely taken for granted. In the city, the adult might find cause to contrast the greyness of a working day by returning to play, trusting in the provisions that are provided by the overarching governmental and infrastructural forces and devices. Do these somehow serve to stand in as an adequate mother, to whom we might turn in our hours of need (so that the consumer centre functions as a kind of social support and measure against the emotional fragility that the unfamiliar arouses?). Is the city modernity's locus of personal reassurance, like a stroke on the forehead and a familiar and gentle voice that tells us everything will be alright. The city hopes to validate us with its industry, award ceremonies and retail outlets. We go about our business, seeing how other people dress, what gadgets they possess, what food they eat for lunch. Silent comparisons take place all of the time.

When the city takes on the role of a space of play, something quite peculiar happens to that which it might be seen to provide, to our negotiation of the industrial revolution as the purveyor of built environments. It is not simply a place of shops, of brightly coloured and carefully decorated rooms in which the individual may peruse shelves in search of a new shirt or album, a toy or novelty fridge magnet, but the sum of its parts, a veritable giant game board around which we move, as if they were nothing more than the miniature icons of Monopoly or the plastic pie pieces used in Trivial Pursuit, navigating ourselves in line with the widely acknowledged and dominant rules of play. From this claustrophobic point of view, it seems that there is very little to counteract an impression of the city as a kind of dead space in disguise, occupied by distinctly non-creative and unthinking drones of the kind that have found feature in such films as Fritz Lang's Metropolis and, to a certain extent, Ridley Scott's Blade Runner for it is here, too, that the streets are dull in their emptiness, empty in alienation.

Thus it would seem, if it can be said that the City of Melbourne is putting out a call for 'flâneurs'—showcasing itself as an opportunity for dérive— that, to a certain extent, I have found myself responding gleefully to its mass televised voice. I have found appeal in the appeal and, though my decision to relocate to Melbourne was made before the city's campaign and with more than this consideration in mind, I cannot deny that I feel some further justification for it. I also feel some justification for my choice to dérive whenever I can in the time after my arrival—as if I had answered the call of the city sphere already drifting through the ether (though this retrospective interpretations is more to do with personal mythology than with a testable and material reality).

The dérive, as a supposedly aimless wander, is a way of interacting with a built environment; with our cultural habitat. But what happens when we walk? Answering this question helps to make further sense of the dérive. It helps us explore its potentially political dimension. The first step in this process is looking at the role that thinking has had in walking and to recognise the close relationship that has been shared by the two.

Walking, especially when it takes place en masse, has long since been recognised as a force to be reckoned with. In France, on the 14th of July, 1789, the starving poorer classes did not storm the Bastille from the discomforting and squalid conditions of their brothels, taverns, workplaces and homes. They marched to the controversial prison, collecting around 30,000 muskets from the Hôtel des Invalides along the way, and challenged royal authority in Paris and, having arrived at the gates to the fortress, demanded its surrender.[59]

It is easy to see how walking and thinking go hand in hand and this is one example in which critical thinking, criticism of royal authority in Paris,

---

[59] C. Hibbert, The French Revolution (London: Penguin Books, 1982), 75-80.

was enough to motivate people to step out onto the streets in a gesture of civil solidarity. Collective walking remains a central gesture of the protest movement as well as for the communication of values, beliefs and ideas. Paris has certainly had its fair share of public demonstrations of many kinds. Human rights, women's liberation, gay rights, are among many cultural concerns that have motivated walking in many cities around the world. Protest marches, for example, such as the march on Washington on August 28, 1963, organised by the American Civil Rights Movement in opposition to racially motivated employment discrimination in the defense sector, or those anti-war rallies that took place in over 600 towns and cities around the world, from Baghdad to Chicago, across the weekend of February 15 and 16, 2003.[60] In the context of the protest march, walking becomes a signifier for community empowerment – for social movement. Elsewhere, we can see how Oxfam Australia's 'Walk Against Want', a 40 year old event that has raised over $10 million for long term development work in 28 countries, aims to combat poverty and injustice.[61] The National Walk for Values events that were organised by the Sathya Sai Organisation of Australia and PNG took place on Saturday, April 12, 2008 in Brisbane, Sydney, Canberra, Melbourne, Adelaide and Perth. Their goal was not to raise funds, but to exist as a gesture of commitment to Love, Peace, Truth, Right Conduct and Non-violence.[62] The Gay Pride parades that take place each year in cities around the world are, yet, more examples of the power of walking as the vehicle for the manifestation of the desire for human empowerment, more often than not in the face of conflicting societal norms and institutional forces. Tiananmen Square, 1989, is not the only example in recent history where thinking and walking have provoked strong reactions.

These examples entail acts of walking that have been motivated by thinking; a kind of 'thinking *for* action'. But the system is cyclic (the dynamism of reflexivity), for on the flip side we have return from action to thinking, action as being '*for* thinking', for other people to thinking about something in a different way, a call bidding them to stop being confined to thinking about the matter from only ever their point of view. Calls for compassion fall on deaf ears when the power of whoever's in charge is threatened, and called into question, by that call.

And so, addressing this from another direction, in demonstrating what I am saying, attention can be drawn to examples that show thinking being motivated by walking; a kind of 'action *for* thinking', and there is a very good reason for this. It is a reason called *endorphins* and by looking at the role

---

[60] BBC News, "Millions Join Global Anti-War Protests," *World Edition*, Monday, 17 February, 2003, Accessed July 10, 2012, http://news.bbc.co.uk/2/hi/europe/2765215.stm

[61] http://www.oxfam.org.au/act/events/walk-against-want

[62] http://www.nationalwalkforvalues.org/

played by endorphins in the relationship between thinking and walking it is possible to arrive at a physiological foundation for a creative cultural practice such as the dérive.

Endorphins are any group of peptides (from the Greek πεπτίδια, meaning "small digestibles") that occur in the brain during exercise, and various other forms of excitement, and that promote a sense of well-being in the individual. The release of endorphins during exercise makes people feel more awake, alert and, importantly here, better able to think. Endorphins counteract the resting state of the brain and associated feelings such as sleepiness. Walking helps you become more alert. It sharpens your senses, not least of all by invigorating your mind.

There is an image of Nietzsche from The Bettman Archive that has been endlessly reproduced and which, for example, has been used on the cover of The Portable Nietzsche, a text edited and translated by Walter Kaufmann. In it, Nietzsche is sitting with his right elbow resting upon what may well be a desk or a table, the right side of his face resting in his elevated hand. Nietzsche does not look towards the camera but, instead, peers out to the side, off into the distance at some indeterminable end. Upon first glance, it would appear that the image is supposed to represent Nietzsche 'the thinker', and yet I wonder just how well this aim is achieved because, when the weather and his health permitted Nietzsche, the self-proclaimed 'first' European, was an avid walker, often strolling for hours at a time through the Bavarian countryside, taking in the crisp, clean air, weaving his way around the dense forest, working his way along the edges of cold, trickling streams. In this sense, the very notion of a 'portable' Nietzsche seems entirely appropriate.

An image that has been used as the cover for editions of Nietzsche and which has, thus, been closely associated with the romantic characterisation of Nietzsche, is an oil painting by German artist Caspar David Friedrich entitled *Der Wanderer über dem Nebelmeer* (The Wanderer above the Sea of Fog) created in 1818. The Wanderer is depicted, having reached the summit of the mountain, peering out into the mist filled distance, into the future, pondering nature. If we are to follow Michael Gorra's interpretation of this painting that the Wanderer is engaged in a Kantian self-reflection then it can be said that it is most likely 'human' nature and the human condition that is being subjected to deep contemplation.[63]

For Nietzsche, experiencing the outdoors was a celebration of the gift of life. When the weather and his fragile health permitted it, it was Nietzsche 'the walker' who adopted an aphoristic writing style, preferring to jot down short bursts of thought, perhaps his revelations that occurred to him as his legs moved, as his blood increased the speed of its circulation, as his brain

---

[63] M. E. Gorra, *The Bells in Their Silence* (New Jersey: Princeton University Press, 2004), XI-XII.

released enough endorphins to increase his alertness, and fuel his trains of thought. In Nietzsche's book *Twilight of the idols*, an aphorism in "Maxims and Missiles" reads, "A sedentary life is the real sin against the Holy Spirit. Only those thoughts that come by walking have any value."[64] The fact that Nietzsche was notoriously scathing of religion suggests that his reference to walking has as much of a figurative meaning than it does a literal one.

Nietzsche was not alone in praising the power of walking. Aristotle, an Ancient Greek philosopher who lived between 382 BC and 322 BC, was taught by Plato and he, himself, went on to teach Alexander the Great. Apparently, Aristotle made a habit of walking while giving lectures and his disciples, known collectively as the Peripatetic School (*peripatetic* adj., meaning: itinerant, travelling, wandering, nomadic, migrant), carried on with the practice of walking whenever they wanted to think.

Predating Heidegger's solitary treks through the Schwarzwald, Nietzsche's participation in walking *for* thinking might have found him, on many such occasions, alone on a winding trail, enthusiastically scribbling down his latest revelation. But Nietzsche's belief in the virtues of walking for a philosophical life found him in good company, by placing him within a tradition in which individuals have used walking as a catalyst for critical thinking.

On the one hand, the notion of the wanderer provides us with a metaphor for 'pushing forward', in a very physical sense. There are obvious physiological benefits that can be gained from any form of exercise. In the case of an aimless stroll through a built environment such as the city, walking can be an opportunity to forget about the stresses of the day, wander around and enjoy light conversation with a friend or even while walking the dog. Sometimes it is enjoyable simply to feel the breeze on your face, the sun on your skin, and listen to the sounds of the birds that can be heard whistle away in the tree tops as you walk by. Walking for pleasure puts no pressure on the individual to theorise about the world; to stop at each bend in order to write down his or her personal thoughts and recollections. Of course, thinking will likely take place, even if the thoughts that we experience on a leisurely stroll are simply thoughts about the day that we have had, memories of a conversation with a friend or colleague, or speculations about what we might like to eat for dinner.

There is also another side to thinking and walking that Nietzsche, Heidegger and Aristotle's merry gentlemen encouraged; walking as an opportunity for 'critical' thinking. They used walking as a stimulus for critical considerations, regardless of their capacity to bring pleasure to the thinker. In this sense it might be said that "philosophy walks" sound a bit like hard work but, if walking is something that supports mental activity, it makes sense to expose oneself to conditions under which the two are put together. While

---

[64] F. Nietzsche, *The Twilight of the Idols and The Anti-Christ: or How to Philosophize with a Hammer* (London: Penguin Books, 1990), 36.

people might experience very varied running speeds, it is much easier to keep up with someone who is walking. In this sense, going on a 'philosophy walk' is something that can readily be shared by two or more people. The only limits are the ideas to be discussed and the individual aptitudes for following them through.

I am very fond of certain memories that I have from a recent trip to Perth—the time spent during a couple of 'philosophy themed' walks with a friend I was staying with. At a strong and steady walking pace (it's nice to find someone you can walk with) we enjoyed a shared enthusiasm for creative cultural ideas. Our own took us along a path that found us gradually weaving through the quiet streets near her home. Though neither of these were the several hour long solitary hikes that Nietzsche or Heidegger would have endured, they were just as important. They were an opportunity to clear the head, experience the day, breath some fresh air, and take time out to mull over some of the theories, ambitions, and what we are concerned with. It doesn't even matter that some of them aren't particularly enlightening, that don't have to be in order to seen as valuable (what's new about tradition, after all, and yet many people continue to find great value in their familiar practices, at times perhaps only because they are familiar). Some thoughts were harder than others, but it was just so good to talk along, getting caught up in our conversation, sharing experience, being critical of ourselves as an encouragement to keep going forward.

A powerful relationship between thinking and walking means that even the chatty urban meandering can become an important part of how someone makes sense of the ideological and material conditions in which they live, as well as fostering fitness and fun. This is the kind of walking that the *Peripatetic School* participated in.

## Praxis

Thinking critically 'on the move,' is a key prerequisite for making theory actionable. The practice of 'thinking about things' is not only about thinking; it is also about acting in the world in a way that puts our thinking to good use. If we agree that thinking and action are two sides of the same coin, that the absence of one if the poverty of the other, than we can start to see a pathway leading back to the flâneur who dérives *dans la ville*; the person who wanders through the city streets and alleyways in search of new people, places, and things; who ventures out creatively in search of new ways of seeing and experiencing the built environment that frames him or her.

If we are to think of the notion of the dérive then, in its practice, we must also consider what it does; how does it impact on a person's experience of a material reality? What we have at hand is the question of a form of praxis—the application of a theory to everyday activities.

The notion of praxis, denoting a concern with actionable theory can be traced back to the classical world and the Greek philosopher Aristotle. A student of Plato and teacher of Alexander the Great, Aristotle lived between 384 and 322 BC. Still, today, he is considered as one of the ancient world's great thinkers. In fact, Aristotle studied and contributed to so many fields that, in their book called *The Philosophy of Art*, Neill and Ridley suggest that Aristotle was probably the last person to know everything that there was to know in his own time.[65]

Aristotle argued that there was a relationship between having skills that transformed the way in which the world was made, and realising that there was an ethical dimension to using that skill, understanding that there should be a relationship between thinking about the world and how we conduct ourselves within it. It is this relationship between thinking, making and observing the social and ethical consequences of making that he characterised by the word *praxis*. As mentioned in the introduction, praxis can be defined as:

- a mode of activity whereby practice is "informed by theory and also … theory is informed by practice."[66]
- "the practice of a technical subject or art … arising out of the theory of it."[67]
- "a whole mode of activity in which, by analysis but only by analysis, theoretical and practical elements can be distinguished, but which is always a whole activity, to be judged as such." [68]

Until a theory is tested it is nothing more than a hypothesis. Through its application in a material reality—for example, by using everyday life as a means to critiquing it in some way—we find theory being pushed across this threshold from hypothesis to participatory practice. We find that praxis is, almost necessarily, 'dyadic'. This is a deceivingly simple equation for it is much harder to "walk the talk" than to keep on talking, and it is precisely this "walking talking" or, alternatively, "talking walking" in which I am concerned with here, and which will characterise the next part of this book.

In the 1920s the philosopher Antonio Gramsci developed the idea of praxis as the working method of the 'organic', or public, intellectual.[69] In

[65]A. Neill, Alex, and A. Ridley, *The Philosophy of Art*: Readings Ancient and Modern, 1st ed. (New York: McGraw-Hill College, 1994), 488.
[66] Williams, in R. Johnson, et al., *The Practice of Cultural Studies* (London: Sage, 2004), 90.
[67] L. Brown, ed., *The New Shorter Oxford English Dictionary*, Vol. 2 (Oxford: Oxford University Press, 1993), "Praxis," 2321.
[68] Williams, in R. Johnson, et al., *The Practice of Cultural Studies* (London: Sage, 2004), 90.

Gramsci's view, traditional intellectuals' actions were 'justified by the political necessities of the dominant fundamental group'. But if we think about praxis as being the engine that could drive cultural production, then this conservative, restraining function of the intellectual evaporates. The public intellectual operates in an open dialogue with his or her chosen audience. In other words, praxis can be seen as the way to making theory actionable.

Praxis comprises a critical negotiation with the cultural environment. It involves seeking 'other' solutions (the solutions to be found in 'otherness', the unknown, the unfamiliar, even, the strange), it is based on dialogue and discussion and, therefore, on the possibility and the opportunity for cultural change. Praxis implies a conscious decision about what strategies are best suited to resolve or clear the interactions between theory and practice. We can detect this sentiment in the way that Gramsci sought to foster organic intellectuals in the public sphere, and it is worth remembering, how the ancient Greeks referred to term 'praxis', as "an activity of people who are free, who are able to act for themselves."[70] For Cornelius Castoriadis, participation is critical to developing universal autonomy:

> Praxis is a type of action which involves taking others into account and regarding them as autonomous beings capable of developing their own autonomy....The revolutionary project builds upon the creativity and autonomous aim of *praxis*. It is, in essence, the project of a radical transformation of society with a view to the autonomy of all, 'the reorganization and reorientation of society by the autonomous action of [people].'[71]

The question of education, then, is critical to this kind of socio-cultural project. Thus, in addition to Gramsci, we may now give due attention to Paulo Freire. Freire was a Brazilian educator who lived from 1921 to 1997. He grew up in Brazil and, living in a middle class family during the great Depression of 1929, he grew to become very familiar with poverty and hunger. He suffered harsh conditions as a child, but later went on to study law and philosophy and to develop ideas about education that were influenced by his childhood experiences. He became very influential by advocating the need for a kind of education that was not simply an extension of traditional education and that did not simply reinforce the dominance of the colonizers. Here we

---

[69] N. Crick, "Rhetoric, Philosophy, and the Public Intellectual," *Philosophy and Rhetoric*, Vol. 39, Number 2, (Pennsylvania: Penn State University Press, 2006), 127-139, DOI: 10.1353/par.2006.0012

[70] M.K. Smith, (1996, August 26, 1999). "Praxis: an introduction to the idea plus an annotated booklist," http://www.infed.org/biblio/b-praxis.htm#praxis/ Accessed February 12, 2010, par. 8.

[71] Cornelius Castoriadis, as quoted in E. P. Thompson, The Poverty of Theory and Other Essays (New York: Monthly Review Press, 1980), 19-20.

might think about those dominant groups, in the mass media perhaps, who help to colonize the meanings we have in our lives through advertising, through globalization, through the propagating of ideology. We can relate Freire to us in this way.

Freire pushed for praxis to be accepted as an emancipatory method— not for the benefit of an elite few, but rather for use by a broader cultural sphere. We may take praxis as the capacity for a collectively developed revolutionary practice that open up the way towards alternative possible futures— alternative solutions made available to accommodate the needs of a group of people. This philosophy was behind Freire's opposition to the notion of a 'banking' education. This is a kind of education whereby students were treated as though they were empty accounts to be filled by the teacher. His opposition expressed itself in his criticism of the idea that teaching was just about transferring facts and so fails to account for individual differences. Freire's opposition to the 'banking' model of education led him to advocate democratic learning environments in which the teacher could learn and the learner could teach. This approach aims to foster an active learning community.

In short, Freire's view suggests that praxis comprises of a cycle of action-reflection-action that is central to liberatory education. In his terms, the characteristics of praxis include self-determination (as opposed to coercion and subjugation), intentionality (as opposed to reaction), creativity (as opposed to homogeneity and standardisation), and rationality (as opposed to chance). This means education that was geared towards liberating rather than domesticating students. There is a difference between providing a service and fostering empowerment. The 'service' constitutes a "performance of duties,"[72] whereas empowerment means endowing "with the ability or power required for a purpose or task."[73] When someone serves you dinner, it means that you don't have to do it—you are hailed into a passive role. Empowerment means doing it for yourself, that way you can. Freire wanted to affirm and empower students as, what he referred to as "subjects of decision" to reinstate their freedom to prosper as organic intellectuals.

## Cultural Reflexivity

People acquire autonomy through self-conscious reflection. Taking others into account when practicing vision empowers them to question themselves, to critique social structures, and to image new realities. People learn best by doing; visioning creates autonomy. The practice of social criticism through vision is emancipatory. It dares the imagination, challenges assumptions, and declares its independence from traditions.

---

[72] L. Brown, ed., *The New Shorter Oxford English Dictionary*, Vol. 2 (Oxford: Oxford University Press, 1993), "Service," 2789.
[73] Ibid., "Empowerment," 810.

Visioning is not for the nervous. Problematizing the present through vision erases the security that springs from the taken-for-granted.[74]

It stands to reason that the kind of vision required for a person to develop a sense of autonomy in culture must be a cultural vision. In other words, to the extent that 'autonomy' denotes self-sufficiency, independence, self-determination, it is impossible to work towards autonomy without a conception of the social self firmly in mind. What is more, this conception requires effort in an ongoing way, rather than as a quick-fix approach. If autonomy must be earned, then it must also be maintained and becomes another aspect of day to day life that is at risk when it is taken for granted. Autonomy entails risk taking, stepping into the unknown by challenging the comfortable boundaries that cradle us into complacency, and passivity. Autonomy requires action based upon cultural information: information + action = change.

A discussion of praxis is close to a discussion of cultural reflexivity. A person who conducts his or herself in a culturally reflexive manner is already participating in a form of praxis. In a dynamic late modern age, reflexivity denotes a critical responsiveness to the contexts in which a person carries out his or her everyday life. Reflexivity is defined by Appignanesi & Garratt as "an immediate critical consciousness of what one is doing, thinking or writing."[75] But, of course, self-conscious reflection may be applied in the course of whatever activity is at hand. To use a sporting example, a footballer who engages in an immediate critical consciousness of what he is doing might not simply be aware of the football hitting his boot, of the numbers of points needed to win this discrete game. To be culturally reflexive, a footballer would also be mindful of the institutional dimensions of football, the role it plays in national identity, the paradigms of masculinity that are privileged by sporting stereo-types, for example. Reflexivity means broadening one's awareness of this world beyond the limits of self-concern and entitlement. It combats the narcissistic impulse in that such an impulse undermines a 'self and society' mindset. We may be doing no more than watching an advertisement on the television, or nothing more than taking a leisurely stroll around the built environment, but there are ways of making our actions more useful than the sum of their immediately gratifying parts.

Sampson argues that "selves, persons, psychological traits, and so forth, including the very idea of psychological traits, are social and historical con-

---

[74] W. L. Schultz, "Sliding Into Our Futures: Provocation as a Path to Critical Futures Fluency" [excerpted from *Futures Fluency: explorations in leadership, vision, and creativity*], (University of Hawaii at Manoa, 1995), 2.
[75] R. Appignanesi, & C. Garratt, *Introducing Postmodernism* (Royston: Totem Books, 2005), 73.

structions, not naturally occurring objects."[76] Thus, being reflexive means asking of ourselves "How do our actions reflect trends or perhaps find us responding to broader social conditions, ideals, political relationships? Where are we located within this multifarious and complex thing called human culture? In working towards a deeper understanding of our 'location', we also further appreciation for our cultural subjectivity—the person we think we are. If a person's sense of autonomy and empowerment to act in the world translates as the expression of that self, the capacity to exercise personal choice, then cultural knowledge is instrumental in supporting that self-sufficiency. With a richer and clearer understanding, we may communicate better with each other, and cultural action is always more powerful when conducted in numbers.

By leading us to recognise our 'embeddedness' in culture, cultural reflexivity also promotes the insight that we are social constructions. A comment on tradition explains this point. Inglis makes the observation that "modern culture involves a questioning and relinquishing of traditional ways of doing and seeing things .... [It] seems to dissolve and destroy traditions, constantly replacing them with ever novel phenomena."[77] He adds that traditions are merely cultural constructions:

> What we take to have been traditions handed down from generation to generation ... have in fact been quite self-consciously assembled by certain politically motivated groups .... promulgated by elites and taken on by a mass public eager for a sense of historical stability and continuity.[78]

The understanding that culture is constructed, and not a manifestation of absolute truth, discloses an assumption about a notion of knowledge that underpins cultural reflexivity—the principle of 'radical doubt.' Giddens makes the claim that modernity

> institutionalises the principle of radical doubt and insists that all knowledge takes on the form of hypotheses: claims which may very well be true, but which are in principle always open to revision and may have at some point to be abandoned.[79]

---

[76] E. Sampson, "The Deconstruction of Self", in K. Gergen & J. Shotter (Eds.), *Texts of Identity: Inquiries in Social Construction* (pp. 1-19) (Newbury Park, California: Sage, 1989), 2.

[77] D. Inglis, *Culture and Everyday Life*, The New Sociology, series (London and New York: Routledge, 2005), 65.

[78] Ibid., 66.

[79] A. Giddens, *Modernity and Self-Identity: Self and Society in the Late Modern Age* (Stanford, California: Stanford University Press, 1991), 3.

Radical doubt impacts upon what we know and on how we conceptualise knowledge—regardless of whether the focus of such knowledge is self-interpretation or another other areas of life. To approach through the eyes of radical doubt means no longer recognising knowledge as stable and finite. By asking that knowledge remain open to revision at all times, radical doubt ensures that knowledge is thought of as a puzzle with multiple possible outcomes. These may, in turn, be constructed and reconstructed as new information comes to hand. In the case of traditional cultural practices, this means that they no longer be seen as hard and fast modes of behavioural discipline, obligation, convention. Traditions, such as marriage, may be approached, assessed, and reconfigured in the light of new ways of seeing them. We are very much used to the way that contemporary cultural values have significantly challenged the heteronormative dimension of marriage. The push to legalise same-sex marriage, for example, is but one instance in which the shackles of 'taken for granted' and routinised behaviours are under timely interrogation. This is all a part of the reflexivity—the self-critical dynamism—of late modernity.

Radical doubt invigorates the potential for people's cultural knowledge to evolve—a point that returns us to the importance of critical action over cultural passivity. The key point here is that, in light of radical doubt, cultural knowledge lends itself to reflexive organisation. Giddens' suggestion that the "reflexivity of modernity actually undermines the certainty of knowledge" tells that reflexivity can feed directly back into the ethos of radical doubt.[80] Cultural interpretations of the external world, of natural phenomenon, and of issues pertaining to the project of the self, may each be reflexively negotiated.

In the notion that "the reflexivity of modernity turns out to confound the expectations of Enlightenment thought"[81] we find a pathway leading us from the notion of cultural reflexivity back to the theory of the dérive— towards an 'at odds' negotiation and interpretation of the built environment. Reflexivity makes a call for a person to entertain a 'big picture' view of his or her lived experience by recognising how other experiences and pieces of information impact upon it, how he or she may act in light of these additional considerations. As a comment on the demands of industrialisation, of the modern city, the dérive opens the doorway to critical engagement in this broader context, not least of all in psychogeographic terms. Once again, this critical dimension of the dérive is unavailable to the viewer during the course of the *Lose Yourself in Melbourne* advertisement. We cannot read the mind of the woman with the red wool, or her character, just what is evident to us. Thus, from what we are shown (the carefree, non-confrontational, and apolitical stroll) the advertisement's content is conducive to the assumption that

---

[80] A. Giddens, *Modernity and Self-Identity: Self and Society in the Late Modern Age* (Stanford, California: Stanford University Press, 21.
[81] Ibid.

passivity is enough. The woman is moving her own body around the built environment, but there is no evidence of activity in terms of critical thinking. Some might say that there needn't be—because it's 'only an ad.' But, to the extent that the historical precedents of the dérive evoke greater critical engagement, the broader critical context warrants articulation. An active engagement in the historical contexts of the dérive leaves little doubt that there is much more to take into account than the mass media tourist-package suggests. There is much more that enables us, with the power of that information, to theoretically and practically reinstate the dérive's critical content. By de-emphasising the self-serving countenance of the broadcast, in practice, the theory may be put to a far more reflexive and sustainable purpose.

The knowledge we shall call *phenomenological* (or, to speak in terms of currently active schools, "ethnomethodological") sets out to make explicit the truth of primary experience of the social word, i.e. all that is inscribed in the relationship of *familiarity* with the familiar environment, the unquestioning apprehension of the social world which, by definition, does not reflect upon itself and excludes the question of the conditions of its own possibility.[82]

Significant attention has been given to contextualising the notion of the dérive, both in a historical and in a contemporary cultural sense. Passing mention has been made to the dérive as a strategy that a person may use to break, if momentarily, out from their habitual behaviour in order to see their built environment in a new way. It is now time to pay more attention to the notion of defamiliarisation by considering a modest selection of its champions. Just as history was mined in our search for precedents that could inform our reading of the *Lose Yourself in Melbourne* advertisement, we may also look to history in order to better understand just what defamiliarisation is all about, not to mention how we might come to think of the dérive as a context in which defamilarisation might take place. We shall explore how the practice of dérive and defamilarisation in the built environment might be enough to enrich our own cultural lives.

Above, we find Bourdieu posing a problem, but how might this problem be addressed. This need for a method of interrogation is one with which David Inglis is concerned when, in his own words, he asks:

How might we go about examining the ways in which cultural forces, together with social factors, influence, shape and structure our everyday activities? A key aspect of both sociological and anthropological responses to this question is to emphasize that one must take what is routine and very familiar to one, and try to defamiliarize oneself with it, making it seem strange and peculiar, rather than ordinary and banal.[83]

Inglis makes the point that the habituation of everyday life fosters its uncritical negotiation, something that I have given voice to throughout this

---

[82] P. Bourdieu, "Outline of a Theory of Practice" (tr. Richard Nice) (Cambridge: Cambridge University Press, 1977), 3.
[83] D. Inglis, *Culture and Everyday Life*, The New Sociology, series (London and New York: Routledge, 2005), 11.

book. However, Inglis adds that uncritical countenance of the familiar may be weakened when a person makes steps to disrupt his or her comfort zones. One such strategy, that to which Inglis refers, is 'defamiliarisation.' From the outset, it is important to clarify that defamiliarisation is less about a person actively positioning his or herself 'outside of' the 'normal' operations of an industrial society, for if we did not know better this might be taken as an opening for unethical behaviour. Or, to anchor this insight down in Nicholas Mirzoeff's statement "there is no outside to culture."[84] Given this, it stands to reason that defamiliarisation, far from a motivation to 'escape' the sphere of cultural influence, instead calls for a person to position his or her self in a way that is essentially 'at odds' with it. The following case studies shall consolidate this approach by ascertaining just how this 'at odds' has been achieved.

## Viktor Borisovich Shklovsky (1893-1984)

To offer some background to this practical strategy, defamiliarisation is a term made famous by the Russian Formalist Viktor Shklovsky, who coined the term in his seminal paper *Art as Device* (1917). Shklovsky used 'defamiliarisation' to denote a strategy of conscious re-engagement with those conceivably banal and ordinary everyday practices that by way of their habituation tend to fade into transparency and, once hidden in plain sight, can readily slip beneath the radar of critical thinking. Shklovsky wrote that

> [h]abitualization devours works, clothes, furniture, one's wife, and the fear of war. 'If the whole complex lives of many people go on unconsciously, then such lives are as if they had never been.' And art exists that one may recover the sensation of life; it exists to make one feel things, to make the stone *stony*. The purpose of art is to impart the sensation of things as they are perceived and not as they are known. The technique of art is to make objects "unfamiliar," to make forms difficult, to increase the difficulty and length of perception because the process of perception is an aesthetic end in itself and must be prolonged. *Art is a way of experiencing the artfulness of an object; the object is not important.*[85]

In the second sentence of this passage, we detect an echo of Socrates' bold assertion that "an unexamined life is not worth living."[86] This philosophical and historical grounding frames defamiliarisation as a way of enriching everyday experience. Defamiliarisation entails treating the taken for granted in a self-conscious way; fostering a fresh perspective on familiar ways of

---

[84] N. Mirzoeff, *An Introduction to Visual Culture* (London and New York: Routledge, 1999), 23.
[85] J. Rivkin and M. Ryan (eds.). *Literary Theory: An Anthology.* 2nd ed. (Malden: Blackwell Publishing Ltd, 1998), 16.
[86] Socrates, *Apology*, 38a.

thinking. Maybe it is the process of going outside to check the letterbox, or the process of making a sandwich. I don't think it matters too much which example a person chooses; I say this because it is possible that someone might view one option as being too boring to consider, such as raking up leaves, or hanging out the washing. There is much about day to day life that passes by without so much as a glance; as if it were almost entirely void of meaning. Often, the most boring and unlikely instances are the most pertinent.

The familiarity and perhaps, consequently, the conceived monotony of our routines means that the contexts in which we operate transform into a kind of cultural white noise. A person might act as he or she always has. What more is there to say? However, by defamiliarising aspects of what is taking place, the routines what we are already engaged in, we activate our capacity to counteract the monotony that we conceive these to embody. By fostering a critical consciousness of what we are doing or saying, defamiliarisation supports a mindfulness of our built environment and its impact upon how we think, feel and behave.

An example of this push to liberate the 'spectacle' from the chains of normalcy (and invisibility) can be detected in the theatrical Verfremdungseffekt—the 'distancing' or 'alienation' effect developed by German playwright Bertold Brecht. For Brecht, defamiliarisation meant increasing the opportunity for political and intellectual engagement by actively discouraging an audience's emotional connection to the dilemmas of the characters of a play.[87] To demonstrate this, we may take, as an example, Brecht's epic theatre production *Mother Courage and her Children*, a tragedy of war written in 1939 (and, typical of Brechtian theatre, created for the working class). While watching a performance of *Mother Courage*, Brecht's audience would be discouraged from becoming emotionally attached to the characters of the story. Brecht's orchestration of audience distancing and dissociation (known as die Verfremdungseffekt "defamiliarisation effect") would be attempted by way of various techniques, including titles on placards shown at the beginning of every scene that tells the audience what is going to happen, actors changing costume and character on stage, as well as the use of songs to reinforce key themes and Brecht's socio-political messages. This practice of using defamiliarisation (estrangement) works as a means to alerting the audience to the cultural implications of individual complacency. By disrupting the audiences absorption in the illusion of a play, his aim was to ensure that the audience were given the opportunity to remain critical of the social realities that were being represented.

*Mother Courage*, as produced by the Western Michigan University Department of Theatre, is an interesting contemporary take on Brecht's play.

---

[87] A. Bennett and N. Royle, *An Introduction to Literature, Criticism and Theory* (United Kingdom: Pearson Longman, 2004), 35.

The question of how to integrate modern technology into the performance without it detracting from the play itself led to the decision to screen a digitised game, based on the play, behind the actors while they were performing *Mother Courage* onstage. As media designer Ken Abbott explains:

> We thought the fit was very, very good because we were looking also for a method to get the audience to disassociate themselves at times. Brecht tried to use distancing effects to keep the audience from becoming too emotionally detached to the show and we thought that, by taking the show and putting it in a video game form at times, at a certain level trivialises the show itself and hopefully pushes the audience back and also, I think, makes a commentary on contemporary media by taking a look at how we tend to trivialise war and combat in video games.[88]

To the extent that Brecht tried to counteract a human tendency to exhibit ambivalence towards social struggles, *Mother Courage* demonstrates a role that defamiliarisation can play as a critical method for creative practice; defamiliarisation challenges a person by requiring him or her to confront habitual ways of seeing and experiencing the world. But defamiliarisation needn't be easy in order to become productive.

In this sense, I should like to build upon Shklovsky's insight and Brecht's demonstration of this, by sharing a personal anecdote. When I was younger, I spent several years learning to play the violin. One of the most important lessons for me came at a point in time, about three years into my study, when I commenced lessons with a different teacher. Almost straight away he identified a problem with my playing posture that was impacting negatively on both the sound of the notes that I was playing as well as on my capacity to play for an extended period of time. There was too much tension in my shoulders, which affected how my arms and hands worked. My teacher pointed out that, although my handling of the violin had sufficed so far, in order to progress to the next level of playing it was necessary for me to take stock of my technique and make some changes. While this all made sense, by my third year of violin tuition I had become accustomed to playing in a certain way; I had made a habit of playing with a faulty posture. I was so used to playing in this way that, upon picking up my instrument, I would promptly adopt that posture without a moment of conscious consideration. My habit meant that I no longer felt its affects; they continued to impact upon my playing, but they, themselves, remained virtually invisible to me.

As a result, it was always going to be difficult for me to break the problematic routine and progress to the next level of technical proficiency. And

---

[88] WMU Theatre promotional video for Mother Courage and Her Children, 2009, Accessed 10 July, 2010, http://www.youtube.com/watch?v=oeYwFzBNk2k&feature=related

yet, something that my teacher said to me was instrumental in making this positive change: "Just allow it to feel different." What might have seemed to be a simple suggestion on the surface was, in fact, a crucial insight. My improvement depended upon my ability to resist the comfort and security of established modes of behaviour. My progress—my further empowerment as a violin player, necessitated an active resistance to what had been, for me, nothing more than an uncritically held habit. By taking the time to stop what I was doing—by engaging some timely self-criticism—gradually, I found that I was able to play with less tension, less effort, for better and far more sustainable results.

This personal anecdote is useful in that it demonstrates Shklovsky's point that defamiliarisation is not a quick fix, but rather it is a long term process of phenomenological recovery. At the core of this recovery is the sensation of life by way of those activities that comprise everyday experience. But it is counter-productive to force-feed this kind of 'help' (at the risk of replaying a critical scene from Charlie Chaplin's *Modern Times*); a person's adoption or rejection of pre-established modes of conduct is only meaningful and sustainable when this stems from personal choice. Being passive and comfortable and secure is all well and good if you take what you are and what you have to be entirely fulfilling. But we do not inhabit a fixed world, a world in a vacuum. Rather, our lives are continually pressed against uncertainty; we don't know what is ahead of us. We don't know who we will meet in the future or what roles they might play in relation to our own experiences. So it is unlikely that the conditions under which we live now will remain unchanged. In turn, it is unlikely that the information which we use to make sense of our day to day experiences will remain static, stagnant.

Thus, defamiliarisation can be taken as an exercise in resiliency, whereby we force change, encourage it, embrace it, and explore it. Living in a world of flux is surely reason enough to engage in a life strategy that accommodates flux and that capitalises on its negotiability. It makes sense to adopt a strategy that sustains a prolonged process of perception, As such a strategy, defamiliarisation serves as an exercise for recovering what Shklovsky might also call the artfulness of life.

Building upon Shklovsky's train of thought, one context of experience that prompts an intensified state of defamiliarisation is tourism. The stranger in an unfamiliar land is, perhaps, the visitor to an unfamiliar city. Not quite orientated, the buildings seem unusual, as might people or the language, the customs. Detached from the monotony of his or her native environment, the tourist finds his or her self detached from the blinkered comfort of familiarity, from the motivations in light of which they might usually conduct themselves, their passage through an urban setting.

It is as if the tourist has the eyes of a curious alien. Something that we need to keep reminding ourselves is that, as communicators, we operate within a cultural system, consciously or unconsciously. We have been born into a pre-existing industrialised society. But that does not mean that we need to let ourselves get swept up in the currents, the trends, the popular sentiments, without really knowing how these function or why they have come to function in the first place. As Giddens observes, while culture acts upon us, we also have the capacity to act.[89] Our actions and interactions can be enriched and strengthened through studying our cultural system.

Some might hold the opinion that they are not influenced by the culture in which they live and work. But perhaps that view is itself a reflection of how deep-seated those influences have become. Perhaps such a view simply reflects how institutionalised and embedded into the industrial world that person has become—the very invisibly that defamiliarisation works hard to confront. If we were not significantly influenced by our culture, why do we have the hairstyle that we have? Why might we be wearing jeans instead of a loincloth? Why are we clothed at all? Why aren't we going out into the bush and hunting down our own dinner? Why is it so hard to get a job without having a tax file number? Why might we find appeal in one kind of advertisement (such as an advert of a woman wandering around the city with a big red ball of wool) instead of another? And so on.

By addressing these kinds of questions, we become more adept at seeing how our culture continues to influence us. Being influenced does not mean that we are just passive and disempowered. In fact, it is by acknowledging how we are influenced that we can become more independent as members of a culture. Being ill-informed about our culture does not make the impact that it has on us go away. It simply finds us more susceptible to coercion.

Engaging our capacity to act requires a critical self-consciousness. Perhaps there have been times when you have driven down a road between your workplace and your home, one that you have driven countless times before, and all of a sudden found that you have driven for a few kilometers without even thinking about it. Familiarity interferes with our awareness of what is happening around us. Once we have passed this period and have taken our mind out of autopilot, we might look back critically at the last few kilometers and think how lucky we were that nothing jumped, or drove, out in front of us, disturbed at how unprepared we would have been if something unexpected had happened.

The potential to 'zone out' in this way is alarming. If familiarity can impair how we operate a motor vehicle, it can certainly impair other areas of life. We can also take the example of people getting caught up in the hype of the new-year department store sales. In the crowded moment, we might feel totally fired up at the thought of being amongst hundreds of people, falling over each other just to spend money (also known as 'saving'). That evening, the news reel might show footage of the event and remind us, now at a dis-

---

[89] A. Giddens, *Modernity and Self-Identity: Self and Society in the Late Modern Age* (Stanford, California: Stanford University Press, 14.

tance from the scene, how irrational or even dangerous it actually was. According to Shklovsky, in order to defamiliarise something, we need to stop seeing it as something that is normal, and start to see it as something that is quite peculiar.

## Craig Raine (1944-)

A source of inspiration for artists and thinkers throughout the last hundred years, the notion of defamiliarisation was given centre stage via Bertold Brecht's theatrical Verfremdungseffekt. For Brecht, defamiliarisation encouraged an audience's political and intellectual engagement by discouraging the viewer's emotional connection to a performance. This is something that interested English poet Craig Raine in the 1970s and 80s.[90] It is with this in mind that Raine coined the phrase 'Martian poetry' to refer to a kind of English surrealist poetry that aimed to free itself from the familiarity of the English literary tradition. At odds with what Raine conceived to be a conservative and stifling literary canon, Martian poetry was the creative context in which he frequently described everyday objects in unusual and inventive ways. For example, in his poem *A Walk in the Country*, Raine describes a sewage farm as being 'like a tape-recorder, whose black spools turn night and day' (Poets graves, glossary). Raine thought that it was the role of the writer to challenge experience and perception. Thus, through his Martian poetry, Raine encouraged writers to see the world afresh, as if through the eyes of a curious alien. Raine once stated:

> What the poet does is as ordinary and mysterious as digesting. I question. I break life down. I impose chaos on order. For instance, we think we know how food is ingested, digested, divided into energy and excrement. The neat theory, however, is one thing; control of the process is another; consciousness of the process yet another. Are we aware of protein in the stomach being acted on by pepsin, the appropriate enzyme? Digestion, thinking and breathing are all functions we perform without knowing how we perform them.[91]

Raine's statement offers a model for thinking about culture and everyday life—a person's long term negotiation of his or her historical circumstances and cultural conditions. We can think about what it takes to digest culture, to put it in our mouths and consume it. It seems simple enough to live and breathe an industrialised culture. But how often do we stop to think about what makes up this culture in the first place—what it is that we are really in-

---

[90] M. Booth, *British Poetry 1964 to 1984* (London & New York: Routledge, 1985), 114.
[91] Author Statement retrieved from "Contemporary Writers" website produced by The British Council, and in association with Booktrust. http://www.contemporary writers .com/ authors/?p=auth212#authorstatement

haling, digesting? What is that culture that also consumes our everyday experience?

By making things seems odd, Martian Poetry exposes our commonplace perceptions as limited assumptions. And it is important to challenge these because, while familiarity might make for a streamlined and seemingly predictable daily schedule, it does not allow for much innovation or self-growth. Raine's Martian poetry explores the spaces beyond the square—beyond that which is conventional and 'given.' It shows us that we can be active in the construction of personal meaning. In his poem, entitled *A Martian Sends a Postcard Home* (1979), Raine described books and their effects upon readers as...

> *mechanical birds with many wings*
> *perch on the hand*
> *cause the eyes to melt*
> *or the body to shriek without pain*[92]

Raine's unconventional approach to describing the world provides us with an important cultural insight—if our understanding of the world is unfixed, open to alternative solutions, then it is not natural, normal, or inevitable. To the extent that our behaviour is informed by how we think, so too is culture something that we construct. After all, as Jeff Lewis confirms, culture begins within the human mind:

> Culture is constructed by humans in order to communicate and create community .... Culture begins with an imagining of the world about us; these imaginings are represented in some way .... formed in discourse, language, symbols, signs, and texts – all concepts applied to meaning systems.[93]

The constructedness of culture enables the proliferation of cultural difference—a plurality of religious faith, politics, personal ambitions, a choice of chocolate flavours, and yet the practicalities of daily life often find us treading the same paths every day. What does this routinisation of everyday activity say about the types of people (self-identity), the kind of culture (national identity), that we make manifest? One could say that the decision to stay in bed would be a sure sign of laziness. But maybe it is just as lazy for someone to make the choice to get up and go to work again and again, perhaps unthinkingly, like any other day. Perhaps the acceptance of this routine to the point of monotony is as lazy as the alternative, because how easy is it to do

---

[92] C. Raine, *A Martian Sends a Postcard Home* (Oxford: Oxford University Press, 1979), 1.

[93] J. Lewis, *Cultural Studies: The Basics* (London: Sage, 2002), 13.

the same thing over and over again? How easy is it to wallow in the sense of safety and security that this predictability seems to promise?

If defamiliarisation prolongs and complicates perception, a risk managing culture might find nominal value in defamiliarisation, in the capacity for a loyal employer to wake up and have the courage to say "today I am going to do something different, something that challenges precisely who I think I am, who I think I would like to be, to make the step required to approach the world in a slightly different way, to experience it from an alternative perspective, to break out of the self-made mould I call 'myself.' However, I find the appeal of habit counter-intuitive, even life-negating to the extent that the uncertain, the unknown, the unfamiliar, is what we essentially step into with each passing moment, ever stepping into an abyss of the future. This dabbling in uncertainty, the risk of being existentially adrift; is this not part of our human condition, the foundation for all those habits that we pile on top of everyday perhaps as a way of denying life's conceivable aimlessness? Without getting too far into poetry, for me, defamiliarisation is close to life; it seems reflective of what it is like to live in, and explore, a material reality, like a curious child who looks in amazement at the phenomena of day to day life with undisciplined eyes. Not yet initiated into the adults world, but not against it either, the child 'at odds' slips aside many of the conventions and associated expectations to which other 'trained' people can comply without thinking. If stepping into the unknown is what we need to do in order to invigorate self-growth, why not make this central to our life-political routine?

I am reluctant to agree with Shklovsky's claim that, as a process, defamiliarisation "transforms perception into a kind of transcendent activity.'"[94] Perhaps this is simply a matter of semantics, but if we are to take this as the raising of awareness above the numbing effects of habituation, then I shall agree with him. But, in this sense Shklovsky seems to imply that art is separate from everyday experience, I am inclined to suggest that, in the context of the dérive, defamiliarisation provides a means by which the flâneur may come 'back down to earth'—to return from the lofty ideal of the sacrosanct. In any case, for each of these creative people, baring the devices of everyday life meant remaining wary of the silent asphyxiations threatened by habitual experience.

In short, it can be said that defamiliarisation "makes things 'strange' to make them truly visible".[95] By turning our attention to Georges Perec, it will become clearer that this is easier said than done; that defamiliarisation not only entails the slowing down of experience but also an increased difficulty in the processes of observation. For pleasure seekers, this may well find it rein-

---

[94] G. L. Bruns, *Modern Poetry and the Idea of Language: A Critical and Historical Study* (University of Illinois: Dalkey Archive Press, 2001), 76.
[95] P. Waugh, *Literary Theory and Criticism: An Oxford Guide*, (USA: Oxford University Press, 2007), 216.

forcing the comforting appeal of familiarity in all its promise of immediate gratification. For the culturally minded, defamiliarisation means an opportunity for reflexivity by fostering "an immediate critical consciousness of what one is doing, thinking or writing."[96] The subject of our next case study, Perec's writing demonstrates how fruitful this can be.

## Georges Perec (1936-82)

> What's really going on, what we're experiencing, the rest, all the rest, where is it? How should we take account of, question, describe what happens every day and recurs every day: the banal, the quotidian, the obvious, the common, the ordinary, the infra-ordinary, the background noise, the habitual?[97]

Overall, our approach to defamiliarisation has been to recognise it as a platform for a person's estrangement from a kind of 'familiarity as anesthesia.' Thus, it would be unfair to talk about defamiliarisation without acknowledging the work of prolific French avant-garde writer Georges Perec—he who plumbed the much overlooked depths of the 'obvious' while smoking himself into an early grave, we regret. Perec's writing invites us into a world of enlivened banality. I mean this in terms of Perec's ability to focus in on those things which we might take for granted, largely because we treat them this way. And so Perec, in the first pages of *Species of Space*, and under the heading "A few other banalities," reminds us that "We spend more than a third of our lives in a bed" before proceeding to explore the "body in the bed."[98]

We are left with no doubt that what is under investigation is his body, along with all the beds he has slept on. This use of the self as a source of data, making much of Perec's work autoethnographic, suits the playfulness with which he observes. For sure, there is much to be said about not taking oneself too seriously. But this aside, Perec's methodical, purposeful articulation of what others might consider 'goes without saying' means that he catches up to much of what modern society learns to overlook. It is what John Sturrock calls Perec's "unusually concrete mode of literary sociology."[99] We can understand this notion of the 'concrete' as pertaining to Perec's interest in making that abstract solid or, at least, drawing substance out of the everyday; of in-

---

[96] R. Appignanesi, and C. Garratt. *Introducing Postmodernism* (United Kingdom: Totem Books, 2005), 73.

[97] G. Perec, *Species of Space and Other Pieces*, J. Sturrock, trans. (London: Penguin Books, 1999), 209-10.

[98] Ibid., XIV.

[99] G. Perec, Species of Space and Other Pieces, J. Sturrock, trans., (London: Penguin Books, 1999), XIV.

vesting, in the 'overlooked' and the 'taken for granted', a certain density through his literary style.

While I view Perec's as an attempt to write his material reality life back (reminiscent of Shklovsky's 'recovery' of the sensation of life), his elaboration on the 'bleeding obvious' is far from his trying to squeeze blood out of a stone. For the very abundance of text that Perec generated goes a long way to suggest that his project was a fruitful one, that there was so much more to what he was doing than simply generating text. His reporter-like stance is essentially communicative, albeit often difficult and drawn out. That, too, is part of the project, where the reader is forced, as Perec continuously forced himself also, to dwell on the things that our industrialised modern age encourages us to skip across, perhaps because they are the material realities that take time and effort away from the modern ideal. Of course, his self-conscious discussion about how a person uses their bed, talking about the place of leisure and rest, surely flies in the face of a broader society's avid organisation around human productivity and financial viability. But his time spent on thinking and classifying, on how many ways there are to arrange books, for example, feeds into his oeuvre of what it means to:

> question the habitual. But that's just it, we're habituated to it. We don't question it, it doesn't question us, it doesn't seem to pose a problem, we live it without thinking, as if it carried within it neither questions nor answers, as if it weren't the bearer of any information. This is no longer even conditioning, it's anaesthesia. We sleep through our lives in a dreamless sleep. But where is our life? Where is our body? Where is our space?[100]

Perec's acute and lucid observational style cuts to the quick of the things that we value and to how much is lost in the process of our evaluations. He is anxious, I believe, about this loss which he sees all around him, taking place not only as a part of everyday life but as a condition. Which is why I suggest that Perec's writing traces a path of personal proof, a documentation of anecdotal evidence that, I imagine, enabled him to find his way through this condition. His literary sociology can be taken as a method for cementing objects with words before he loses sight of them. He draws up this insurance policy with word plays, puzzles, intricate descriptions, even a detailed list of postcard messages that he'd received from friends and family over the years (collected under the heading 'Two Hundred and Forty-three Postcards in Real Colour', from *L'infra-ordinaire, 1989*). By itself, this collection is an intriguing but exhausting feat of classification (from 1961-1978 Perec was employed as an archivist at the Hôpital Saint-Antoine's *Neurophysiological Research*

---

[100] G. Perec, *Species of Space and Other Pieces*, J. Sturrock, trans. (London: Penguin Books, 1999), 210.

*Laboratory*). To give you some idea of the content of Perec's postcard collection, the reader finds: "We're roaming around in the Greek Islands. All the sea urchins we're eating! The people are being really nice to us. Yippee! And to think we've got to come home!"[101]; "We're traveling through the Balearics. Beautiful and we're stuffing ourselves into the bargain. I've got sunburnt. Expect to be back a week on Monday."[102]

Perec was a hoarder, for sure, and yet he managed to keep an incredibly comprehensive inventory of the objects that he had placed and piled up around himself in his Parisian domicile—that co-habited the spaces of his life. His was a seemingly inexhaustible curiosity with regard the nuances of such subject/object co-habitation. As Perec observed:

> What we need to question is bricks, concrete, glass, our table manners, our utensils, our tools, the way we spend our time, our rhythms. To question that which seems to have ceased forever to astonish us. We live, true, we breathe, true; we walk, we open doors, we go down staircases, we sit at a table in order to eat, we lie down on a bed in order to sleep. How? Where? When? Why? Describe your street. Describe another street. Compare."[103]

We might sense a 'before it's too late' trailing off the end of Perec's call for the reader to make comparisons in his or her own material reality—as if his call announced an urgency for others to join him in exhausting their subjectivity, to work it to the bone, to never take it for granted—the sensation of life that his parents had taken from them in the formative years of his life (Perec's father died while serving the French Army in WW2, his mother died in the Nazi Holocaust). In a late modern age, we are accustomed to seeing war being played out on the television. The Australian national media expresses uproar when, after almost a decade in the Middle East, the death toll reaches 12. Our comfortable lives entrap us in complacency. We might feel privileged to know very little of the kind of motivations that Perec, certainly Shklovsky and Brecht, would have had as a result of their proximity to military conflicts.

But why wait for war to find one's motivation? Both Perec and Schklovsky posit the quotidian, the 'everyday,' as a viable target for interrogation. Perec echoes Shklovsky's sentiments entirely in his regard for the way that work, clothing, interpersonal relationships, even domestic furniture, is devoured by the habitualisation of everyday life, with the city being a prime target of such appeal, such anxiety at the thought of life being consumed by

[101] G. Perec, *Species of Space and Other Pieces*, J. Sturrock, trans. (London: Penguin Books, 1999), 236.
[102] Ibid., 223.
[103] Ibid., 210.

itself. With this broader cultural concern in mind, Perec understood the importance in literature that "starts with yourself and goes towards others. It's what I call sympathy, a sort of projection, and at the same time an appeal!"[104] This level of cultural mindfulness ensures that Perec's elaborately detailed explorations of the quotidian are not confined within the limits of the personal; they maintain cultural use-value on a broader scale. He does not simply talk to us, but urges the reader to get up, go out, and try some of these worldly exercises out for his or her self. His indulgence in the banalities of day to day social behaviour is an indulgence in the practice of creative cultural thinking—perhaps equivalent to the diver who straps enough weight to his or her diving belt to over-ride the body's natural buoyancy and, thus, effectively sinks below the visible currents to the ocean floor.

Much like a diver, Perec dwells in the depths and in the gravity of things, *les choses*, where the light is different and the terrain looks different, where the colours of coral and strange fish surprise human eyes and enrich the experience overall. What Perec calls 'sympathy' we can also call sensitivity, vulnerability, concern, softness, discernment, difficulty, or fragility. No doubt Perec would have enjoyed compiling a significantly longer list of associated words.[105] By diving into the materiality of everyday life (admittedly, the notion of diving into 'the concrete' shows the peculiarity of this metaphor), Perec's writing documents his news that there is treasure down there, below what we are used to seeing, below the collective allure of the horizon or, more to the point, hiding in plain sight. On the flip side of Perec's compulsive analyses, is a genuine desire to share the spoils. His meticulousness, when it comes to creating an inventory of his cultural world, is much more about obsession than possession. We may consider Perec's step by step account of "the number of operations the driver of a vehicle is subjected to when he parks merely in order to go and buy a hundred grams of fruit jelly"[106]:

— parks by means of a certain amount of toing and froing
— switches off the engine
— withdraws the key, setting off a first anti-theft device
— extricates himself from the vehicle

<hr>

[104] G. Perec, *Species of Space and Other Pieces*, J. Sturrock, trans. (London: Penguin Books, 1999), 153.
[105] "Species of Space," offers the reader two prime examples of what I am referring to: the first is a list of words relating to their heading, "Moving in" (pp. 35-6); the second is located at the end of Species of Space, under the heading "Index of some of the words used in this work" (pp. 93-5). Not for the faint hearted, there is a third example; "Attempt at an Inventory of the Liquid and Solid Foodstuffs Ingurgitated by Me in the Course of the Year Nineteen Hundred and Seventy-Four" needs no further explanation (pp. 244-9).
[106] G. Perec, *Species of Space and Other Pieces*, J. Sturrock, trans. (London: Penguin Books, 1999), 51.

— winds up the left-hand front window
— locks it
— checks that the left-hand rear door is locked;
    if not:
    opens it
    raises the handle inside
    slams the door
    checks it's locked securely

In the course of documenting my own defamiliarising dérives, it shall soon become very clear just how difficult it is to break out of a kind of domestic blindness played out in the broader social sphere. It seems near on impossible to see everything, to do total justice to the materiality of a moment. Impossible or not, Perec gained a remarkable amount of ground.

Perhaps you too will sense a jovial bemusement in his comment on fashion included in *Penser/Classer*:

Fashion might be as much what distinguishes as what begins together: the sharing in some superior quality, 'happy few'-ism, and so on. That is at least conceivable. But at the risk of being taxed with elitism, I shall continue to ask myself why so very many people take pride in showing off handbags bearing the monogram of their manufacturer. I can understand people attaching some important to having their initials on the things they are fond of (shirt, suitcases, napkin rings, etc.), but the initials of a supplier? That really is beyond me.[107]

At the risk of stating the obvious (though this explicatory approach is most certainly one that Perec held in high regard), he is not opposed to, but rather 'at odds with' the object world as it is experienced by a consuming mass. Perec was also a consumer, but his eyes sought depth in the 'commonplace'—in those things that had been repeated so many times that it was if they had been emptied for their meanings (like the childhood language game).

Perhaps in my construction of this bridge between the past and the future, perhaps in this moment between the theory and is practice, I should take heed of Perec's proposed urban method in trying to create something meaningful of one's cultural world, of trying to have what Socrates might have thought of as being a life worth living. Perhaps Perec gives us a clue in *Species of Spaces* when he says that:

---

[107] G. Perec, *Species of Space and Other Pieces*, J. Sturrock, trans. (London: Penguin Books, 1999), 157.

you must either give up talking of the town, about the town, or else force yourself to talk about it as simply as possible, obviously, familiarly. Get rid of all preconceived ideas. Stop thinking in ready-made terms, forget what the town planners and sociologists have said.[108]

It's not just boredom at the thought of the ready-made, perhaps one such as Duchamp's poor-man's fountain, which is striking in this passage. For Perec entertains an uncertainty principal that steps before all claims to knowledge, not least of all sociological knowledge. We can also say that Perec is asking us to forget about, moreover to feign our forgetting. He effectively implores us to pretend we are a person visiting a city for the first time (our city for the first time); to step into that stance of receptiveness to the unknown and to see what it contains. As he points out at the beginning of *Species of Space*, the subject of that book "is not the void exactly, but rather what there is round about or inside it."[109] Perec shows that he is aware of 'talking up the obvious' from the sink-hole of common-sense. In using the word 'familiar', he emphasises the importance of 'accessibility' in matters of the human conditions; he seeks to disclose ourselves to ourselves, and pursues this disclosure without ego getting in the way.

By defamiliarising the familiar, Perec's concrete writing style also encourages us to adopt the eyes of Raine's curious alien. Thus, what better way to see the town or, by extension, the city? In Perec, we can detect a dérive aesthetic, a nomadic aesthetic, the potentially subversive scope of culture (due, in part, to one's sensitivity to—a hunger for—that which is under threat of invisibility). When we talk "of" and "about" the city, just as we might talk of wandering through the malls, arcades, and alley ways, about the bustling streets, the historical reference points to which I have drawn attention highlights creative responses to modernity as a historical circumstance and as a cultural condition. In other words, not only in terms of changes in a material reality but also in terms of how certain cultural figures have interpreted and responded to these changes. The dérive is one way of making the theory of defamiliarisation actionable.

## Jim Henson's 'Uncle "Traveling" Matt' (1983-7, c. 96 episodes)

Shklovsky, Brecht, Raine, and Perec all explore unique and creative approaches to the interpretation of everyday life. We can appreciate them not only for their imaginings of society but also for their willingness to share these insights as a means to enriching the everyday lives of other people. For the forms that they occupied, we may say said a book about the theory of art, a political theatrical performance, sophisticated poetry and intelligent word

---

[108] G. Perec, *Species of Space and Other Pieces*, J. Sturrock, trans. (London: Penguin Books, 1999), 61-2.
[109] Ibid., 5.

playing, are best suited to an adult audience. To the extent that culture is taught, and despite the acknowledgement of the playfulness of the dérive and of defamiliarisation, there is one audience that has not yet been considered.

Children are curious creatures. It is a convenient coincidence that a close male friend, a reasonably new father, has shared his amazement at how fascinating it is to see the world through his daughter's eyes. "The things that she sees, the things that she says", he recalls, "always blow me away. It's like she's visiting from another planet and I'm just tagging along for the ride." There is much to connect Raine's notion of the curious alien to the child who is seeing so much of the world for the very first time; for a child, numbers and letters are strange. A child must learn how to write his or her own name, that difficult formation of lines and curves that is meant to stand for his or her self. New foods, new clothes, the first hair-cut or trip to the dentist. What an amazing and terrifying place this unfamiliar world must be. How wonderful to be experiencing life without the baggage of past experiences (or with the littlest of bags), presumptions, assumptions, knowledge that set up expectations, judgments, definitions, and classifications.

The implicit connection between 'alien eyes' and 'young eyes' is one of the main reasons why I have chosen to consider one of Jim Henson's creations for the final case study in this chapter. Best known for his Muppet Show, Henson used the world of puppetry to create funny (Fozzie Bear), strange (Animal, Beaker), lovable (Kermit the Frog and Miss Piggy), and cantankerous characters (Statler and Waldorf). He entertained audiences by showing them the world through the plastic eyes of countless alien-like characters. Of particular interest, however is his series called *Fraggle Rock*.

*Fraggle Rock* is a children's television program that aired for four seasons between 1983 and 1987 in the United States. It also aired on Australian television and proved very popular across the country. The program centred on the day to day lives of several humanoid creatures with a height of approximately 50 cm's. The Fraggle puppets inhabit a place called Fraggle Rock having adventures and singing songs together. Fraggle Rock is the home of many characters, in particular Gobo, Mokey, Red, Boober, and Wembley.

The unfamiliar world beyond the comforting familiarity of Fraggle Rock is often a risky one. Two exits from the rock are worth mentioning. One leads into a garden belonging to the Gorgs—big hairy and oafish creatures (approximately 6.7m tall). There are three Gorgs, a father and mother, who believe that they are the king and queen of the universe, and their son, Junior. This small reclusive family think of the Fraggles as pests, perhaps equivalent to the way that suburbanites might regard mice or rats. As a result, they pose a great threat to the Fraggles.

Another exit from Fraggle Rock leads directly into the workshop of a human called Doc. He is kept company by a shaggy dog called Sprocket (Sprocket has seen the Fraggles, the true nature of which his master remains unaware). What's strange for Doc is that, every so often, he receives a postcard in the mail from someone called Uncle Traveling Matt. With no knowledge of anyone by that name, Doc routinely throws the postcards into the waste paper basket.

Of all the *Fraggle Rock* characters, it is Uncle Traveling Matt to whom I should like to give special attention. This is because Uncle Matt experiences the outside world (which he refers to as 'outer space') as if through the eyes of one of Raine's curious aliens; there is something very telling, and rather moving, in the way that habituated cultural phenomena such as an Aussie BBQ, young people blowing bubble gum, kangaroos, planes, getting a hair-cut, riding a rollercoaster, and going to the library, for example. In each case, the phenomena at hand is seen for its apparent arbitrariness and peculiarity.

Uncle Traveling Matt is the uncle of one of the main Fraggles, Gobo. It is through the postcards sent by Matt to his nephew that we hear about the strange things that Matt encounters. In order to learn of his uncle's adventures in 'outer space', Gobo must first venture into the Doc's workshops to retrieve them from the bin, and take them back into the rock—where he reads them out to his friends and, in turn, to the show's audience. The 'String Creatures' monologue, included below, comprises one of these rescued narratives;

'The String Creatures'
Today I made contact with a mysterious tribe of beings that I call the "String Creatures". It's curious, but right away I was drawn to them. It was almost as if I saw some kind of family resemblance. These small creatures spend their lives attached to strings that join them to the hands of the larger silly-creatures. It is not entirely clear to me why these two creatures would spend their lives attached to each other with string; there surely must be some mutual benefit. The silly-creature leader of this tribe was such a charismatic person, and soon I was won over and under his spell. Soon I found myself initiated into the tribe, as I too now have stings attaching my limbs to the leader of the "String Creatures". This lifestyle may prove to be a little strange. And somehow I just don't feel in control anymore. I'll probably go off on my own again, just as soon as I find a pair of scissors.[110]

So far, we have been dealing with defamiliarisation as a practice by way of which an adult can disrupt the monotony of everyday life. Of course, the fact that defamiliarisation is 'seriously playful' means, perhaps, that it is well suited for a younger demographic. We might go so far as to say that, because culture is taught, creative engagement with cultural notions and common-sense is pregnant with comedic potential. The curious and coded mono-

---

[110] J. Henson, "Fraggle Rock," *The Finger of Light*, Season 1, Episode 12, Nick Abson et. al (dir)., Canadian Broadcasting Corporation (CBC), 1983.

logues featured on Uncle Traveling Matt's postcards provide us with a creative, but critical, negotiation of this potential.

What is useful about Uncle Traveling Matt's postcards, certainly for the purposes of this discussion, is the way that they defamiliarise our own late modern cultural environment, given that 'outer space' is clearly the industrialised minority West. A stranger in a strange land, Uncle Traveling Matt is a perfect opportunity to see the world through the eyes of a curious (puppet) alien, providing access to ways of seeing that wouldn't have the same impact if they were simply being recited by a visible human being. After all, human beings are often the very objects of investigation. For the purpose of savouring its ethnographic content, a postcard from Uncle Traveling Matt would likely never have been discarded by Perec (especially if it turns out, in actual fact, to have been sent my one of Raine's curious aliens).

## Reflecting Upon Defamiliarisation

> The central characteristic of and life-world is its pre-reflective, taken-for-granted nature. People exist for the most part in their life-world like fish in water. So 'natural' does the life-world seem for each person that they do not generally experience it as anything other than 'just the way things are'....Thus, when we are defamiliarising ourselves with our everyday routines, what we are doing is, as it were, 'escaping' from the life-world and coming to look at it 'from the outside', as if it were foreign to us.[111]

We have seen how three curious individuals, and a puppet, have put the theory of defamiliarisation into practice. Once more, we have accessed valuable precedents that further inform our understanding of this idea. Perhaps their relevance becomes even more acute, particularly the case of Uncle Traveling Matt, when we ask: "How can we achieve this 'at odds' in a way that also puts Baudelaire's poetic, romantic figure of the flâneur, the Situationist preoccupations, to good use? The answer to this question emerges from our willingness to participate in behaviours that, without transgressing ethical boundaries, go against the grain of habitual behaviour—by taking paths less travelled, entertaining thoughts less considered, accessing the limits of everyday life in some way so that we may more clearly observe where they begin and end; by negotiating their limits. In this way, everyday life may be more closely engaged in and, in so doing, critiqued. This might sound good in theory but, still, we are in need of a context in which to make this theory actionable.

A desire to fulfil this need is precisely why I return our attention to the dérive. The dérive, such as that represented in the *Lose Yourself in Melbourne* advertisement and which has precedents running through the evolution of

---

[111] D. Inglis, *Culture and Everyday Life*, The New Sociology, series (London and New York: Routledge, 2005), 12.

modernity (of people's critical responses to the historical circumstances as well as the cultural conditions of industrialisation) provides us with this required context. For the way that it promotes a renewed and revised engagement with the built environment, it can be said with confidence that the dérive sets up the conditions for a defamiliarisation of the familiar; the dérive provides us with a suitable strategy for the constructive and critical estrangement of everyday life. To view the *Lose Yourself in Melbourne* advertisement is to observe a performance of defamiliarisation taking place in the context of a dérive. It is a fabrication of the theory, a representation and, to this extent, it is also imbued with its theoretical ideal. In general, we can say that the defamiliarising dérive is relevant, but not limited to Melbourne—that it is also applicable to whatever alternative geographical location a person might choose to experience. In particular, there is still room to see how a person engaging in this historical information, making use of it in their contemporary cultural climate, might engage first hand (or 'first foot', for that matter) with this information in his or her own streets. It would be hypocritical for me to discuss, at length, how dérive and defamiliarisation may shake up routinised cultural experience and, therefore, enrich everyday life, without practicing that of which I speak—to accept my responsibility not only to talk the talk but also to walk the walk.

# CHAPTER 6
# MAKING THEORY ACTIONABLE

The best thing would be to write down everything that happens from day to day. To keep a diary in order to understand. To neglect no nuances or little details, even if they seem unimportant, and above all to classify them. I must say how I see this table, the street, people, my packet of tobacco, since these are the things which have changed. I must fix the exact extent and nature of this change.

Jean-Paul Sartre, *Nausea* (p. 9)

## 'Qui Vive?' at the Entrance to the City

In my dream, I am walking along a forest path, near the edge of a mountain—high up in the thick of it all and yet light headed because of the thinning air. As I walk along the path, I notice countless dead and dying pine needles littering the forest floor. I also notice how some of them have been trodden into the dirt by hiking boots, though there is nobody to be seen. I walk around a bend in the path and, in doing so, catch sight of an old tree stump. A man is sitting on it. He has a bushy moustache and a distant stare, his cheeks red by the chill of the mountain air—reminiscent of the misty morning air of the Schwarzwald. He is alone, writing in his notebook like a man possessed. I continue to walk and, even as I get nearer to him, he doesn't look up or stop what he is doing. Nevertheless, the forest is quiet enough for me to hear him mumbling to himself as I pass: "Wenn du in einem Abgrund blikst, blikt der Abgrund auch in dich hinein."[112] Upon hearing these words I suddenly feel that I am lost in the forest, but feel good from exercising my legs. The endorphins pump through my veins as I cut through shrubs and branches. Finally, at the end of a long and tiring journey, I reach the peak of a ridge, as if to re-enact Casper David Friedrich's painting *Der Wanderer über dem Nebelmeer* [The Wanderer above the Sea of Fog] (1818), and peer off in to the distance; finally I have reached the city limits—like a quasi-Nietzschean lover of long walks, albeit with more obvious signs of exhaustion, and improper footwear.

At last I can see the gateway to an alternative, possible future. I make my way to the gates that comprise the city's entrance. Sentinels stand to attention on strategically placed look-outs, keeping an eagle eye out for suspicious looking individuals. Other sentinels are on active patrol, pacing systematically and repeatedly up and down the perimeter. They are soldiers who

---

[112] F. Nietzsche, *Beyond Good and Evil: Prelude to a Philosophy of the Future* (H. Zimmern, Trans. 3rd ed. Vol. 12), (London: T. N. Foulis, 1911), 97. [Trans. "If thou gaze long into an abyss, the abyss will also gaze into thee."]

have been posted here to keep watch and prevent any unauthorised access into the precious interior. They specialise in the apprehension of evil-doers and unfamiliar bodies. The responsibility of maintaining the city's security is theirs, and they intend to do a good job.

As I approach the entrance, I am met by the guards; each one of them is dressed in a scarlet greatcoat, boots and hat, and carrying a bayonet as well as other military standard issues. A few of the soldiers approach quickly, encircling me. One of them stands directly in my path to block me from going any further. Poker faced, he looks me straight in the eyes and, with a firm voice, bellows "Qui Vive?" in order to find out who I am and where my loyalties lie. His phrase is a challenge to my word, my intentions, even to my reason for being in this place at this time. I am now required to show official papers that prove my name, my origin, my business in general. If I am found to be a friend, I shall be allowed to pass without incidence; if not, it's true I may be done for.

"Qui Vive?" he bellows once more. "What is your business here?"

"Why, Sir," I answer politely, if a little bemused "this is where I live now".

Now, in my dream, I can read the man's badge; Althusser. He looks tough; his silvery grey hair is combed back on his head, dachshund wrinkles hang underneath both of his eyes, a black and brown pipe is poised at the corner of his mouth; jowls pulling gently either side of his long world-worn face. He has an air of cynicism, of 'no kidding around.' Just as I think that he's going to detain me, he starts talking to me about gifts. He seems to think that I have brought something with me. He starts talking about the weight of these gifts that I was given as a child, perhaps at the precise moment that I was born. He says that I could not see them then, just as I may not quite see them for what they are now. As he continues to speak, I realise that he is speaking of my name, my language, my nationality, my assumptions, my education, and other such aspects of my cultural subjectivity. He points out that I carry these gifts around with me as if they didn't weigh a thing; that I would have taken them with me wherever I chose to venture. He has become more forceful with his tone; he wants to know just how much they really weigh.

## Idealising a Nomadic Aesthetic

Though born in England in February 1975, two years after the country's major oil crisis, I have grown up in Australia. As a three year old living in England, I would routinely sit on the lounge room floor in front of the television and watch Open University on the BBC (who can tell how much of an impact academia had in this infant-developmental process?). Beyond the domestic sphere, my experiences of the world have been framed by a late capitalist society comprising the ideological circumstances and expectations of a post-war population—built upon the assumption of certain material conditions, particularly the availability of cheap and abundant fossil fuel. However, in light of decisions made by the Organisation of Arab Petroleum Exporting Countries (OAPEC) to affect an oil embargo, the early 1970s saw this assumption greatly challenged; the oil crisis meant that the nation would suffer a significant rupture in the totalising and colonising modernist aesthetic it had inherited and further institutionalised.

Each time I sat on the lounge room carpet, watching educational content about the outside world (outer space) on the television, my learning was taking place in a period of steady socio-economic decline. This decline manifested itself as a decline in Britain's national confidence—something that can still be seen today. But, more to the point, it can be taken as a time when what had been taken for granted, what had become familiar and commonplace, (normal, natural and inevitable), was suddenly exposed for it constructedness, its instability, is opposition to nature, to the natural world. By putting a spanner in the works and forcing people out of their day to day complacency, by denoting a set of circumstances that were inherently at odds with the population's sense of entitlement and material expectations (this cultural arrogance), the oil crisis instigated a period of cultural defamiliarisation.

Mindful of their personal and parental responsibilities, keen to hang onto the comforting embrace of materiality, my parents packed up their late capitalist belongings and moved our family to Australia. They migrated in search of a new life (what would also entail my new life) in a country still dubbed nationally as 'the lucky country' (where this tourist-targeting ideological notion was taken as a material truth). With three children under the age of seven, the locus of my basic trust stepped out into the unknown in search of better opportunities, alternative solutions. They put into practice what Sharon Wegscheider-Cruse theorises as the "risks of self growth [that] involve going into the unknown, into an unfamiliar land where the language is different and customs are different and you have to learn your way around."[113] Thus, from a very early age, this notion of risk and of a trust in the unknown has, to greater or lesser degrees, underpinned my sense of self.

To experience the unknown is to experience everyday life; this idea has always been important to me. But for my entire adult life, university has played a central and anchoring role in my self-identity, with my PhD degree consolidating this trajectory. The PhD was a veritable training ground for institutionalised labour, and I used it as an opportunity to research cultural representations of the 'abyss' metaphor (also known as the unfathomable void, the indeterminable, the unknown). In this sense, my research project

---

[113] S. Wegscheider-Cruse, *Learning to Love Yourself: Finding Your Self-Worth* (Florida: Health Communications Inc., 1987), 82.

was entirely concerned with the cultural value of notions of the unknown, and yet this concern was at odds with the day to day routine of travelling to and from the built university environment and performing a range of institutional chores in the interim. My choice to stay engaged in these chores was a sign of my appreciation for such opportunities. Of all the jobs I could be doing, this was up there with my most desired. But this engagement is also central to critical self-questioning.

Anyone who works in academia will know how easy it can be for academic life to (be allowed to) take over a person's life. Such times have made me question my place in relation to that well-worn dichotomy of either living to work or working to live. My entry into academic life has entailed my questioning how to negotiate it in a rewarding and sustainable way without this investment impacting negatively my extra-academic potential, for example. For three years, my PhD was one of the most important things in my life. After its completion, once I had found time to clear some head-space to accommodate other considerations, I began to re-assess my place in the world. It was an important time to reflect upon the past three years and make a plan going forward. I recall David Foster Wallace's comment on the perils of academic life:

> Probably the most dangerous thing about an academic education—least in my own case—is that it enables my tendency to over-intellectualize stuff, to get lost in abstract argument inside my head, instead of paying attention to what is going on in front of me, paying attention to what is going on inside me.[114]

Relating these thoughts to my own experience, a personal investment in the nuances of institutional validation sets the scene for my departure, for the need to observe the world beyond my own concerns. Ideally speaking, PhD's provide people with a training ground for a long-term academic career, but ideals aren't always practical. You can't create demand out of thin air. I have said elsewhere, with reasonable cynicism, that business is business even when it is the business of education. The humanities are well aware of the implications of the economic squeeze—where the life of a discipline is often determined less by cultural value than by monetary value. A couple of months after my doctorate had been conferred, I finally had the head-space to think about what I might now do with my exciting new title; my piece of paper. What did academia now mean to me? Who was I beyond the familiar embrace of my student status? I gradually built up academic teaching responsibilities and enjoyed these. Being a sessional employee meant that I was only

---

[114] D. F. Wallace, *This is Water: Some Thoughts, Delivered on a Significant Occasion, about Living a Compassionate Life*, 1st ed. (New York: Little, Brown and Company, 2009), 48.

useful during the teaching semester, which meant that I was spending almost half of the year unemployed.

The institution was where I had discovered by cultural value. My expectations were high enough for this to affect my self-esteem. So long as I could use the university to feed this self-esteem, things were fine. Off the clock, I struggled to renegotiate my work/life balance. I had always valued academia, but being specialised meant that I now needed it too. Slowly but surely, I began to resent this dependency. Fortunately, my destabilised sense of cultural worth was propped up just in time (saved by the bell) when, six months after completing my PhD, the opportunity arose to coordinate and lecture the first-year Cultural History and Theory core units. This would be my chance to make the most of my enthusiasm for teaching and learning, my desire to demonstrate academic self-reliance and use this to help hundreds of students negotiate a world of ideas. I had hit the ground running, updating an existing core unit alongside writing an entirely new one. On top of this, starting with my first semester in this capacity I was also responsible for coordinating and providing educational material for students both on campus and overseas. My tendency to over-prepare was as much as sign of my ambition and ability as it was a direct reflection of my academic inexperience. Fourteen weeks later, the semester would end and I'd be unemployed again, wondering if another contract would be on the table.

Being an emerging researcher meant that this 'time-out' was just what I needed to be able to concentrate on writing some articles and developing a peer-reviewed publication track record. Whatever my short term circumstances would be, I was well aware that some investment had to be made towards my long term ambitions. Between teaching commitments, spanning 2007 and 2008, I wrote my first four peer-reviewed articles and a book chapter that soon appeared in its second edition. On that level, this was a very challenging and rewarding time for me. However, as an employee, I couldn't help but feel worn down by my academic liminality, and guarding these feelings so as not to give the false impression that I lacked commitment. However, with no end to this cycle in sight I lost faith in the process and left, moving from Perth to Melbourne—on the other side of Australia.

While it wasn't the deciding factor in my decision to relocate to another city, the *Lose Yourself in Melbourne* advertisement was being screened at a time when I needed to reinvest some creativity in my day to day behaviour. I had already enjoyed several years of intermittent holidaying in Melbourne and often entertained the thought of moving there. The vibrancy of life that I perceived it to embody was more attractive to me than the idyllic sleepiness of Perth's clean but culturally lack-lustre atmosphere. I felt like I was retiring before life had even really started. This was mostly my own fault, but if moving to Melbourne was what I needed to do in order to defamiliarise myself to myself, in order to wake myself from an everyday slumber, then so be it.

My pre-occupation with the rather romantic notion of drifting around the streets of Melbourne, apolitically represented by the sentiments of the *Lose Yourself in Melbourne* advertisement, can be said to reflect a desire to relocate myself beyond the built environment in which I had been invested. Upon arrival in Melbourne, there were a few jobless months during which I felt "existentially adrift," a trait that Foster Wallace attributes to someone "without a meaningful identity....no idea who he [or she] is."[115] In fact, I spent the first few weeks of my new Melbourne life adrift in a very corporeal way, conducting quasi-Baudellarian/Situationist dérives around the city streets and shopping malls. These active attempts to embrace the peculiarity of the city space—to confront myself with the unknown—were part of an attempt to re-discover the concrete side of experience. It was as if, by wandering aimlessly around the built environment, and treating it as a space of play rather than commerce, I would be somehow able to resist the gravitational pull of 'career-mindedness.' I hope it is a coincidence that this notion of 'the concrete-ness of experience' was echoed in the building materials with which the city has been largely constructed. In any case, While physically exhausting, the dérives expressed my desire to become who I wanted to be, who I thought I needed to be in order to grow—to locate my authentic self. Taking the dérive as a context of critical engagement with my cultural environment, I was very much still interpreting my everyday life through the application of an academic mindset; this was also a critical engagement in personal freedom and self-reliance. What better place to test my education than in a geographical and cognitive space beyond the institution—a space where I could challenge my own navigation and interpretation of the supermarket dream that defines our Western world, that commodity context in which we can see just how "modern capitalism melted all solids."[116]

When it came to the matter of self-direction, life-trajectory, path, personal choice, or whatever you would like to call it, a desire for the unknown underpinned both my decision to move to Melbourne and my decision to begin my 'orientation' with a series of disorientating dérives. For me, the unknown was a context in which I could re-vitalise the risks of self-growth rather than indulge myself in contexts of novelty and entertainment. In fact, while dérive and defamiliarisation have playful sides (that are certainly privileged in the Lose Yourself in Melbourne advertisement), my awareness of the historical contexts of both theories meant that, from the outset, strolling around Melbourne would be about work, essentially. It would be a job that I set myself not only as a reward for assessing my previous situation and doing something active about it, but also as a chance to begin a new life on a critical

---

[115] D. F. Wallace, *A Supposedly Fun Thing I'll Never Do Again* (London: Abacus, 1998), 31.
[116] Z. Bauman, *Community - Seeking Safety in an Insecure World* (Oxford: Polity Press, 2001), 30.

foot. I didn't come to the city just to find new and exciting ways to slip back into complacency. I came here to avoid that stuff, to give myself a cold shower. Having forced myself out of my comfort zone, away from the friends that I loved and respected (that I still love and respect) it was only fair that I practice what I had been teaching. Among my friends and colleagues, during conversation, it was common-place for us to theorise the risks of self-growth, the boredom and routinisation of everyday life…and we kept touching on these ideas, repeatedly; we continued to teach them from the comforts of our classroom desks and lecturns. But I kept asking myself how I could teach defamiliarisation and praxis without providing the most accessible example; without putting myself to the test and risking myself? I had reached the point where there was nothing left to do other than test my own assumptions, ideals, practices, to see not only what it was like to think these things, but also what it was like to feel them too. My writing had become my new means of expressing cultural creativity, but it was life itself that I thought needed to be the focus of my praxis. Increasingly, I felt the need to enrich my contribution to our cultural conversation. Ultimately, this search meant leaving the familiar rock and, like Uncle "Travelling" Matt, venturing into outer space for a good look around, to find the strangeness in things that I could go on to share with others.

With this in mind, it would be unreasonable to think that people negotiate theory on an intellectual level without also experiencing them on an emotional one. Taking certain features of modern French theory/philosophy into the streets that would frame my new everyday life, meant subjecting my day to day activity to critical consideration—defamiliarising my self-interpretation, what I wanted to do and be. The perils of routine have been discussed at length and, for the most part, in general terms. But, by demonstrating my engagement in a form of creative cultural praxis, this part of the book explores its auto-ethnographic dimension. Now, it's time for me to share, with you, in order to make them as useful as possible to everyday thinking, both my intellectual and emotional negotiation of these journeys.

Getting all of my things from A to B doesn't concern me. I'll throw out the junk and wrap the rest up in newspaper before strategically packing them in large cardboard boxes. Lengths of packing tape will seal the cartons shut, while numbers written in black on the outside edge will match a master list and remind me what is inside. Maybe, in six months' time, I will have misplaced the list and fail to remember what I've put where. My memory will be put to the test in due course. For now, I am about to take a leap of faith into the unknown, reach out to embrace the abyss of potential (hopefully I will realise more creative potential than destructive potential), Cristin recounts Heidegger when he asserts that "[w]e speak of the abyss when, having been separated from a basis of support and having lost a point of support, we go looking for one on which to rest our feet."[117] But I haven't yet lost anything. In fact, maybe I have nothing to lose, nothing to regret other than the regret of looking back from some future moment and not having taken this chance. As Gayatri Chakravorty Spivak phrases it, "[t]he fall into the abyss…inspires us with as much pleasure as fear. We are intoxicated with the prospect of never hitting bottom."[118] The logistics of moving house seem straight forward enough, but I'm yet to discover just what lies ahead. I shall just have to keep my fingers crossed that it all works out for the best. Merde à la puissance treize![119]

## A 'Pilot' Walk Around the Belly of IKEA

*Friday, 28th November*
Already, I am more tired than usual; there seems to be a lot more visual stimuli for my brain to process now that I am experiencing an unfamiliar place. Perhaps it is akin to the primordial hyper-vigilance required to ascertain whether there are any threats around; whether something might want to eat me or cause me some other kind of harm. I fell like a caveman entering a new cave, ready to have a look around but knowing, all the while, that something could jump out at me at any second. For me, the cave is the built environment—a massive cave that contains a myriad of much smaller caves. Together, they comprise a row of houses, shops, the city streets. There is so much to see, out of the instinctual necessity of self-preservation.

Maybe a set of blinkers would come in handy—a kind of civil inattention that is also applicable to inanimate objects. If this is to remain a project throughout which I write my experiences of defamiliarisation, then when might I know if I have reached the end—when it's time to stop and move on to the next self-set pre-occupation? How might I recognise an unfamiliar conclusion? Perhaps the end will come when my surroundings no longer seem strange to me and when, having trodden the same paths many times, find myself no longer lingering on their finer details. Perhaps I will know when I realise that I have joined the other people around me in allowing these finer details slip below the radar and, in that way, disappear into the everyday. Maybe I will know the end only in retrospect having, through my own diminishing 'observational mode,' found that I missed it completely. Maybe the end to the project will come when this place starts to feel like home—when I start to feel comfortable walking around the streets during the day or the night. This point in time, this stage of my negotiation of the built environment will mark the beginning of a different kind of challenge,

---

[117] R. Cristin, *Heidegger and Leibniz: Reason and the Path*, Gerald Parks, trans. Vol. 35, (Dordrecht: Kulwer Academic Publishers, 1998), 49.
[118] G. Chakravorty Spivak, quoted in Jacques Derrida, *Of Grammatology* (G. C. Spivak, trans., (Baltimore and London: The Johns Hopkins University Press, 1976), LXXVII.
[119] This is a French idiom, equivalent to the English "Good luck!"

beyond the sweet meat of novelty that I am feeling now. That will be the time, I imagine, when I have to find ways to keep my eyes wide open, prising them like torturous tooth-picks or like a stick in Dali's paintings, over which a face or clock is slumped. I might have to reach back into the sleepiness of my subconscious in order to drag familiarity out from the warmth of the doona, giving it a sobering cold shower before the day starts afresh. I will need to find an alternative means to use my eyes—to place them, once again, at odds with whatever monotony threatens to draw them shut.

For now, there is other work to do. Having been accustomed to the luxury of having my own car (at my disposal and awaiting my every beck and call) the task of setting up a new home in a new city without a car requires creative planning. Julie and I organised a hire car once we had arrived at Tullamarine airport in Melbourne but, so that we didn't spend too much on it, we decided to limit our hire to 24 hours. The idea was that this would give us enough time to drive from the airport to the real estate agent's office, collect the keys to our house, drive to the house for a quick look around, and head out again to do some serious grocery shopping (staple foods and other miscellaneous items such as a dust pan and brush, a broom. It is incredible just how involved a process like buying a broom can be when you have been exempt from the task for almost a decade, well accustomed to the 'old faithful' forever leaning against the laundry room wall. The task of buying a new broom means having to check for such invaluable qualities as bristle strength, do some price comparisons with the two alternatives (one's capacity to exercise personal choice, at this stage, falls far short of overwhelming). I find myself trying to think of a whole range of possible future broom usage scenarios as if this will help me in some way to make the most informed final decision.

I find it hard to believe that something as conceivably insignificant as a broom in fact requires this much thought. It just goes to show that, if buying a broom can be a serious business, so too can buying a dust pan and brush among other presumably obligatory grudge purchases (aluminium foil, cling wrap, Tupperware for putting things in, a packet of chocolate biscuits to put in the Tupperware). I take a moment to look shamefully into my trolley, casting my eyes upon the pseudo-necessary plastic products and wondering just how much crude oil went into making them. Teflon, plastic wrappings, aspirin, nylon, polyester, garden hoses, and compact discs are just a blip on the list of affordable everyday items, the production of which crude oil has enabled—I start to feel queasy, not least of all because I still feel that I need to buy them. The chocolate biscuits at least offer some superficial affirmation that, despite the myriad of un-fun and environmentally questionable items, the trip to the supermarket has been completely without reward, not entirely devoid of pleasure.

Having the rental car also meant that we would be mobile until noon the next day and, as a result, have enough time to drive out to the IKEA furniture store with our meticulously compiled list of house space/alcove dimensions so that we might buy suitable furniture to fill them with. One thing that strikes you about these 19th century terraces, those that have been subject to renovations or other modernisations, is their distinct lack of storage space. Keen to make the most of our time, and all tooled up with a limited budget, IKEA seemed to offer the solution that we were looking for.

We got up and organised this morning, sitting on the phone to our internet representative trying to set up our access. This process would have gone a lot quicker and smoother if it had not been for the fact that, in the dishevelled process of untangling, arranging, and connecting some pretty coloured IT plugs and cables, we had overlooked our error of plugging the phone line into the wrong socket. One of the good things about living in the same house for years is that you get to go through the rigmarole of settings things up once and then forget about it (the more things stay the same, the more you have to take for granted, the less you have to think about). The problem with living in the same house for years is that, having gone through the rigmarole of settings things up, time goes by and you tend to forget how it was all done. At the point of change (moving house for instance) and having taken everything apart, having disconnected each and every dusty plug and cord at 'point A', you reach 'point B' and realise that you have absolutely no idea how to put it back together again. You have lost touch with the rigmarole, the steps in the process, how things 'should' be.

Once this hurdle had been successfully overcome, and with now only a couple of hours remaining until our hire car was due for return (only a short while before we would, once more, be car-less), we rushed out of the house and, street map firmly in hand, drove to the IKEA store located a few suburbs away. The idea of shopping at IKEA has never held any appeal for me. The affordability of the products doesn't seem to quite make up for the 'furniture for the people' subtext that underpins its 'philosophy' and which does well to reflect how the Swedish unashamedly strive to be the same as each other (ref. Swedish IKEA show).

But, as that clichéd and capitalist expression goes, "Money talks", and so there was every chance that I would be at least partly converted by the time that I reached the checkout. While I was well aware of this possibility, what I had not taken into consideration was that, in our mad rush from the house, we had left our list of painstakingly compiled dimensions on the living room floor. Much to my dismay and my frustration, it seemed at first that our 'outing' was over before it had even started. But we are not quitters, not a couple who are likely to shy away from adversity (resiliency is the key), and so we sucked up our pride and ventured into the store.

Perhaps it might have been wise to bring with us a packed lunch, for the store appears more like a 'consumer maze', though a 'maze of torment' is also a very real possibility. This, however, is more an emotional impression and not a rational one because mazes contain numerous dead ends and present a complex challenge for anyone trying to find way out, whereas IKEA has a very definite through route, making it more akin to the labyrinths of the classical world. What is more, IKEA has free maps to assist a customer's shopping experience, their monotone appearance screaming simplicity at you as you stand, unconvinced, in a veritable no-man's land between the outside world and something far more bizarre, the inside of IKEA, the many coloured belly of the flat-packing beast.

The claim to simplicity is one thing, but it is a very different story when you are actually in the midst of it all. It is a bit like watching a show on some historical event, taking it all in on an essentially passive level and, perched on the couch in front of the television, feel confident that you have captured the knowledge. This confidence remains, of course, until such a time as you are required to be active with this information, required to recall the historical details, the names of emperors and heroes only to find that you didn't take in as much as you had thought. I look over to see the girl at the information desk giving out store maps and am tempted to ask her where I might find a place to kill myself. But the generic smile on her makes me change my mind for it, like the IKEA map itself, gives me a sense that everything will be okay, that this shopping experience will be smooth and stress free and, most of all, it will mean that I can get everything I need without bringing my budget to its patched-up knees. For those customers who have been bold enough, either through necessity or some kind of masochism, to come to IKEA with their children, the store map promises order and efficiency—the promise that the parentally guiding customer will not have to deal with distracted and tired children for any longer than is necessary for a series of financial transitions to take place.

Reassurances of this kind must surely provide IKEA with its key sales point given that the first thing that a potential customer sees, as they enter the store, is the Smaland play area on the left hand side and the cafe/restaurant zone on the right. I pass a late thirties couple who are both looking unblinkingly in the direction of the play area, at the children who are gurgling and giggling among the brightly coloured plastic balls and fun slide. I presume that one or two of the children are their own as they, steadily devouring their one dollar hot dogs (perhaps as a way of allaying their hunger for a little time out), appear to look without watching - fulfilling the basic physical requirements that are associated with parental supervision while finding deep and secret relief in the safety net of somnambulism.

I find some miniscule but entertaining sense of achievement in having calculated the possibility of eating for 21 dollars a week, three oblong meals a day, 7 days a week, might make perfect sense until your organs start to shut down. The immediate acknowledgement of the store eatery offers itself up to the tentative shopper as a gentle reminder, "Don't worry. If you can't find our way out, we have enough food to feed you until you do."

Somewhat dazed by the unnaturally bright fluorescent lighting, I make my way down the pathways that direct me through various signed departments. In doing so, perhaps another one of those pesky gaps between the ideal and the reality will be exposed—a gap between what is expected and what is produced. This gap might become manifest as a discrepancy between what is experienced by the man, woman, or child who feels as if, with each uncertain turn through the products, they are being reminded of their poor orientation skills (perhaps wishing they'd taken more notice on Scout camps, as I do). The arrows on the floor of IKEA seem to suggest my own stupidity for not knowing where I am, for not knowing where I am going. But I'm not asking for much—just a shelf, a couple of chairs, and a damn cupboard. The question of whether or not I should be adding a desk lamp to this list fades into insignificance as I gravitate towards a table piled high with finger puppets and make a beeline for the one that is meant to look like a frog. My train of thought drifts as I become preoccupied with trying to have as much fun as possible while, at the same time, wondering how long I can keep this up before self-consciousness sets in and I drop the puppets back onto their collective pile............eight seconds. I wander off, slightly disappointed—already suffering the birth pangs of shopping boredom.

I wind my way through the living room department, already heady from the visual pollution that comprises of countless shiny signs hung from the ceiling, price tags and intermittent sales posters, conceivably exotic sounding Swedish product names, none of which I understand. I could go on forever recounting the way that the space is broken up either to fit more in or to create the illusion of there being more stock than there is—more, at least, to get yourself lost in, step by step disconnecting you from any clear sight of the end or the beginning  the store that lasts forever now surrounds you, no more north, south, east, or west, just the black arrows painted onto the floor that, after a long and weary journey, are designed to lead you straight to the cash registers. The arrows are probably my only saving grace in this place, each subsequent sign pointing me, and all the other soul crushed customers, in one seemingly endless direction.

It is as if they found IKEA providing some acknowledgement and, with it, some pathetic consolation for the confusion and/or bodily damage that it may have caused. I think back to images that I have seen of the Mongolian nomadic tribes that live together in well insulated Yurts, or 'felt tents'. It has been a long held Mongolian superstition that it is bad luck to walk around the Yurt in an anti-clockwise direction, but I cannot help wonder whether this is a rule with a more practical basis, that being the desire to minimise head bumping incidents in the dark of night, once the flames of the camp fire have dwindled. The superstition works well as a take for granted system of human organisation, a way of coping with the limitations of a material reality that, over time, has soaked down a peg or two, embedding itself in the commonsense of the people, that unthinking level of day to day behaviour that affords it its most effective disciplining of social action. In the realm of belief, as a superstition, it is placed at a safe distance away from critical thinking and, in this way, remains free from the threat and the inconvenience of being challenged.

Bodily discipline and social organisation, for the benefit of the system in which they are operation, are notions that move to the forefront of my mind as I try to make sense of my experience in this consumer centre, as I step across the black arrows that cover the floors of IKEA, the labyrinth's main arterial pathway that extends from one end of it to the other. Not quite as exciting as the yellow brick road in The Wizard of Oz but perhaps laden with the promise of something equally as rewarding; together the black arrows mark out IKEA's 'preferred route', officially decided upon on behalf of the browsing and buying public now far removed by way of their negotiation of this constructed environment, from all signs of the natural world beyond it.

This is not a place of nature, but of culture and, more specifically, the minority world that is 'industrial culture', governed not by the climate, by bio-diversity, but by the self-justifying and perpetuating catch phrases of 'consumer demand': convenience, novelty, entertainment and immediate gratification. My mind flashes back to the Smaland play area located reassuringly inside the store's entrance. If Guy Debord's notion of dérive had not been "the rapid passage through various ambiences" but, rather, "the rapid passage through various retail departments", the 'situations' he sought to create would have taken on quite a tone more akin to the shopping ecstasy that is 'on display' in Zola's modernist novel *Au Bonheur des Dames* [The Ladies' Paradise].[120]

Less pressing than financial limitations at this early stage of my relocation, are the limitations encountered as a direct result of having had all household items packed and loaded onto a crate a few days prior to our departure. For we are currently without use of a fridge and shall continue to be so for the 14 days that it will take for the freight to get here. Until that time, we are relying on a modestly sized plastic esky for keeping essentials such as margarine, milk, and beer at a constantly cold temperature (with much help from the two bags of ice that we have broken open and moulded around these items. They will have to be replaced every two days to ensure minimum wastage.

The fridge seems so necessary to me that I often take it for granted. I don't know if I could live without a fridge. I did live without one for six

---

[120] "And, elbowed and jostled by the growing masses of women who had little to spend and were rushing towards the inexpensive woolens, they went into ecstasies over the exhibition of carpets....First, pale satins and soft silks were gushing out...Next came the thicker fabrics...[then[ velvets....Women pale with desire were leaning over as if to look at themselves. Faced with this wild cataract, they all remained standing there, filled with the secret fear of being caught up in the overflow of all this luxury and with an irresistible desire to throw themselves into it and be lost." É. Zola, *The Ladies' Paradise*, Oxford World's Classics, Trans. Brian Nelson (London: Oxford University Press, 2008), 103-4.

months in one of the share houses that I lived in as a student. My housemates and I bought the smallest quantities of things like cheese, milk, and meat so that what we brought home was what we actually needed to eat that day or very soon after. I remember feeling trapped between a rock and a hard place on one occasion when, with a hunger growing in my belly, I walked up the road to the local independent supermarket. The supermarket is a veritable Aladdin's cave, but brick and concrete instead of rock and geometrically shaped, not organic—so that it is not really like a cave at all but more like a big unnatural block in an urban setting, an industrial artefact filled to the brim with all manner of other industrial artefacts. Nevertheless, it was my cave and my forest, my Serengeti plain, or wherever it is that animals find their food these days—a food place decorated in brightly coloured signs, like the gorgeous wings of a prospective mate being placed on show for the aim of my arousal and, if all goes well, for the propagation of our species. It was here that I could find my food, low prices guaranteed—that place where I could hunt it down, walking back and forth along the aisles, competing for the best deals with all of the other animals present, looking carefully and closely for suitable and affordable prey, casting my gaze with eagle eyes up and down the multi-tiered shelving. From beneath the surface currents, down in the dark and rarely seen depths, to the highest of lofty peaks, I searched the shelves for my food, my sustenance, my over-eating and gluttonous, colours and preservatives, pleasure.

Sure, this process didn't entail the same levels of danger or even fear that might be experienced in the wild, but the survival instinct was still going strong. I spent a few minutes contemplating the possibilities when, all of a sudden, I found myself looking into the discount meat section and there it was—a packet of fifteen chicken drumsticks on sale for the low, low price of $3.25, pre-cut and wrapped in crude oil-derived transparent plastic film, and it is here that I came face to face with my dilemma. For I was hungry and, with access only to a limited budget, I knew that every cent would count. But then there was the matter of the fridge or, at least, the matter of its absence. I stood motionless in the cold produce as the questions flooded through my mind, as I started to wish I had worn some warmer clothes to the supermarket. Should I buy a smaller pack, knowing that I could not safely store any excess food and effectively pay more for less, or should I buy the drumsticks, run the risk of being the only person at home this evening to eat them, and rack myself with guilt as I throw out what I cannot eat? Within a minute or so I had come to my conclusion, one that I felt ticked the necessary boxes. I would buy the cheap bulk pack, return home, cook and eat them all in one sitting. As it turned out, it was not until I started to chew on drumstick number ten that the fear finally kicked in.

While it is possible to live without a fridge, it sure sucks to have to, but what rings louder than this acknowledgement is the cry of entitlement making the whiny claim that luxuries are necessities. The absence of a fridge might not seem like enough to rule out its usefulness but, then again, we have only removed the fridge from the kitchen, and not the expectations that had been surrounding it and which, still, might be conceived to remain hovering vaguely about a rapidly warming void. When the point of view of the fridge as an unquestionably deserved device is adopted, you know that you are dealing with one narcissistic complainant, or more for that matter. There is nothing to say that whole societies cannot be founded upon a sense of entitlement that wildly overlooks those who may never even see a fridge, a toaster, a coffee maker, in their lifetime.

The void in the kitchen where the fridge might once have been (the fridge that I am merely privileged to once more, one day, see again) is an absence that has been culturally constructed, primarily, by way of the expectation of a presence. Sartre once touched on the idea of absence, in a way that can be useful here, by saying that the conception of absence emerged because of the unfulfilled expectation of a presence. He described this idea by using the example of a man who is waiting in a café for his friend to arrive. The friend in question, Pierre, should be arriving any minute. The 'should' in this assumption is where we can locate the expectation. But, the thing about using words like 'should' in claims is that, in the event that they are not fulfilled by some future event, they can lead to negative feelings. In other words, the more I think about what should happen next, the more I set myself up for disappointment when things turns out differently which, and let's be honest, they usually do. Sartre is also experiencing a growing disappointment when Pierre does not arrive. The man waits for a while longer but Pierre still does not show. For Sartre, it is here in Pierre's absence, in the illusory shadow of presence, that a glimpse into nothingness becomes possible, opening up like a void and chasm that is akin to, it might be fair to say, a rather existential emptiness.

That was Sartre in Paris in the post WW2 period. In this part of Melbourne, some half a century later, absence resides in my new home, its nothingness resonating through the empty rooms and lengthy passageway. Where it might not be so readily found is on the city streets, in their abundant 'visuallity' (a seemingly inevitable by-product of dominant Australian practices being consumer practices), for there are signs, images, and sounds present all around me. Their individual contributions to the overall impression of visual and auditory pollution filling every nook and cranny available. It is as if everything were here, at once in this moment as it was in the last—everything, all the time, feigning nothing short of a perpetual presence and in a way, it might seem, that defers the confrontation with nothingness, thus, with the challenge of existential questions about what it is to exist, not simply in the world, but in this small corner of the world, in this space, at this time, in our cultural contexts.

The challenge of nothingness, even if we are to take this challenge as the question of what we would do if it were not for all of this STUFF what we pile up around us, all these devices and gadgets and buildings and cars and whatnot. For to accept the challenge of the absence of these things would surely be to remove the many distractions that keep us focussed on ourselves and not on our capacities to collectively engage in the inequalities and indifferences that exist everywhere in the world, including in the so-called lucky country. Driven away from the realm of collective political action by the glossy and novel appeal of the latest mobile phones, such so-called consumer 'luxuries' are perhaps mere props in the task of keeping the public confined to the solitariness of their own materialistic concerns. The more people use their hands to clutch iPods and play-station joysticks, the less chance they will put them to more productive social causes and in much the same way that the act of praying places a person's manual dexterity way away from any critical function.

There is little doubt that the stereotypical image of a 'kid in a candy store' evokes all the joy and madness of a society experiencing childlike awe in the face of the seemingly unlimited possibilities afforded by mechanisation and mass production. However, if we look beyond the window displays and sticky coloured sweets, we might also find just cause to ask whether late modernity's consumer preoccupations find individuals, each day, treading a treacherously fine line between empowerment and enslavement.

No wonder, as a new-comer negotiating the 'big city' scene along with its surrounding areas, it proves to be an extremely tiring process. There is simply so much to see that, at times, I also feel like that child in the candy store but not necessarily overwhelmed with joy and wonderment, but more like simply overwhelmed. No sooner have I noticed an advertisement on a shop window over here, but I see the brightly lit neon of a sign over there, this building, that smell, the sounds of trams, buses and cars rushing, and brushing, past the edge of the sidewalk, an attractive girl passing me by, two people talking words that I can't hear, a big black woolly dog lapping water from a silver bowl beside a demountable newsstand. The problem of multiplicity is partly to do with how disorienting it can be to the individual who is in the midst of it all, or at the very least believes that they are experiencing a business around them. But tiredness also comes from trying to make the most out of this process, by trying to understand it in a culturally reflexive way, that is, in a way that recognises and articulates various points of dynamism between the individual and the cultural institutions that surround that individual.

If I were to limit my reflection to the documentation of subjective description that would be fine but it might be missing out on an integral part of the narrative, and integral part of the scope of meaning that can, over time, be made. With this in mind, while there may well be echoes of self-concern here, let there also be seen an attempt to share a glimpse into the broader social context in which such descriptive elements as well as my own needs, wants, desires and so on, exist. Going beyond the limits of description finds description being brought into the fold of something that is conceivably more useful. This 'going beyond' marks a shift away from narcissism, in the direction of critical reflection.

Having left IKEA with a roughly compiled shopping list, and intent on returning later that day, Julie and I dropped off the hire car at the depot and headed into the city centre. First on foot to a tram stop some 2 blocks away, we then rode a tram up to, and along, Bourke Street, getting off at Swanston Street having decided that it be suitable point from which to begin having a look around. This new sense of connection with the environment in terms of actually feeling it beneath our feet rather than having the tyres of a car do the feeling for us, this 'pedestrian mode' is far different to that which I had become accustomed, that being the decidedly 'vehicular mode'. I have been quite looking forward to moving my body outdoors more.

I felt completely lost on more than one occasion which, because Julie is usually better with directions than I am, meant that I kept falling back into relying on her to guide us around. As a new person in a new city who is trying to find their own way, their own sense of place and, in turn, of identity, meant that I was experiencing great frustration at myself for this shortfall. Making this frustration known to Julie, she suggested that we stop and that I take a moment to calm down and simply have a look around. "Just stop" she said, "and see what you can recognise. Maybe look for landmarks or something like that." "There is too much to see at once. Try to focus on one thing at a time." I took her advice and looked around for anything that might jog my memory in some way and, hopefully, help me get my bearings.

To my surprise only a minute had gone by before I was able to mention about eight things that I recognised, the gallery that way on the distance (Federation Square), St Kilda further away but in that same direction (despite not being able to actually see it from the city) and the tram that could take me there, the tower block around the corner on Little Lonsdale Street in which we once stayed, the grassed area in front of the library up the road a little. All these material points of reference were there and ready for the picking in my mind's eye, but how quickly they seemed to vanish into thin air as I got caught up in trying to take it all in at once or, perhaps more to the point, not yet being able to successfully block much of it out. But it is this 'blocking out' that can be problematic in everyday life because it furthers familiarisation and, like its spoilt cousin, encourages the taking of so much for granted. With all of the distractions and the ultra tiredness from an abundance of visual and auditory stimuli, perhaps what is needed is a set of blinkers, the kind that you might find on a service Clydesdale, or else the knack for a kind of civil inattention that is readily applicable to a vast array of inanimate objects.

It is here that I find a trace of defamiliarisation's antidote, a dose of which might help me keep my wits about me. Inattention is also a trap, treacherous in such a state if you are not careful—the kind of trap which I am actively working against in my own time, at my own pace. The trick then,

I imagine, is to remain focussed in a culturally reflexive way, to consider the strands that weave together the different parts, a bit like considering the social fabric, the 'cultural con-texture'—not being distracted by every little detail while not forgetting that such details nevertheless exist.

We eventually got around to having some lunch, stopping at a Korean restaurant in the city called The Oriental Spoon, on La Trobe Street, where I had my first ever bowl of Kim Chi Spicy Rice, a dish with a handful of vegetables in it that seemed to have been cooked through with the rice itself. It was nice, but finishing off a whole bowl took quite some effort (not knowing what serving size to expect, I had to do my best to avoid wasting food).

After lunch, Julie and I caught a tram back to IKEA, this time with our precious dimensions list firmly in hand instead of our haste. Once again we walked through various departments (consumer ambiences), seeing a few oldies sitting in the café area, enjoying a coffee and some $4 pasta only seconds into our reprisal. This trip has been no shorter than our previous one due to our being distracted by bath mats and miniature cacti. I selected a plastic pack of three to start my new collection.

We were pleased to find that the items we had been drawn to, during our visit earlier that morning, fit in with the dimensions that we needed to work with. In fact, we were pretty much spot on with in terms of the space sizes. The only thing is, once a final decision had been made about what we were to purchase, we still needed to take our 'picking' lists down to the warehouse section, wherein we would have to locate and gather the various boxes. For one cupboard alone, as an example, we needed to locate 4 different boxes, each on a different aisle and, without exaggeration, there were dozens of aisles, all wide and high, tall and long. The sheer scale of the warehouse created the sense that we had entered a far distant land of giants, albeit highly organised and industrialised giants. It felt if we had just reached the top of the magic bean stalk and, now employed in the service of the giant, were begrudgingly condemned to doing his shopping for him.

I suppose the scale and 'boxiness' is a testament to the profitability of standardisation. For there are, of course, piles upon piles of each item, items that might be included in any number of picking lists, multi-purposeful, all prepared with the prospect of slotting neatly together (with a little nudging and banging thrown in for good measure) in perfect mechanical harmony. One problem that became evident quite early on in the piece was the weight of some of the packages—quickly bringing resolution to my question of why we needed to get them ourselves rather than have someone simply bring them to us (it's much more fun when you are the giant…). Even with a large sturdy flat bed trolley at our disposal, there was still the matter of how to manoeuvre a box that was over two metres long and weighed a tonne (I exaggerate here, but only so that you might better get my point) off of the back of the stack and onto the trolley safely (the safety of both yourself and the product in question is at stake).

It was precisely this problem that I was mulling over in my mind when standing, alone, in front of one of the giant's piles. Improvisation was the only recourse and so I decided to make something up as I went along. I began by placing the trolley head on in front of the stack and went to stand next to the pile itself, sliding the long pack out of its nest so that it extended into the aisle. I did this until I had pulled out just more than half of the length of the pack, just enough to tip the balance, enabling the end of the pack to make (gentle) contact with the trolley. I then reached into the shelf to grab the back end of the pack, sliding and then lifting it out (so that the whole scene, including the trolley looked like some ridiculous wheel barrow). Still hold the back end of the pack, and with the other end still resting on the trolley, I used the weight of the pack to help me move the trolley away from the pack so that I could put the back end of the pack down and have it resting flat on the trolley. It was still extending out a long way from the end of the trolley, which would not be practical as we went around looking for other items, so I grabbed the handles of the trolley, and drove it slowly towards the pile of packs once more, this time causing the extended end of the package to connect with its 'own kind' and, with one last determined shove, pushed the trolley in a way that made the pack slide along it into a more perceivably balanced position. Ouila! Perhaps there is some trace of a moral to this narrative, in the notion that a heavy package can be manoeuvred in the absence of great physical strength so long as the creative hand is fit or, as Confucius said, "To pierce through the target does not score in archery; because men differ in strength."[121]

As we progressed through the picking list, ticking of each item as we went, the flat bed trolley became full and then miraculously mutated into two full trolleys. Once these had been steered, precariously, to the nearest check out, they were promptly redirected to the home delivery counter. We had well and truly resigned ourselves to the impossibility of transporting everything home on the tram. We left our load at the store for 'next day' delivery and, with only a bag or two of small, incidental and unplanned purchases remaining, we picked them up and caught a tram home. In review of the day's events, a reasonable conclusion flickered brightly in my mind, like a faulty neon sign alerting me to it meaning, its connotation. That is, one trip to IKEA is bad enough. Two trips in one day is sheer masochism.

## Post-Pilot

It is now Saturday, November 29 and, as promised, our IKEA purchases the next day arrived in a big truck and where delivered into our front room by two men averse to eye contact; in their routinised labour we are merely two more faceless customers—nothing more than an address on a delivery slip, a

---

[121] Confucius, *Analects*, c. 400 B.C.

phone number, even though our wants further demonstrate the pre-condition for the men's employment.

A few minutes later, the front door is closed, at which point Julie and I decide to make an immediate start on our giant sized jigsaw puzzles; we agree that the assemblage of two shelving units will be enough of a challenge for today. I've heard of couples nearly splitting up over the trials and tribulations of furniture assembly and am far from willing to follow suit. But I wonder why such a possibility exists in the first place. Does it stem from some glimpse of an extant gap between the ideology of an easy street to the final functional product, from the promise of an almost instantly available harmonious and personalised home that has become happy and democratic through its 'cashed-up' collaboration with 'everyday' furniture? Does it stem from coming face to face with the factory finished reality of emotionless metal components, that is, with the screws, plugs, bolts and hinges that have each been put into groups and asphyxiated in dedicated plastic pouches?

There is no (free) choice for Julie and me but to accept full responsibility for putting it together. It was made by machines, and so there is an implicit awareness that any mistake will surely be our (fallibly human) own. What is more, perhaps we are somehow symbolically responsible for taking the brunt of our compliance to the ideology of a happy home, the potential backlash of this ideology if an unexpected hurdle should happen to present itself. Is the weight of this all, perhaps, too much for some couples to bear and, if so, what weight is this? If it is the kind of weight created by a formidable void between what is expected and what is produced, the gravity of it all when what is thought to be good goes terribly wrong, then it might also be a weight associated with the fear of falling into this opening and, by way of it, in to a state of confronting self-awareness. In other words, perhaps this weight may well be described as the weight of our own falling bodies.

The call to work together, the implications of taking a chance against this abyssal opening, might lead to a sense of personal success or failure rather than to a questioning of that which has provided you with the rules of play, i.e. the ideology itself. If an individual or couple has bought into IKEA as part of an attempt to achieve 'personality', a failure to follow instructions and/or work together might also be subsumed under the banner of personal failure. While mostly pre-empted by the avowedly fool proof assembly instructions, the assembly manual perhaps only threatens to make the bitter taste of error more disconcerting. Not satisfied with urging 'negative growth' in the relationship department, it were as if IKEA manuals were the duplicitous tools of an institution that taunts us with the additional prospect of making a fool of oneself. We buy the dream but, once home, risk unwrapping something very different as if, in some distant echo of Jacques Derrida's *Pharmakon*, the evasive men had brought to our door both 'poison' and 'cure'.

For some conclusive comments on IKEA, I shall begin by sharing some of the details of a recent festive experience. Over one recent Christmas break,

I was enjoying a semi-traditional Christmas dinner with my wife's family. At some point in the evening, someone carried out a ginger bread house, covered in the many colours of smarties. Very soon, it was being demolished and devoured by children and adults alike. There I was, chewing on the back wall (mainly because of the blue smarties that were stuck to it with semi-transparent icing) when I overheard the others talking about the ginger bread house having come from IKEA. Not only that, but it had been purchased in a flat pack ready for 'at home' assembly. It struck me as odd that here we were eating a pre-fabricated fairytale artefact. It made me question whether nothing was safe from the clutches of a mass packaged culture. It struck me as quite absurd. After all, if this really if 'the future', what's next? Steak and three veg—flat-packed? IKEA styled noodles, or assemble-yourself-hamburgers and chips? In this day and age, so long as it sells, so long as the product is financially viable, I suppose the possibilities are endless.

To be honest, the privileging of compartmentalisation and mass production also seems kind of obsessive, like when a child discovers sticky tape for the first time and then, before too long, everything is covered in sticky tape, or when a person buys a laminator for the first time and will perhaps become entrenched in the preoccupation of wandering the house or office, looking for anything at all that might fit between the alluring heated rollers. The upside to this was brought to my attention by a close friend who informed me that his IKEA shelves were still standing proud, having been bought for him by his mum nearly twenty years ago; he's been using those shelves for more than half his life.

# CHAPTER 7
# CITY WALKING

Many authors…have highlighted the perceived tension between the individual who walked the streets of a city which had been transformed by power and authority, yet who retained an inner sense of alienation and distance from the signs of power inscribed in the city. Baudelaire's fruitful depiction of the flâneur—the alert urban stroller—was built around this notion.[122]

## Phase One

*Monday, 1ˢᵗ December*

Monday morning, the beginning of a new working week. Today is the first day, since my move to Melbourne, which I shall be spending by myself. What better time than this to commence a series of dérives that engage with the built environment as a context of industrial discipline in a novel and creative way. Julie has already left for her first day at work and I will take this opportunity to be the flâneur and go on a series of dérives around the city and surrounding streets of Melbourne - to treat it, that is, as a space of play. The city, thus, becomes a potential space, not for the known but for the unknown to come into awareness, as if each walk were a dance, the appeal of which rests in its capacity to reach out into unfamiliarity and, in this way, to resound with the prosperity of the abyss. As Baudelaire put it, "We wish to plunge to the abyss' depths, Hell or Heaven, what does it matter? Into the depths of the Unknown [sic] to find something new!"[123]

In the context of my lineage, the appeal of self-dissolution has a certain historical precedent. I remember listening to my Uncle, a couple of years ago, talking to me about his experience of joining the British Army as a young man because he wanted to get lost. I realise that moving to Melbourne and 'having a look around' means that I have chosen a far less gruelling option, but perhaps the principal behind our decisions is not so dissimilar.

I must admit that I'm feeling a little nervous about leaving the house. I mean, what do I actually do with my time? I become aware of the clock ticking in the next room and know that the challenge to make the most of my time and my life has already started. It is most certainly a creative (albeit slightly anxious) project, this 'making the most', and so it would make sense for my 'leaving the house', to be conducted as part of a creative endeavour. Already these white walls have come to form something of a protective co-

---

[122] C. Jones, *Paris: Biography of a City* (London: Penguin Books, 2004), xxiv.
[123] C. Baudelaire, "The Voyage," in *The Flowers of Evil*, William Aggeler trans., (Fresno, California: Academy Library Guild, 1954), 459.

coon, a place of safety and security, and so it must be that the perils of familiarity are already beginning to sink into the space, into my thinking and, in
turn, into my behaviour. I am sitting at the laptop typing and am happy to
continue doing this because it has an air of productivity about it (I can feel
assured that I am doing something – privileging thinking but legitimising it
through its translation into text). But there is a limit to how useful self-
referentiality can be, and the whole point is to communicate this experience
in a way than is useful, that is, in a way that finds the narrative conveying a
subtext of collective responsibility and not narcissism.

For this reason, the time has come to get showered and changed and go
out into this little corner of the world, to become lost and found and lost and
found again—to see where the day takes me but to keep my eyes actively
open and, as Xavier De Maistre makes the distinction in "A Journey Around
My Bedroom", try not simply to 'look' but to 'notice'. This will entail my use
of the Dictaphone, notepad and camera to capture that which captures me.
This is the extent of my motivation. This is my entry point into the dérive.

*Dérive Kit*
1. Backpack
2. Dictaphone, with new batteries and a spare tape.
3. Two pens (in case one runs out)
4. Note book
5. Digital camera
6. iPod and headphones
7. Water bottle
8. Watch
9. Mobile phone
10. Metcard for travel by tram and/or rail
11. Cash
12. Credit card
13. Personal Identification
14. Street Map (If you are intent on getting lost, keep a map on hand
    just in case getting lost loses its appeal and you want to be found
    again).
15. One Tram guide
16. Two Chocolate biscuits

The problem of where to go in a city that is unfamiliar is somewhat re-
solved by the decision to go wherever the eye is directed. But this is not
simply a passive process for it is important that you keep your eyes open for
things that are of interest, for new directions in which to develop the dérive
further. I begin my dérive with the expectation that it will be conducted on
the pathways and verges of the city, rather than going up no entry areas and
through private property. The point is to be open to exploration but this

need not entail ignoring ones collective responsibility. Respect for privacy can still be maintained in the course of a dérive unless we are to claim that a dé-rive veers into the unethical, that is, and I am not sure anyone is going to put his or her hand up in support for that claim.

[11:30am]

Given that it is Monday morning and, for all intents and purposes, the beginning of the working week, there is something pleasantly perverse, thus rewarding, about the fact that I see no better time than this to commence my dérives, aimless wanderings, walks that resist the urge to settle, nomadic, drawn along in this or that direction by the luxury of whims. If the built envi-ronment is a context of necessary labour and wage slavery, of industrial disci-pline (for the conditions of our minority world urge us to behave and to communicate in certain unnatural and peculiar ways, acting in a way that might seem peculiar to the general consensus, I should imagine, puts me in good stead for some kind of respite. It is possible to express some resistance by behaving differently in this space, that is, by approaching it in a creative manner, a space of play, a potential space in the sense that I attempt to hold myself open to potentialities, to the possibilities of colliding with the unex-pected, by embracing not the known but the unknown, whereby each walk represents my venturing in to the abyss, the unfathomable to come.

I start to walk down my road and pass all of the terrace houses that line the street, each one slightly different from the last, some more so than others if they have been modernised, repainted and renovated. I near a roundabout, lined with trees with a small tavern on one corner. The question of whether or not there are any good 'locals' around here has already been met with an amused chuckle for, to the locals, it is common-sense that good locals are many and close between. It is an element of common-sense that I am yet to learn for, in these parts at least, I am not yet common—closer to a dedicated tourist than other subjectivities. But being a tourist affords one a sense of distance that is useful in these situations. Like the overseas visitor, perhaps from France or Belgium, with the exotic accent, there are certain things than one can get away with (knowingly, usually), certain tolerable liberties, that may not be to one who is familiar, who should know better. I am yet to find myself in an interpersonal situation wherein I need to draw upon this differ-ence. Though it must be said that if I did I should need to remain mindful that to take too much advantage of it would be to act in an interpersonally exploitative manner and this, let me make clear, is a narcissistic personally trait, signed and certified in the diagnostics and statistics manual found on many a psychologist's book shelf.[124]

---

[124] While the DSM-IV is widely used, some psychologists prefer to use an ICD-10 (International Classification of Diseases).

I near the end of Church Street and my attentions turn to the directional signs that add to the overall visual pollution around me. I capture several in one photograph, though I am sure that this is merely scraping at the surface. If I find myself in the city, the subject matter in this image shall surely pale into insignificance. But, for now, I turn right and head down Brunswick Street. This, admittedly, is one street that I have been down a number of times before and so, self-conscious of this fact and keen not to undermine the process in which I am currently engaged, scroll through points of difference in my mind, those which confirm the unfamiliarity of this are. Firstly, I have never been this far up Brunswick Street before. Secondly, I have never derived here before (something that can be taken for granted with regard to any street I come across). This is enough for me, at this stage, to feel like the integrity of the process is being maintained though I am careful not to dwell too much on this detail because it could mean that I run the risk of looking without noticing, caught up in thoughts about the theory of things while failing to recognise their implications in this material reality.

Brunswick Street offers one the main tram routes that head between the city and the outer suburbs. It is a popular destination for all kinds of artistic types, latté sippers and gourmet pizza eaters. The roads are lined with various architectural styles, most of these being quite old and, as a result, conceivably dirty. I guess this 'grunginess' is the price that you must pay, if not part of the initial attraction, for having various examples of Victorian architectural history around you, not like in Perth which is a very clean city but usually, I feel confident in saying, because everything is just bulldozed and rebuilt. This might make for a fresh appearance but I am not sure it does much for maintaining a sense of coherence with the past, with the sense of place or even of identity that comes from seeing the artefacts of times gone by still standing around you, punctuating your passage through the streets, housing whatever life it is that you choose to lead.

It is an appreciation for a living history that stays with me as I continue southbound down Brunswick Street. It is an appreciation that is reinforced through the contrast that exists between the old and the new, between the dark brown paint and terracotta bricks and the concrete coloured block of flats that are visible in the distance, towering above all else, announcing their presence in the landscape, altering the horizon line, confirming that this truly is a place in which Modernity has left its footprint. I approach a public toilet to my right. Its roof line is sharp and dynamic with countless lean lines. It is built from concrete slabs that are joined by two grey metal sheets running horizontally between them and which form the roof—grey metal doors provide entry and exit points in this functional but soulless industrial form. From the pathway, it is possible to see into one of the inactive cubicles. The open door is unsuccessfully inviting. I wouldn't go in there unless I was desperate. Even though there is a space between the top of the door and the roof, all you have to do is get the sun in the wrong place and there you are, in the half darkness, trying to relax enough to pee while the afternoon breeze blows around your privates. While the random comments left by compulsive scribblers are sometimes amusing, it is well known that you can catch Herpes or Chlamydia just by sitting down on a public toilet. One of the few ways to get around this risk, other than by avoiding the vicinity altogether and holding it until you get home, is by covering the toilet seat in a few carefully placed layers of scratch-your-bum toilet paper, and then kicking them off with your shoe so that they fall into the water when you're done.

Signs are to be found all along the streets, instructing cars where to go, where not to go, fulfilling the same task for pedestrians. There are times when I am not quite sure who the intended audience is. For example, I arrive at the end of a little street only to see a sign on a wooden pole that reads, No Entry and am not all together certain whether this is meant for vehicles or for any person who might otherwise be thinking of going down it. A police station can be seen a short way down and so I wonder for moment whether this might be an official zone, hence my confusion. In the end, I decide that I shall look around in any case, thinking that I may be able to draw from my aforementioned and presupposed 'tourist privileges' if need be.

One thing I have noticed (although my self-imposed hyper-vigilance may mean that I am exposed to a little paranoia) is how people tend to look at you when you are walking around taking photographs of this and that. The objects that I am capturing in my lens, because they seem interesting to me for whatever reason, may well be those very same things that the locals see every day and which, as a result, are nothing but invisible icons, landmarks, trivial objects, mundane at best. By being seen everywhere, every day, it is as if they have lost all colour, all character and slowly, silently, slipped into the background—hence, out of sight from the eyes of passers-by. It is as if, with each day to day glance, the life of a thing it taken piece by piece, with 'looks that kills' but it is a slow kind of death, like a sickly cancer or gradual decay. It is a less desirable alternative, a quick death like passing peacefully and painlessly away in one's sleep. No. This, I suspect, bears some resemblance to the kind of extraction of life that some ancient cultures believe takes place when a person's photograph is taken.

Part of my ambition to experience the life of the day means that I must resist one of my forces of habit, that being the tendency to walk around with my eyes to the pavement. There must be some irony, then, in the fact that I am taking photographs of some of the things that catch my eye, as I find myself unwittingly exoticising the buildings, the incidences of graffiti and the countless boring utilitarian road signs. Maybe I, too, am killing these sites, these artefacts for, my documenting them, am I not also contributing to their familiarisation, their repetition, thus, their vanishing? Am I not inevitably, by the very fact that I am wandering around the streets, even without an intentional destination, even without the kind of motivation that might lead me to one, heading towards a certain familiarity and, with it, towards the death of my surroundings? If this beginning is merely the inevitable beginning of the end, then the least that I can do is to make the most of it—so that this death might not be in vain, one could say in a sombre but decidedly sentimental tone. For the beginning of the end, as it happens, still constitutes a beginning.

I stroll down a series of roads, Brunswick Street (205 onwards), all the while taking photos of various things. I am caught on the colours on Moor Street as I walk along the empty sidewalk; a pink wall, white wall, blue bin, yellow VW Beetle, red sprinkler alarm. A "No Entry" into Young Street is tempting and, turning right down it, I continue on until I reach Condell Street and the Town Hall. I veer left off of the pathway and head through the park until I come out the other side at Wood Street. The rusty street sign sits above a drawing of a flower, drawn in this black marker on the cream painted bricks. I turn right, back onto Moor Street again.

37°48'07.03"S  144°58'50.75"E[125]

With the sun behind it, St Mark's Parish Church appears to be half in silhouette, a tall point reaches the crucifix up into the air.

37°48'07.06"S  144°58'53.21"E

House number 202. The one with a nameless cat who pokes its head out from under to green metal gate when I stopped to say hello. It sniffs at the air in my direction then, keeping its head still, sits awhile for the sun to warm its furry face. The cat just sits there, staring blankly at the world going by.

37°48'07.53"S  144°58'55.48"E

Left onto Gore Street; I look across the road and see a cream coloured concrete building. The corner of the building is missing. Instead, there strands another diagonal wall. Its main feature, by far, is an arched window, perhaps either as some reference to ancient Roman architecture, or else to the problem of multiplicity confronted in Play School. There is a reflection in the arched window—of the building that sits diagonally across the road, somewhere over to my right. The building is a 19th century red brick terrace that is flanked by other just like it. I don't turn around to see the real thing; I remain transfixed on the reflection of history, caught within the metal frame of modernity.

---

[125] "Space seems to be either tamer or more inoffensive than time; we're forever meeting people who have watches, very seldom people who have compasses." G. Perec, *Species of Space and Other Pieces*, J. Sturrock, trans. (London: Penguin Books, 1999), 83.

37°48'07.44"S   144°58'57.06"E

I turn right down Hodgson Street, noticing the big yellow chemist in the near distance. The façade of an old building guards a void where the rest of the building has been demolished.

37°48'06.13"S   144°58'57.41"E

A man in a grey jumper walks past a burgundy vintage car. I've got no idea what model it is but it has the words "Equipe – Soixant Neuf" painted in orange calligraphy along the curve of the white roof.

37°48'06.00"S   144°58'57.67"E

Right onto Smith Street

37°48'07.43"S   144°59'01.02"E

[12:15pm]

A passer-by comes up to me and asks "Excuse me buddy. Have you got any spare change?"

"I haven't got any. Sorry," (really, I don't).

37°48'11.96"S   144°59'00.33"E

Just before the Webb Street corner I stand to look at a large poster on a yellow wall. It's of a female face and is mostly black and white, except for her metallic red lips and blue eye shadow. They stand out greatly against her lily white skin. I continue along Smith Street.

37°48'14.49"S   144°58'59.99"E

There are four red steel poles above a Mountain Designs outlet. They are affixed about a metre I front of three upright rectangular stone windows. Each window wears a triangular hat. All of the glass is still intact. It's clear enough for me to be able to see the brick wall that abuts the façade. People inside the top room would see nothing more than an uninterrupted wall. The brick wall keeps the façade excluded from the site. The characters 'AD 1872" are painted in burgundy near the top of the façade at 86a Smith Street.

37°48'17.45"S   144°59'00.01"E

I turn right at Gertrude Street. A taxi and scaffolding take up space just beyond the Gore Street corner.

37°48'22.38"S   144°58'55.23"E

It seems that I have been walking in a street lined circle. An electricity box on a metal pole catches my eye, before I turn left up Little George Street.

37°48'22.06"S   144°58'48.26"E

I walked past a garage door, comprising five horizontal sheets of grey metal, all of which are covered in colourful icons and scribblings. There is a sky blue man icon, like those you might see on toilet doors, a pink stylised shape of a woman, her arms straight down to either side to bracket a knee length skirt. Another pink female has wings and another male symbol is much thinner than the first. Two black cats face each other far below three black bombs, heading directly for earth, just as the right position for the peace symbols that they sport to be right way up. Each peace symbol looks to be strapped to its respective missile. A little further up along the wall, I see more human symbols in their stereotypical colours (even paint has a gendered role in this society). When stencilled onto the wall, they have been positioned so that they look to be holding hands. Further up, again, more people have been stencilled onto garage doors, a brown woman, an orange woman, a yellow man, and a brown woman in a corset, a blue man with wings, a dark blue man, and two more pink women, one with wings and one without. The winged figures are painted higher up than any of the others.

37°48'25.14"S   144°58'47.66"E

A yellow pedestrian sign directs me the keep left as opposed to turning right up an alley way. I turn right to satiate the curiosity that the sign provoked, to see a corrugated fence, half rusty, with rusty barbed wire for hair. I turn right up a lane that takes me to Lt. Victoria Street, past a balcony filled with flower pots and dry plants.

37°48'27.30"S   144°58'47.22"E

At the base of a wall, some create person has stencilled a drumming teddy bear in white with a black border. Nearby, a budgie rocks out on a flying V electric guitar. There's an amp and an effects pedal about to get stomped. Everywhere I turn, another wall has something to say. I have to look all around me to see where I am going, though I have tried to lose myself as well. Right up Napier Street.

37°48'27.02"S   144°58'45.46"E

I have now lost all sense of direction (perhaps tracing my route on a map would make this clearly apparent). The camera batteries are running low and I am down to one chocolate biscuit as I turn left up Gertrude Street.

37°48'21.74"S   144°58'45.65"E

The road is busy with traffic. The solitude of the backstreets has been broken by a passing tram, the horns of impatient drivers, and the gesticulations of frustrated cyclists. Turn left along Brunswick Street (photo of Brunswick Street from Lt. Napier Street corner).

37°48'21.16"S   144°58'38.28"E

"Ben Emil" can be read in the façade on the top of a building (big home).

37°48'25.96"S   144°58'36.63"E

A couple are kissing goodbye next to a car. She is going somewhere without him. "Ciao...." She says, though I can't make out his name.

37°48'26.59"S   144°58'37.18"E

A blue wall occupies the left hand side of my peripheral vision, as I stare off towards the Gothic Cathedral. On the right, a multi-storey building bares red brick and white concrete, horizontal strips. Directly ahead, an illuminated orange arrow directs the traffic to turn right. In any case, all motorists have no choice but to comply or else drive into a utility vehicle that has been parked across the out-of-bounds section of road.

37°48'27.74"S   144°58'37.13"E

The black and white image of woman's face consumes an entire wall, approximately 3 x 5 metres in size. She has a face but no name, no voice, and no third dimension. Her face is a metonym for her entire body, almost entirely absent. She is a poster on the wall, publicly disembodied, publicly silenced. All she has left is a look, her white face contrasting the blackness of her eyelines, eyebrows, lips (including the shadow beneath the lower one), and the cavity of her left nostril. In this context, these features are the extent of her definition.

I walk down to Victoria Parade and look left down the tram line as I cross it. Concrete and steel extend into the distance, lined by green leafy trees and rusting power poles, steel cables strung between them—suspended over the tramway. A truck, parked on the left hand side verge, has a green and yellow cabin—the same colours of the tram that I can see rolling off in the distance.

37°48'29.96"S    144°58'36.77"E

I walk past a parking lot of a private business and notice the four yellow metal men that have been positioned, bolted to the concrete ground, in such a way as to prevent unauthorised parking. They have red and white reflective waistbands, brass padlocks piercing their foreheads, and each one has its right metal arm reaching into the air as if to have been captured in the middle of a welcoming gesture, or perhaps a gesture of "Good-bye, and don't try to park here again!" They have no feet or hands, but what they do have are screws where we might expect their eyes to be; these screws are meant to hold on rubber stoppers to prevent the yellow paint being scratched when the parking spots are needed and the metal men end up temporarily face down on the ground. Two of these metal men catch my attention, both of which are missing their right-eye side rubber stopper: on one, someone has drawn a black line so that it appears to be smiling; on the other, perhaps the same person has drawn a little Hitler moustache accompanied by a short straight black line for a mouth. Whoever drew these must have thought that the extended right metal arm resembled a different, and much less favourable, kind of gesture altogether. In any case, it's incredible what lengths people will take to keep their space exclusive. It's Monday afternoon, the beginning of the working week, and here is a large slab of concrete currently home to four yellow figurines that all stand to attention, blocking the way, with not a single car in sight.

37°48'32.02"S    144°58'36.76"E

I look up towards the grey cloudy sky, and see a 'P' sign at the top of a tall cream painted building on Morrison Place. Without a signifier of such high visibility, the passerby might otherwise mistake it for another generic towering construction, with no windows or external distinguishing features. "Here I am" says the 'P', "modernism in all its glory—another example of the 'non-places' that unites efficiency with population density and that you experience as the multi-storey car park."[126]

---

[126] The multi-storey car park falls under the groups of modernist constructions that Joe Moran classifies as 'non-places', along with hotel foyers, waiting room, airport lounges, and the like.
J. Moran, *Reading the Everyday* (London and New York: Routledge, 2005), Chapter 4.

37°48'32.09"S    144°58'37.23"E

The image of a hungry yellow hippopotamus it still visible on the side of a large, blue metal bin. The hippo is yawning in the middle of the long side of this 8 x 2 metre construction. The bin is full to overflowing and a strong gust of wind will be enough to prove it useless. The bin is weathered and rusting in discrete parts. It has its own number—132 955.

37°48'32.90"S    144°58'35.76"E

I turn right onto Albert Street, then left onto the Gisborne Street corner, and continuing down through the Cathedral yard.

37°48'34.97"S    144°58'32.98"E

I walk past the statue of O'Connell…

37°48'35.28"S    144°58'35.81"E

…past an arched wooden doorway, and stop at a row of miserable look-ing faces, carved on stone, flanking the inset cathedral windows with their morose and nose-less countenances. One, in particular, catches my eye; an orange browed male face with cavities for pupils stares blankly into the dis-tance behind me, over me. His mouth is turned slightly down. The weather hasn't done any favours to his podgy cheeks, embedded into the cathedral exterior maybe 10 feet up—stuck for an eternity between rock and a hard place.

[12:55pm]

Gisborne Street becomes Mac Arthur Street and I continue along it.

37°48'38.29"S    144°58'31.89"E

A small green wooden hut is juxtaposed against the modern environ-ment just before St Andrew's Place.

37°48'42.02"S    144°58'29.74"E

Having passed the Treasury Theatre, I walk all the way down Mac Ar-thur Street to where it becomes Spring Street.

37°48'47.55"S    144°58'25.65"E

Once here, I turn right down Collins Street and veer left into Collins Place (Arcade). The triangular ceiling holds anodized purple, yellow, and green balls hang from the complex structure. The 13 Christmas decorations perhaps serving to remind the people walking below that a holiday is not too far away.

37°48'49.29"S   144°58'23.20"E

At 13:12, I walk around Level G, peering down onto the people having a coffee break on the Lower Ground level. Underneath their glass umbrellas, workers from the central business district unit for coffee and conversation. I go up to the top floor and am directed back down again by the sterility of the snobby noses and austere décor, various items of furniture carefully positioned along the walls of empty spaces. Upon my return to Collins Street, I continue down in the direction that I had been going in before, past Exhibition and Russell Streets, and left down Swanston Street.

37°48'56.10"S   144°58'01.35"E

Left again at Flinders Lane and turn right into the initial undercover part of Chapter House Lane (along the side of the Alphaville outlet) along to where it opens out into the St. Paul's Cathedral car park and which, at the top of the steps, allows you to look out over the road to Federation Square. There seems to be an event taking place there and so I walk down the steps and go to have a closer look.

On the way down the steps I see, down below and next to the stair way, the empty sleeping bags of homeless people, crumpled and dirty and littered with various indistinguishable items of clothing. After the steps, I walk along the pathway and past a red door on St. Paul's Cathedral to my right.

37°49'04.27"S   144°58'03.49"E

I continue onwards to the Flinders Street roadside across from Federation Square and wait patiently for the green man to indicate my safe passage across the road. When he arrives, I walk over to where all the action is. I arrive at Federation Square and, given the sleeping bags that I had seen not one hundred metres away, am struck by the irony being played out before me. I stand in astonishment at the festival/spectacle of the "56 Nations, one goal event", that is, the "Melbourne 2008 Homeless World Cup" taking place from today until the seventh. The allure of grand views, the desire for a global perspective sure seems empty when it obscures a clear view of the doorstep!

I am always suspicious of calls for world-wide unity. They seem decidedly religious and, in this sense, disturbingly white-washing to me. It takes me a minute to figure out how to actually enter the square given all the partitioning and fencing that has the whole place cordoned off as ajar from plain sight. I spot the constructed tunnel-like entrance, like the walkway into an ancient Greek or Roman arena, the sense of entering a different place and, I turn out to be justified in saying, an ideological space. Walking through it, I feel like a cow in a farm shed. 'Soon to be' audience members are being herded through the construct like livestock.

Having finally reached the guts of the crowd, I arrive just in time to hear the some of the opening speeches. A man is at the microphone, making the most of his technologically driven power to project his voice, as he communicates participant instructions. He shall be saying "Welcome to the…" and asks the crowd to complete the sentence by coming in with a collective "new world". I wonder where the new world is and about what kind of 'order' might be found to underlie its operations. I guess that the new world must be around here but I can't say that I have been able to locate it yet. Maybe I am not looking hard enough—looking, that is, without actually noticing. Maybe I am not looking in the 'right' way but turning this notion over in my mind just arouses more cynicism and the crowd is successfully disorienting enough, cutting off my view of the world beyond the stadium with a giant digital screen that displays close ups of the internal going's on. I say 'interior' because the 'games area' does not take up the entire square but, instead, exists in a frontal pocket of it, confined within its own additional mesh-fencing, maybe ten metres high and extending around the exclusive zone.

In Russia, for example, it has long been the case that if you do not own any land, you are considered a 'nobody', without rights, without any visibility. For this reason, homeless people in these two places are removed, by law, from any kind of social support, any recognition of their plight. Russia's participation in the Homeless Games, as a way of raising their international profile and building their image, forced them to change this section of the law and, effectively, give homeless people some rights. In this sense, the event has been successful.

On this point of the 'new world' I would have thought that, given that our living and production arrangements are only 200 years old, perhaps what he means by the "new world" is this world, the world around us now. Perhaps what he means by the "new world" is the privileged minority world. Perhaps the vocalisation of this sentiment, now backed by the light pub rock tones of musicians on stage, is truly a kind of industrial music.

The chant has evolved into "Welcome to this new world"—an appeal to late modern culture's demand for novelty and entertainment, 2 modes through which ideology is communicated, transmitted to the masses. The following slogans appear in a repeating sequence on the large digital display: "Free public event…supporting grass-roots football in 56 countries"; "Using the power of sport to change lives"; "70% of players experience significant life change."

These are confident claims reflecting the power of the organised dissemination of ideas to colonise the cultural meaning, a sense of identity and, with it human behaviour.

"Join the fan club, make a donation, buy the t-shirt" As Terry Eagleton says, "meaning, like everything else, is expected to be instantly consumable."[127] Here, there is a call for the public to consume ideology. The three components of this last statement each connote a key term "belonging", "giving", "receiving". The call to give is sandwiched between two calls to 'get', thus softening its implication of the consumer going without.

I leave federation Square and, walking back onto Swanston Street, sense another motivation, to find food. I choose something to eat at the Subway store and find a quiet place to eat; a bench next to the window that looks out into the arcade walkway. While it is an ideal spot for people watching, I cannot help feeling like a window display; like I am the one who's on show—a free advert for all of the potential customers walking by. I function as a picture of the product in action, its consummation and confirmation as a viable choice despite the numerous others on offer. My presence in the window says "Choose Subway...not for the benefit of the company but as a way of expressing your personal freedom. You too are free to do as I have done, to make the decision to eat here instead of somewhere else."

I continue to eat my words as pedestrians walk by, every now and then looking in at me, as well as at other customers, through the window from the arcade. I wonder whether what they see is anything more than a billboard covered in crumbs, struggling to control to steady flow of sauce that sneaks an intermittent drip or two out of the side of the package. I feel like I have paid to provide the company with a free commercial.

37°48'59.87"S   144°58'01.43"E

[2:20pm]

I finish my food and head back out onto Swanston Street, continuing in the direction of Collins Street. I notice a young boy of about nine years old walking past me, and am amused by the cardboard wrap around hat that he is wearing (the kind of hat that children sometimes wear at fast food restaurant birthday parties). The front panel has been cut out in the shape of a reindeer with the brand name David Jones written in bold lettering on both sides. The reindeer is on the front, so I guess that is what is most readily seen when you look straight at it but, on the city streets, no-one really ever looks straight at anyone. Instead, people are continuously walking past each other, on the move, and so much visual contact is spent in the mode of side-stepping, dodging, overtaking. The side of the head is a very prominent feature.

---

[127] T. Eagleton, *Literary Theory: An Introduction* (MA: Blackwell Publishing, 2008), p. xi.

One of the ways that culture is taught is through object-use. These days, assumptions about what is valuable or not are communicated through consumer items. A David Jones sign located on a child's head next to the cartoon of a reindeer has the purpose of triggering specific associations in people's minds—the innocence of childhood play, fun, hijacked by the cut throat world of advanced capitalism. I am astonished at a parent or guardian would consent to a multi-national corporation using their child's head as free advertising space, turning a living and walking being into an unwitting canvas for corporate branding, wherein the ideal of the former is put to work for the reality of the latter.

[2:50pm]

I cross Collins Street and turn left down the pathway, but it is here that my first walk ends. My new motivation is to meet Julie on Lygon Street at 4:30pm, by which time she would have completed her first day at work. Even though I still have some time left between now and then, the unmotivated walk has concluded. I shall begin again tomorrow, returning first by tram to this location where I shall alight, pick up where I left off and, in doing so, take the walk into a second phase.

## Phase Two

*Tuesday, 2nd December*
I have returned to the place where my walk concluded yesterday. On the way, I had a small task to complete; that is, become a member of the Victorian Writer's Centre. Being new to the state, and keen to find ways of furthering my writing, means that this appears to be a favourable decision. I enter a small arcade, passing the window of Subway with its sauce faced lunch munchers on the way, and walk up the stairs to the VWC office. After a brief chat with the receptionist, I pay the fee and return to the street below.

My second walk begins to the sound of two trumpet buskers fumbling through notes of what resemble Christmas carols, dressed in festive green salvation army t-shirts and black trousers. A music stand, holding the scores in place, is all that sits between them and a third companion; a self-standing red poll capped with a donation tin. Every now and then a pedestrian slots in some spare change; the sound of coins make a quick sharp metallic sound, disrupting the rhythm of the music. I think that I could probably do without this soundtrack—'as the saints go marching' perhaps becomes the ideal cue for my departure from this corner and my entrance into the next unmotivated walk.

[12:15pm]

I move westbound down Collins Street, past a poker faced woman in a power suit, and along a line of boutique clothing outlets. Country Road, David Lawrence, Cue, Kookai. The names mean nothing to me. Looking up at none of them, her poker faced gaze is as though fixed upon a mental image of her destination, this 'elsewhere' place that determines her route.

A group of people forms one at a time at either side of the road, at equal points along it, gathering with one group facing the other across the way. The number builds steadily, slowly, patiently, as if in anticipation of a kind of anonymous and pedestrian climax, measured by the rhythm of the ticking sound that, once it shifts into a rapid fire, results in their movement onto the road, towards the other side, the two groups crossing each other's paths somewhere near the middle of the asphalt but depending, of course, on the pace of their gaits. They meet and cross, civilly inattentive, but aware enough to dodge and weave a safe passage to the other side, ensuring that it is reached without falter. The crossing is complete. The groups disperse from the roadsides leaving them almost empty but for one or two loners. Then 3, 4, 5, 6. The numbers begin to mount once again in preparation for the next public climax, the next population dispersion. For, while the faces are different each time, the motions remain distinctly the same—a collective necessity forms their habituation.

A slim school girl of about fifteen or sixteen, and dressed in a navy green uniform, sits by herself, silently smoking a cigarette. Straights locks of long black hair grace her shoulders. She peers down onto the sidewalk around her feet, a dead stare, deep in thought as the smoke trails into the air above her head and disperses into invisibility. I stop walking for this moment and wonder what her name is, what she is thinking. She doesn't know that I am over here, seeing what she is doing without reason for any sense guilt. It doesn't matter anyway. Maybe if she looked up and caught my eye I would quickly look away and pretend that she had merely captured the end of my momentary glimpse, the passing eyes of a stranger disappearing inside the body of the busy crowd. Maybe I would stand my ground and smile, testing the waters of anonymity, pushing the boundary, pushing against the distance between us. But nothing is happening apart from what exists in my mind. She does not break her stare. She does not look up at anyone let alone me, and why should she? Why should her glance take my presence into account? That might be what breaks the magic of this moment. Besides, I am nobody in the city, anonymous, invisible amid the faces as I stand on the footpath, staring into space; staring into infinity.

Three more girls sit behind her, looking in the other direction and not smoking. Instead, they are talking to each other, one at a time and all together depending on the cadence of the conversation, also inside the limits of their own world, a shared paradigm. I do not care for how they look or what they are wearing but, instead, am struck by the way that their conversation seems to be conducted without sounds, merely by the movements of their mouths, by the shapes that they all make. Throwing shapes into the atmosphere, shapes that have fallen completely apart long before they have reached the other side of the road. Their low level chatter lost entirely amid the sounds of cars, trams, buses, once more the ticking beat of a cross walk can be heard from one of its many locations. All these join a range of other indeterminable sounds as the pulse of the public finds them weaving past each other, stretching compressing, dispersing, collecting—the social formation, the cultural fabric, spills out over the road ways and paths of this built environment. The industrial organism breathes life into itself, self-perpetuating the new habitat of modern human beings. The city's noise drowns out the differences of all things within it. But, plugged in, switched on, wired up, scratching their noses and bums in a collective communication of their consent, their regard, for our progress into the digital age.

What does it mean to be free in the city? Free to roam? Free to spend hour upon hour shuffling through the contents of your desktop in the middle of the central business district? What would be left of freedom if were guided only by city approved paths, adorned with our various conceivably appropriate attires, pin striped and pushing buttons while shuffling shoes. The rustling of shopping bags just loud enough to contribute to an industrial deafness Are these the signs of success? Here, perhaps. But, beyond the city? Well...that might be a totally different matter altogether. At least there remains enough scope for a dandelion to float effortlessly past my face, moving both in and out of my peripheral vision in a moment. Nature seems so out of place amid this culture.

37°38'49.16"S    144°57'54.59"E

I find an available metal bench on which to rest for a minute, to collect my thoughts on the page before they go the way of the dandelion. Having stopped to look around, taking myself out of the general flow of traffic so that I might achieve a certain perspective of it, I know that anyone who has watched the first Matrix movie will understand why I sit here, half expecting to see a woman in a red dress walk by at any moment.

Fabricated silver stars decorating the gaps between the buildings, filling the voids with artificial space, starting a few metres above the road. They are a sign that Christmas is on its way and that it, once again, is the season to spent lots of money (the season to be jolly in the city). The notion of the star has great appeal. Many people want to be stars, to live the lives of the glamorous, the rich and famous. In the biblical story of Christmas, the followers of the star were wise men, travelling to a destination of which they had only a vague notion though they, too, where taken along by their motivation. Thus, a few strings of seasonal 'bling' might just do the trick in reminding us of our aspirations and, by way of the thoughtful positioning of the stars, perhaps we are being shown where we might purchase the signifiers of such arbitrary ideals, that is, in the malls, in the fashion outlets, these status stores as sellers of fantasy lives. Anchored between Optus and ANZ, between a jeweller's and HSBC, Tiffany and Co. and Novotel, and so on, the strings of stars indicate that the festive season is well and truly anchored in the profit margins of the business sector. On this occasion, I too follow the stars, turning left up Collins Street and continuing on my journey.

The string of shop signs extends above my head; Kookai, Cue, David Lawrence, Country Road, and I, thinking now that they mean something to me, know that it is because they mean I am tracing back along my previous path. If I had been walking with the sole purpose of getting somewhere, some location in the city, I might have been forgiven for thinking that I had taken a wrong turn. But I have not. I am both become properly aware of my position and, in having realised that I had been walking along a discrepancy, sense a degree of disorientation, a gap between my thinking and the material reality in which I am currently operating. I enjoy the confusion while it lasts, knowing that I have stumbled into a sweet spot for thinking, an indicator of the success of my aimlessness, but also disappointed by the way that my mind works to overcome it, to iron out the crease as soon as the crease comes to light (my brain kicks in to establishing that I must be heading back up to Swanston Street). I might have been better to walk in the darkness. To never find my way and conscious only of that which I continue to notice, the fleeting glimpses and dead stares (the flight of dead stairs). But alas, the stars have led me back in on myself, back into the known if from another direction.

I walk along 50 metres and see, to my right, a middle aged man sitting in a green fold-away chair. He is still, facing an Asian man who, poised behind his clip-board and sheet of paper, works on a portrait in charcoal of the sitter. His right hand pushes the charcoal over the much finer lines of what seems to be his preliminary sketch. A bracelet of thick green beads pokes out from the end of his white striped and collared shirt. It is tucked into a pair of grey trousers and black belt. His shoulder length straight black hair adds something of an air or the artist to him (however stereotypical this perception may be). He is also sitting on a fold-away chair, though this one seems like it would be much more comfortable than the other one, and beside him rests 2 rows of picture frames, 3 in the back, 7 in the front, each the same and each containing an example of his 'finest' work.

Viewing the frames from behind, I can see how each frame has been propped up on a plastic coloured clothes peg, a blue one, a red one, a blue one, a yellow one, each peg successfully fulfilling the task of holding the pictures in clear view for the pedestrians. The collection of frames is accompanied, at one end, by a thick book filled with photographs of more examples. At the other end stands a tripod, now being used to display a conceivably traditional landscape oil painting, nothing challenging to the eye or mind. Underneath it sits a loosely compiled collage of oil painting images, reduced in size to make the most out of a limited amount of space.

Though mostly charcoal, there are also a couple of the full-sized framed pictures are in colour—a sign of his repertoire. The three in the back row catch my eye. On the far left is a picture of a 1960's Holden sedan. To its left is a black and white portrait of Jesus, including the top half of his torso and complete with long hair and beard. I am rather curious about the cross that has been drawn, hanging down front and centre as if it were a pendant, around this Jesus' neck. Did this symbol not come into play until after the crucifixion? Why would a prisoner on death row wear a t-shirt with the picture of an electric chair on it? Why would anyone draw him with one ex post facto? I am equally amused by the next and last image along, for the juxtaposition that it creates with its neighbour, just described. A colour portrait of Paris Hilton, international woman of 'not a lot of mystery', sporting signature oversized sunglasses and holding in her arms a rodent so hideously deformed that it could easily be mistaken for a dog. The pairing of a modern Western harlot next to a spiritual icon from the ancient East makes for quite the juxtaposition.

I consider the possible meanings that might be read into this scene, the individual sitting among the hustle and bustle, being transformed into a two dimensional representation by a silent stranger—the artist at work. Here, the sidewalk becomes his studio, a creative space, a work place—his process out on public display for pleasure or disapproval. I once heard that if you don't know how to fix pipes you can't consider yourself a plumber, if you cannot lay bricks then you are quite unlikely to consider yourself a builder, if you cannot cook then you will not call yourself a chef, but that everyone considers themselves an art critic. I wonder if this notion is true for the countless people that walk by, taking a second or two to cast their eyes across the pictures while others seem to remain oblivious to them entirely. Perhaps there is some echo in this of that process in which I am taking part, sitting here on a bench not 2 metres away from the drawing, scribbling my notes like a squirrel inconspicuously collecting nuts for the winter. For I too am passed by strangers (this much is both a pervasive and inevitable circumstance of city living), many of whom move along with their eyes fixed on the paths before them, concentrating not on what is taking place around them but on their 'ways to go'.

With a total sitting time of between 10 and 15 minutes, the portrait is now complete and the sitter gets up, now standing next to the artist who remains seated. The sitter smiles at the artist, accompanying it with a nominal nod of approval, and holds the smile still, not moving a muscle in his face as the payment is made. Maybe it is the sceptic, or cynic, in me that wonders whether he really likes what he has bought. Making a payment post completion might give one the impression that the unsatisfied customer is free to leave but both parties have invested time and effort in this creative exchange. For the artist, his time is money in this culture as is the case for the sitter. The collapse of the deal would mean wastage for both of them and perhaps the few dollars is a small price to pay for a sense that it has all been worthwhile.

[1:50pm]

As one moment ends another begins, and an old lady walks in front of me, muttering quietly to herself. She seems to be looking for a place on the bench behind me to rest but I can hear her grumbling about the woman who is sitting having a cigarette. I am able to make out a few words to hear her predict how they (presumably smokers in general) will "all complain when they get cancer". She continues to grumble as she walks back around to my side of the bench, sitting herself down beside me, turning herself in my general direction, and poising herself for a shot at a conversation.

The old lady is not much over 5 feet tall, with short grey hair, a small round face, with ginger stubble spanning the entire area of skin above her top lip (developing into grey stubble around the sides of her mouth and covering her pale and wrinkled chin). She is wearing a woollen coat with brown buttons down the centre, over the top of a pale cream blouse with denim-blue coloured polka dots on it. She continues to sit facing me and starts to chatter away in a gentle but concerned voice. I get the feeling that she is looking for some reassurance as she tells me about how her purse was taken and about she had just gone to buy a replacement. The new item is taken out of a red and white plastic shopping bag—the item, a purple purse reportedly identical to the old one. She tells me about going to the police, the pain she gets in her leg and the name of the painkiller that a lady recommended to her. I nod along sympathetically as she shows me a piece of paper with the word PA-HAMAX written on it in capital letters. She reads the word out a couple of times and I have a closer look at the paper as she holds it out for me to see. I gently take the piece of paper from her hand and, resting it on my still open note book, take to it with my pen, double writing a darkened 'N' over the top of the 'H' so that it reads what it probably should—PANAMAX. "It's Panamax", I say to her so that she has no doubt as to what I am doing, is clear that I am helping her. "It should say Panamax", I reiterate as I hand the corrected piece of paper back to her. She puts it away and recommences the purse story, repeating the same details as before and in much the same order, returning over and over again to the main point, that someone took the purse from her and how terrible it is that it happened. "I had to get another wallet because someone took my old one". She adds that it had been full of money at the time, thus adding to her difficulty, reaching into her bag, once again taking out her new purse, making sure that I had got a good look at the shiny purple replacement, and opening it in front of me—some kind of prop to her telling of the past. This purse is also full of money; twenties and fifties lined up neatly together in one of the longer pockets. I wonder whether it had been under circumstances similar to these that her purse went missing in the first place. What if I was a petty thief or a drug addict in need of money for gear or both? Opening your purse to strangers is not something that I would ever contemplate doing but, then again, she has done it just now and no adverse consequences have resulted. I am not interested in her money or of taking advantage of her age. There are people out there that wouldn't be so forgiving and I guess my assumption about the meaning of this scene stem from a protectiveness, from my belief in the untrustworthiness of others.

37°48'49.33"S    144°57'56.23"E

The French writer Albert Camus observed that the prospect of something bad happening to a good person, as in the case of something good happening to a bad person, is merely a reflection of the absurdity of life as opposed to any of Karma's crossed-wires. Karma or no Karma, this was not the time or the place for mis-deeds. Her hands are covered in sun and liver spots. The right one doing all of the work while the left rests on the handle of her small personal shopping buggy—a light grey painted frame clothed in a tartan cover. I sit for a little while longer, listening, nodding politely in agreement at the inhumanity, feigning by belief in the shock of it all (for it is an unfortunate fact that purses go missing every day and, I am afraid, they no longer make the news). A few minutes pass and I can just about hear her words. They seem to be getting quieter and quieter or perhaps it is my interest that is waning. Maybe the gradual quietening of her voice is her way of testing the genuineness of my attention, a way of answering the question of how much silence she can speak before I cease to nod and retract my support? The walking and noticing has made me tired and so I tell her that I have to go. "Have a good night" she says with her vocal volume resumed. I reply in kind before walking off along the street and turning left down Bourke Street, aware that I shall soon be out of view and keen to be so, just in case she is watching.

When I reach Elizabeth Street I stop. 2:25pm. I feel as though I have been barely anywhere today, trapped in the city. But there is much to see and so it would be unnecessary to judge my activities by the physical distance across which they have taken place. For, geographically, while I have only managed to travel a short distance, it has still taken me 3 hours to do so.

**Phase Three**

*Wednesday, 3rd December*
I start the day unsure of whether or not I will conduct a dérive today. I am finding it hard to lay claim to the unfolding of an unmotivated urban exploration when I am starting to feel quite overwhelmed by the anxiety of unemployment. Fortunately, I can take this as a sign that I am already out of my comfort zone, in which case it might be worth simply continuing with that

which cause me the discomfort, to ride it out in order to see where it takes me. It is precisely this place of agitation that I was hoping to achieve in moving to Melbourne (that 'outer-space' across the cradle of my established limitations), so it makes little sense to back out when confronted by feelings of discomfort and self-doubt—the latter being something that has been prominent over the past few days though only really coming to a head now. All the self-certainties that find support in the familiarity and habituations of everyday life that, once removed or, in my case, left, find the self somewhat adrift. The notion of the dérive has felt like a logical expression of this dislocation and the critical challenges that it brings—the step by step process of finding how I choose to deal with them and, in this way, of acting as a kind of physical and emotional scale by against which I may test my resiliency.

Then I have decided that a dérive is in order after all. Though I do feel as though I am on some kind of paradoxical mission, the sense that I am trying to see as much as I can before I know what it looks like—not in the sense of capitalising on my opportunity to not-notice things but to capitalise on the fragile freshness that the outside offers up before I find myself another face in the herd who goes about their day stepping over the countless wilted remnants.

[1:10pm]

I leave the house and travel by tram to my last 'end-point' in the city.

[1:35pm]

I reach the location where Elizabeth Street crosses Bourke Street, turning left down Elizabeth (roughly Southbound), and watching the other pedestrians as we walk by each other. I think about how my drifting is doing very little to aid instances of interpersonal exchange (human interaction beyond the nimble footed necessities of sidewalk dodgery). The sound of a nomadic sales promoter, microphone in one hand and sales reference brochure in the other, who stands just inside the entrance to a shop while announcing a stream of generic shopping prompts in an effort to help reel the customers in with the promise of Christmas specials. He will be the voice of perfume for the next few minutes before moving to become another store's keynote speaker.

A 'doof, doof' beat, accompanied by a woman singing, fades in and out of my earshot as I walk by a fashion outlet. I seem to be riding the wave of the crowd for, as I reach the Collins Street crosswalk, the little green man starts to blinker and beep away and I, without so much as a second though, find myself following the pack across the road to the other side, coming face to face with the same two fumbling trumpeters of which I made mention yesterday (with the same green t-shirts, same red pole with the donation tin perched on top of it) The are playing a different song at the moment to the one that I heard before, but I sure that this is merely a matter of fortunate timing.

A rapid ticking commences somewhere else but fades as I continue along and down the footpath, struck by the intensity of some bright colours that move towards me, popping out into conspicuousness through their contrast against the myriad gloomy and neutral tones—pink head scarf, bright blue jumper, blue jacket, green (environmentally friendly) supermarket shopping bag. I can hear laughing approaching and look up to see a woman with a wide smile, a mouth filled with glistening pearly white teeth, and way too much foundation for my liking, walking towards me with her female companion. A whiff of perfume streams up my nostrils as they pass by am I cannot help but wonder what kind of smell it is that they are trying to hide beneath the floral bouquet of expensive scent. I decide to cross a minor road, j-walking in front of a police car (a remarkably cheap thrill even for my liking) and continue on to Flinders Street, turning right once I get there.

[2:oopm]

I turn right into University Arcade, attracted like a mosquito to an insect zapper on a barmy summer's evening, to the shiny floor tiles and electric blue interior features. Admiring the blue of the supporting arch extending across the ceiling from left to right, as well as the VU entrance in the same colour, I stop at the VU entrance and peer in, seeing the bright blue LCD words appearing and running along the digital display from right to left before disappearing into the unit just as suddenly as they had emerged from it. "Victoria University" it reads at speed "a new school of thought." I can't stop thinking about the blue, mesmerized like a potential student, softening and priming for institutional consumption.

I reach the end of the arcade, taking the odd photo of the gaps between things, before turning left onto Flinders Lane.

It would seem that my eyes, in their effort to make sense of the multiplicities found amid the visual pollutions, in an effort to find some sense of grounding and anchorage in the aimlessness, and perhaps conditioned by the joy of colour that attracted me into University Arcade, are now conceivably hunting down the colour blue—the blue plastic wheelie bin that I can see to my left and down beside the truck, the blue street signs that are noticeable as I pass Fulham Place, Bond Street, Ryrie Lane, the blue "P" of the car park sign, a Bankwest ATM, a man in a blue work shirt standing on the steps across the road smoking a cigarette, the three blue café umbrellas, the reflection of the blue sky in a glass panelled sky-scraper, the sky itself. Each instance provides me with a potential place of pleasure amid the discomfort of an experience that is taking place beyond the limited confines of familiarity and quality assured comfort, that is, beyond the guarantee of safety—a guarantee so conceivably hardwired in a human beings list of necessities and which, in the end, only the view of the sky can seem to turn my awareness away from it (even though this is not a sustainable solution).

As with my previous experience of being disorientated, having miscalculated my location along Collins Street yesterday, I am once again pleased that I have reached this point in the process—this point of needing a place to rest my eyes, being aware of this urge and, as a result, the opportunity to process this experience in a self-conscious and critical way as it continues to unfold— to heighten my vigilance as I prepare to find out where it takes me and, in turn, what sense I can actively make of it.

Continuing straight along, I cross Queen Street, interested by the reflective qualities of the buildings near the Tavistock Place corner. The tram wires form a web like pattern over the top of the street adding to a sense of being enclosed inside of something, the hint of danger by entrapment, claustrophobia, insularity. The sound of a woman's voice coming from out the front of a café, breaks my preoccupation with paranoid adjectives. Her syntax sounds like a muffled string of syllables against the backdrop of road-works, jack hammers, and general traffic noises that frame them, that make them disappear. It is a mutter that seems to be punctuated, as far as I can hear, by the kind of cultivated half-lisp that I have sometimes heard used by the purveyors of new money sophistication on the back of the city's CBD. It reminds me of the impediment experienced by Charles II, King of Spain from 1665 to 1700. The so-called Hapsburg Lip came to be adopted by the Spanish people as a signifier of prestige and privilege, of the wealth and power of royalty, when in fact it was a hereditary deformity that came about as a result of successive inbreeding. Ironically, inbreeding was favoured by royal families as a means to ensuring the security of pure blood and, no doubt, monetary wealth. Here, I entertain the possibility of the lisp being re-contextualised as a signifier of independently acquired wealth. I turn left along King Street.

[2:30pm]

The last two streets or so have been relatively empty, like an industrial dead zone where people go to work and die. My field of vision is no longer filled with the hustle and bustle of the shopping malls, as it has been so consistently for me in the city so far, but rather dominated by the height and number of the sky-scrapers, faceless as they are, lifeless, inanimate giants towering above the common man. Dead zones.

I turn left at the end of King Street and onto Flinders Street and start to feel a creeping anxiety building up inside of me and which, it seems for now, is drawing me back in the general direction from which I have recently come; slowly sucking me back into the beating heart of the city centre, the pulse of the visually polluting nevertheless feeding a sense of place among the streets and pathways.

It occurs to me that there may be some problem with this, for I am not lost but, in fact, seem to have formulated an assumption about precisely where I am headed and, with this assumption, permitted it to be self-fulfilling. Perhaps the problem does not so much lie with my not being lost, for Debord knew his way around Paris very well I'm sure, but with the fact that my bee-line back to the city's centre has caused me to close my eyes to much of what is around me. In other words, in my growing anxiety, my pace has almost doubled. While I would not go so far as to say that all has come to an end, it does seem as if I have reached a critical part in the process and, what is more, I no longer know what road I am on.

I decide that it is best to continue in this way for a while, paying less attention to the names of roads, and it is as if I have somehow been able to walk myself out of my anxiety—leading me to smile and for this smile to turn into a quiet laugh when I walk past a young boy hugging a giant hamburger for dear life; his arms stretched around the foam suit as far as they can possibly go, and then some—a grin from ear to ear lights up his face in the joy of it all (the kind of smile you might expect to see on a child who adores their pet more than anything in the world and with all the appeal of unconditional love. The man inside the suit might have no other option than to wait for the boy to let go.

I have stopped looking at the street signs and, as I re-enter the shopping malls, find myself seeking signs of other kinds. Did my search for street signage serve as some kind of safeguard against the feeling of being lost? Did it mean that I was in some kind of space between lost and found? What does my decision to ignore the streets, to ignore their names, mean if not that I have passed through a mental barrier? I worry that what it indicates is that my barrier crossing and the shopping malls are each part of the same materialistic beast. I ask myself whether or not my anxiety was partly to do with a lack of people and visual stimuli; a certain disconcerting boredom that arises when there are no more shops to look at. Going from a context of intense business to a place of emptiness within a brief period of time is quite confronting; the contrasts and juxtaposition between an abundance of presence and an abundance of absence serves to intensify my experience of both. But, has my wandering, my deriving, if each day has been the continuation of one winding path starting from late Monday morning, somehow been to the service of the city, that is, a gradual expression of the allure of consumerist centres, with each step of mine as if it were another step closer to being reeled into the captivating vessel?

This might be too much to bear for it puts my sense of freedom in serious doubt. I act as if free but how can this be if it turns out that all the photos and incidental details have merely been expendable and replaceable props in a much greater cultural movement? I look for ways to think myself beyond this disappointment, wondering whether or not the hours of effort have only been in vain. Apart from lunch, I haven't bought a single thing in the city and yet, it would seem, am have still contributed to its perpetuation and, worse, its dominance over human behaviour.

I was lost for a short while and revelled in this fact. But now, now that I have some a sense of location once again, I am not certain that I like what I have found.

[3:15pm - Dérive suspended]

[6:30pm]

Psychologically isolated. Physically demanding/draining/tiring. These are just some of the words that come to mind, as I sit out on the back patio, a glass of red wine placed down on the ground beside my chair, and reflect upon how I might best describe the day's meandering. For, while it's all well and good walking around for no other reason than to find out where I am going, devoid of all directional motivations such as the need to get to a school or a work-place, the shops or to meet with a friend, while I am certainly lacking these particular motivations, there is one overarching but less obvious motivation with which I have been working. It is a veritable meta-motive relating to my own personal experience that, I cannot deny, has shadowed my every step, my every contemplation. What I refer to is the desire to find a sense of place in this state, in this city; a place that cannot be picked off of the production line but, rather, one that can perhaps be described as my 'self-authenticity'.

Perhaps I have spent far too much time considering the geography or, to maybe put it in another way, quite enough time already. In something of a belated response to the psycho-geographical question of how the built environment impacts upon a person's thoughts, feelings, and actions, I believe that I have the birth pangs of an answer. Rapid passage through various ambiences seems to be very adept to keeping one at a distance from everybody else—particularly so in a culture where social directives abound. It has kept me from the experience of interactions beyond the limitations of the fleeting glances that occur between the eyes of transient strangers. Rapid passage, therefore, seems conducive to a sense of personal isolation, a sense of isolation through separation that, while useful for defamiliarisation, is perhaps not so conducive to establishing social networks and enjoying the company of other people. I imagine Guy Debord, having spent many years in Paris, leaning upon such social devices for support at the end of a long day, in times of need, in times of joy in order to allay the alienation of the dérive—the challenge of the day in which he has been intimately engaged. In other words, being already familiar with a place means that you have the privilege of an already well developed sense of place, and so it is not surprising that, for Debord, the dérive presented itself as the opportunity for a kind of game; one that has a beginning and an end—always and end; a life of normalcy, monotony and habituation always exists beyond these two borders; they provide a secure basis to rebel against (perhaps in this way reaffirming their institutionalisation, their immovability, mocking the game in its futility.

The routinisation of everyday life provides respite from the challenges of aimlessness—rest for the walker. But it is a very different thing for these borders to blur (these borders being the beginnings and ends of this peculiar game) or, furthermore, for them to disappear completely. At least in this context, this is precisely what they seem to have done. Without the privilege of having immediately accessible social supports, without the comfort of having already been familiar with this setting, without any monotony to fight or fall back against but only the expectation that monotony will eventually arrive, the dérive becomes a very different game indeed. It is, for my part, under these conditions that the space of play seems to have melded with the basis of the 'everyday', that it has become a game of life. In fact, of this I feel quite sure, for it means that the rules of play have changed, that the game is not one that will simply end, on cue, requiring only the nominal effort of a click of the fingers. Quite the contrary. I may well have to claw my way out of this one, as I fight for a new kind of life.

It seems to be a hard and lonely fight against a familiarity which has not yet shown its face but, rather, has merely made the promise and threat that it will do so, in time, if given the right conditions. Thus I find myself in this current state, playing a game that is no longer a game (for its impact has extended far beyond the preconceived parameters of a beginning and an end). Or maybe, in my tiredness, the line between them is simply too faint for me to see. For now, it would seem that the game has come to be life itself and I am left wondering whether I am just fighting a phantom, or whether I am merely fighting what my past experience suggests I should, what my thinking tells me to.

My aimlessness is an attack on my limits, and this is what I wanted, the challenge and the skills that result from it. But perhaps I am taking heed of this warning to the detriment of other things. It might be largely due to the energy that I have expended through all the walking that I have been doing, that this has proven to be quite a gruelling process. In any case, I have long held the consolatory belief that the things that require more effort to achieve are also more rewarding (a sentiment that has seen me over invest in many a project) and so I guess I shall hope that it will all be worthwhile in the end.

I feel some sense of being marginalised not because of any incapacity to engage in consumerist practices, for there are many ways that I choose, and need, to do so every day. Rather, as a result of going in to the city and spending a number of hours there without actually doing any shopping. If Christmas time is the time to spend wildly, then my behaviour of wandering around the streets without going into any shops might seem quite strange indeed, out of keeping with the general population, and I feel a distance between us in this way. It is not a distance that I wish to bridge, simply it is one that warrants acknowledgement.

I am not discomforted by this distance, though I have experienced many days of going to malls and city centres and, while the people that I am with seem to have very little trouble at all, I, for the life of me, can't seem to find anything that catches my eye. I have an aversion to the illusion of choice for all predilections, for all tastes. I have an aversion to the obscuring of social inequalities (still amazed when I go into Kmart only to hear Christmas carols playing in the elevator. I thought we were living in a secular society). I have an aversion to suffocating the dissatisfactions and instabilities underneath the standardisations and uniformities that are placed on sale (made buoyant) by, and to the benefit of, the determining powers of business and industry. Walking around the city without doing any shopping is something that I am quite used to—and it doesn't take throwing money away to avoid the label of 'miser'.

"How Santa Really Works" is the slogan that I see wobbling around, each word moving independently, in the Christmas display windows of Myer. Small scenes of Santa pointing at a blackboard, written on which are transport and logistics details, further over there is depicted a sorting centre, elves moving parcels around; these imaginative vignettes are an example of, at the same time obscuring, just how insidiously ideology 'really works'. For, if you want to know how Santa really works then you need to take notice of the mechanics of ideology, of the dissemination of values, ideas, and beliefs, of that unthinking basis of everyday knowledge that we also call 'commonsense'.

Santa, as a notion, works by promising children who don't know better, that good behaviour is rewarded by the reception of material goods; not that 'presents' have been produced by human effort (obscuring the power relationships that exist in the processes of labour), but that have been put together in a fantasy land somewhere far removed from the city space, i.e. the North Pole (the thought of such a huge distance is a thought that works to protect the lie, for what child could travel without adult consent?).

It is the classic display of training the (industrial) dog. Where children don't know better, it is usually because their parents are lying to them as well; representatives of the part of the adult world that wants the lie to live and breathe, which consents to the deception because it, too, wants the children trained, because it enjoys the fruits of subordination. Children enjoy the delusion either because they do not realise that it is a delusion or because they are already sick with the fever of presents. The sparkle in the eyes of parents as they watch their children open them on Christmas morning...am I scratching at a much deeper source of joy...a giddiness that stems from the convenient and comforting power afforded to them by the holy 'Spirit of Consumerism'.

## Phase Four

*Thursday, 4th December*

I spend the morning going over some of my journal entries, contemplating the possibilities of where the next dérive will take me, and feeling somewhat disillusioned by the whole process. I have the desire to make goals but am not quite sure which ones to make. Like many others in the industrial world, I have the privilege of personal choice, the ability to do whatever it is that I fancy without so much as the slightest worry. I decide to go the library with the presumption that I will be able to relish in the protective cocoon afforded me by the cloak of self-motivated education, under the illusion that I am along a community of other interested people, minus to pushing and the shoving of the city streets outside, plus the convenience of clean toilets and places to sit in peace.

I remember a character in Jean-Paul Sartre's *Nausea* that, in some English translations, is known as the "Autodidact."[128] Briefly put, this 'self-teacher' makes the decision to learn about the world and so, confident that the library holds everything that there is to know about the world, he goes there, every day all day, with the intention of reading every book that is there. This must be done systematically of course, so that he can be sure not to have missed a publication, and so he decides do read through the books alphabetically, reading everything in order from A to Z.

Given that the library is a cultural construction, a feature in the world and not a representation of it, all knowledge gained by the Autodidact will be second hand. However, we might at least admire his perseverance. To what extent will the limits of other's interpretations become his? He has a rational mind and so, surely along the way, he will be able to think critically of the information that he reads. If reading necessarily meant believing then we would not have such rich cultural histories of written fiction. He will have many an opportunity to compare and contrast, to object previously held assumptions and ways of looking at things, that is, as he works his way further into the collection, as new information comes to hand.

Keen to begin my day of decisiveness, I arrive at the library almost three quarters of an hour early, having overlooked the opening time of 10am and making the misguided assumption that everything opened at 9. I hover around outside, before heading across the road to Melbourne Central Station, a multi-story mall with a bookshop among various other outlets. Now aware that the rest of the city hasn't really woken up yet either (as if the capacity to consume was somehow intrinsically linked to clarity and alertness, the proactivity, of the human mind itself), I go back out onto the sidewalk and wander around the streets until just after 10am, at which I arrive back at the library.

---

[128] J-P. Sartre, *Nausea* (London: Penguin Books, 1965).

Bags are not allowed in the library itself. You are required to turn left as you go through the entrance, and pay for an electrified locker which, once you have gone through the process of attending the main control unit, selected your preferred locker height, chosen a password, read the instructions, inserted your money, a plastic circle on the designated door lights up so that you can look around and see just which one it is. Now unloaded of unnecessary baggage, I enter the main library hall and take a long look around me, enjoying the spaciousness and height, basking in the glory of books.

A quick search through the database leads to me wonder why so many books have can have a request sent for them. Nearly every item has a send request note attached to it. Thinking at first that these are the specially stored books that a person must request before reading, I am left wondering what exactly it is that they have on their shelves. My imagination starts to get away with me. Are the books I seek part of a greater collection of shitty books that nobody wants—the thousands of dusty rejects stored in some secret location? Who knows where this unseen place is, which people cannot reach without proper authorisation; or the path trodden upon only by the select few book fetchers whom, hobbit-like (or perhaps similar to the vault-key masters in the bank in the Harry Potter movie) scurry through the labyrinth of underground tunnels between the master chambers and the customer service desk. Are they, behind the scenes, searching high and low, begrudgingly pulling carts of requested dust behind them? No; not at all.

My mind wanders and I start to think about how moving house often means having to 'make do'. In the spirit of "you don't know what you've got until it's gone", here are some of the things that I have taken for granted which, in their absence (being still in transit from Perth), I am starting to feel a great sense of appreciation for:

1. Fridge
2. Couch
3. Television
4. Washing machine
5. Ironing Board

The fact that I am having an emotional response to the absence of these items just goes to show how industrialisation has impacted upon my life in the most fundamentally of ways. I feel a little queasy that the couch and the television are on this list and, while I greatly miss the company of friends, having already accepted their absence, I would have at least liked some comforts to soften the blow. Not being able to watch the news is something that makes me feel disconnected, even though is am always already 'at a distance', wrapped up in the warmth and safety of my lounge-room, from the constructed narratives that are broadcast into it, ordered into half hour programs, neatly edited and sound-tracked for viewing enjoyment, and taken away again, as quickly as they arrived, so that we can go on as before, sipping red wine from a glass in one hand while picking at a fruit platter with the other. My agitation and disgruntlement reflect the cracking of that shell of narcissism that late modern culture helps us form around ourselves, i.e. an over-inflated sense of entitlement, the belief that one 'should' or 'must' have certain comforts, certain conveniences for no other reason than that is 'how life is' and that, in the event that these expectations are not met, lead to negative feelings. It seems that one set of negative feelings is going to lead me straight to another. My (false) need for these items takes me to a very inconvenient place of self-confrontation and, in this way, to self-loathing.

The fridge is probably the only thing on the list through which I can at least direct my negative feelings to invisible 'others'. So much of what we buy at the supermarket needs to be refrigerated and so, on this account, I feel somewhat rescued by a glimpse of necessity. Herein lies a desperately grasped 'fatalism', one that tells me all about the 'inevitabilities' of our everyday lives. But there is nothing inevitable about how we live, and my failure to be mindful of that would be my own responsibility.

Having previously put the familiarity of my life-world, my 'everyday', into a jumble, having packed its inanimate components into boxes and waved good-bye at its living components from the airport window, I have found that, perhaps, I have packed away some of the supports for my self-esteem also. When talking to Julie about this, she returns to the same solution; "Just enjoy the time that you have off, while you have it." But, for some reason, I don't seem to be able to let go of the feeling that I should have a job, having quite happily relied upon the job that I had for a sense of (institutional) validation. This kind of validation can be really rewarding but does it not just direct us into the winds of status anxiety, even if we only realise the strength of the winds once that support has been dismantled? If the absence of that support leads to this feeling of self disvalidation, then is it a poison or a cure to have it? Is it not simply another reflection of Derrida's *Pharmakon*, with all the individuals still within its grip, sporting sickly smiles? I have had a sickly smile and, looking back on it, it wasn't enough simply to be self-conscious of that fact, to smile ironically. In fact, perhaps knowing about it and consenting to it just helps to spread the fever further.

My Dad has said the same thing as Julie did, about enjoying the time that I have out of work. But I am never out of work, for there is always some task that I have set myself, writing for this or that, documenting the process of relocation in terms of a critical awareness of how I am experiencing it. I have plenty of work; I just don't have a job.

My imagination comes to an abrupt halt as I scan some shelves upstairs and realise that all the books are here, with the request service merely a way of saving legs for those people who are too busy learning to fetch them for themselves. I stand in front of the literary texts from various culture, a few shelves on Kafka, Goethe, others on Sartre and Derrida. I select a book on the history of French literature, keen to soak up some culture, as well as a small book about Simone de Beauvoir, though I don't expect I will actually get around to reading any of it. In any case, I shall make an effort, even though it's hard to say where these kinds of books will lead you. You never know, perhaps I'll end up wandering around the streets, trying to distract myself from the aimlessness of unemployment, trying to make this time as useful as possible before I get settled in, employed, and distracted by day to day habituations. Maybe I'll even write a book about it.

## Phase Five

*Monday, 8th December*

In my efforts to explore the city in a series of dérives, I found that it was mainly heightening my sense of alienation and loneliness and still manages to help me get established and, for want of a less irritating word, settled (I suppose this is my chance to find my feet before I start finding other people's). 'Settled' is what I think of as the doorway to complacency and the deadening familiarity of habitual behaviour. I came here for life. But what kind of life is it to be wandering around the streets, exhausted. If I am to operate in this context in a culturally conscious way then the least that I can to do to start this process is to learn something about the history of the city.

The "Autodidact" conceives of self-directed learning seems to be a solid way of spending time without the nagging feeling that you are doing something worthless, somehow assisting the institution in their protection of knowledge, demonstrating support through attendance, marching around the building like a soldier of information. Unless you are a 13 year old boy having a day out with his mate, in which case you are not marching but rather playing at the top of the 'upward-bound' escalator, challenging the uppermost steps to a battle of wits and balance. I watch as the scene unfolds, first pleased at the sight of the boys bucking the system, trying to go down that which is supposed to take things up, a juvenile but symbolic display of rebellion and, not a minute later, I feel a stupid sense of satisfaction as I watch the female security guard spot the undesirable game and having silently walked over to them, passed on a few calm but clear words that such a practice is unacceptable. There is a sudden quiet as the security of the border is once again ensured, now that the boys have become the subjects of a process of socialisation, disciplined inside the institution, slinking off to the father of one of them who, only three or so metres away, had been peacefully staring out of the window in the other direction—a precious moment of respite and its end marked by a subtle turn of the head to take stock of the boys now standing close beside him, under the wings of their protector; a flaw in his authority to loosen the leash now exposed by the uniformed official.

Like the library, the museum is also a protector of knowledge constructions, of 'versions' of history, not histories themselves but merely their recollection and representation. While my decision of going to the museum to learn about the city's histories is a method that has its own problems, I am sure (from the outset I am dubious by the way that mention is made of "The Melbourne Story" and not "Stories". Perhaps this much is to be 'taken for granted', but then...). Nevertheless, I decide to visit the museum and see what historical construction they have on show.

Once inside the museum, I walk over to have a look at one of Melbourne's first trams. They were pulled along by constantly moving cables or wire ropes, located underground. At its peak, this transport system comprised 17 routes across a total area of 100km and operated by 26 cables. Of the twelve engine houses (steam engines used to keep the cables in motion, one can be seen on the corner of Nicholson Street and Gertrude Street, and another on the corner of Toorak Road and Chapel Street.

After perusing the wooden tram, I start to walk over to my next point of interest, the deep sea creature display. I have seen this exhibit before and actually find quite sad, all those beautiful anglers and the smooth-head blob fish, with their friends from the ocean's Abyssal and Hadal zones, shrivelled and suspend for us to see. The whole 'fish out of water', like a dried one on the beach, resonates with me at the moment, more than it might do under more 'settled' conditions. The information available at the exhibit makes me think about how ridiculous the idea of outer-space being the 'final frontier' is, about how quick we might be to bask in the wonder of things beyond our own planet. If this tendency indicates the assumption that all on earth has been 'mastered', then it is founded in a flawed conception.

With the notion of what we take for granted as being normal, and common (common-sense?) kept firmly in mind, it is interesting to note the following information. If 70% of the earth is covered by ocean, and most of the ocean is more than 1km deep then, (as the exhibit explains) the deep sea is the most common habitat on earth. I read that the deepest part of the ocean is somewhere off of the Philippines. This area is known as the Challenger Deep (almost 11km's deep) and has only been visited by 2 people (Belgian Jacques Piccard and American Don Walsh went down there in the USS Trieste on January 23, 1963). As it turns out, more people have visited the moon. There is also a large exhibit that talks about human emotions and about how people have made sense of them in personal, social, and clinical contexts.

I now reach "The Melbourne Story" and listen to a short film about the 20/30 initiative to bring people back into the city, the city's loss of innocence in the face of the Gangland murders and about the city's ability to adapt to change and be open to many different voices, nationalities. Upon its completion, feel like I am another step closer to making this place my home. For if it is so that our memories endow us with a sense of identity, then visiting these kinds of places, these enduring institutions, and finding out what they have to say about the city, by discovering some of the 'city's' memories however mediated they are by institutionalised subjectivities, nevertheless helps me find a sense of place in Melbourne beyond the limitations of my own immediate experience. It contributes to a sense of who I am or might become for as long as I continue to live here.

I want to build my own Melbourne story, despite my awareness that it may well take me years before my sense of place is completely restored, perhaps this will never happen. Perhaps I will still be here, fifty years on, looking out onto the paths and the people walking by, thinking back on the life that I have lead, thinking about how I always looked for a way to call the city my own but, in all that time, I always felt a bit like an impostor. I hope that this is not how I end up but what would it matter if I did? Who could say that this was not the ideal path for me, settled down in my own alienation, my isolation.

If my wander around the various parts of the museum has any resemblance to a dérive, then at least it had a goal, the motivation to seek out and explore points of connection with the city's past, a past that I shall be a part of but a sense of which I feel will be really helpful in my process of identifying with it, of making it mine in some way. There is possessiveness in 'knowing'. I am aware of that. But it is just another way of a deep sea fish out of water, a creature of the abyss, trying to feel at home in a conceivably alien landscape.

It is strange how, even after only a little while, it is possible to feel the first softening slumber of insularity trying to creep its way into my mind. I have been here not even an entire two weeks and already I notice how I am becoming less and less concerned with the people around me. Upon arrival, my eyes flick everywhere and over everyone. The slightest movement is enough to attract my attention and lead me, surreptitiously of course, to take stock of the action, to find out what I can about what is going on. This is not a matter of nosiness but of a genuine interest in the workings of my new home. But, over the course of even a few days, the sharpness and curiosity evoked by a non-conventional haircut and a pair of leopard-patterned leggings is not so exciting after all. I find myself feeling increasingly self-conscious with regard where and upon what or whom I cast my eyes, as if I had been acting nosily after all and am only just beginning to realise.

But there is a comforting flip-side to this development. For it is as if a reduction in available personal space also meant a reduction in self-consciousness in terms of what I am, myself, doing—perhaps presuming that there exists an unspoken agreement to ignore each other's peculiarities, the same thing that draws my eyeballs inwards, also affords me some protection from the potential gazes of others. The sense of shame that keeps my eyes on hold is a sense that I, perhaps not only in metaphor, 'see' in others.

[10:45]

While I am well aware of the risk I run of stating the obvious, some-times I am really struck by the feeling that I have entered a completely differ-ent life. This much I have been able to conceptualise for a long time, turning the notion over in my head at every given moment. But I think perhaps that the emotional impact of this transitional period is only just starting to peak out from under the logistics. It must also be said that this impact has been expected but I am still surprised by how it feels, like being in a lucid dream, crystal clear as if the night time never arrived, only further hours of light streaming in through the window in my bedroom. Or else, might I compare it to waking up and realising that you are somebody different to the person who you went to sleep as, woken up inside a different life, different job, wife, home, a different set of friends. Maybe that would have been easier, stepping in to a mould that had already been set, established and, I, nothing more than a passive party, would have nothing to do but go through the prescribed mo-tions, doing what the signs tell me is expected of me, whatever that may be.

I am certainly glad that the journey I am on is, and will hopefully con-tinue to be, considerably more engaging and challenging than the kind of cat-alogue lifestyle which I have just described. I have got my first wave of this feeling while Julie and I were being intimate, as if I didn't even know her and, looking up at the moonlight coming in through our bedroom window, the radio playing beside us, the unfamiliarity was quite clarifying. It was as if I had awoken from a refreshing sleep yet could not remember having slept at all and, what is more, could barely even remember waking up.

Tip-toeing through the house at night, learning my way around a differ-ent floor plan, a different set of obstacles, I become hyper alert as I continue to move, trying desperately not to bump into anything, more so because I don't want to wake Julie. The layout of everything is new and so I find myself prone to forgetting where things are if not, in my half sleep, forgetting which house I am in, momentarily disorientated, trying to allay the slowness of my hesitations by fumbling my hands along the walls, my fingers crawling along the masonry as they search for traces of door frames, guiding me along as I precariously make my way from room to room. In the day, everything is fine. I can see where objects rest and the world seems ordered to me. In the dark, all bets are off. The world tumbles into a kind of mental chaos, I cannot see the order of things and so I cannot confirm my confidence among them.

It is a shame that many of the things that have brought me moments of joy and a general appreciation for where I am, are those that I cannot simply go up to and thank. Such as waking up in bed to see the morning light stretching down the length of the alleyway outside my bedroom window. Another thing that has really added to my experience in Melbourne so far is the sound of one of the birds that lives around here. It has a seven note song that I can hear when I'm sitting outside. I am sure there are many birds of this kind but, mostly due to the fact that I don't know which species it is, not able to identify it as anyone of the birds that I see, I continue to hear the song as coming from the beak of one bird and one bird only—the species, invisible in the face of my ignorance, condenses into one chirping expression, a single unseen bird, a kind represented and letting me in on its call. I could never thank the bird for making me feel welcome, at home—it could never understand me and, in any case, my comfort surely would not have been one its intentions. Perhaps I am as invisible to the bird as it remains to me—audible, but invisible.

[2:30pm]

"THANK YOU FOR BUYING WEIRD SHIT" reads the slogan on my receipt from Polyester Books.

I stop by at my favourite bookshop and see a book on a table among many others. "Astonish Yourself!" it urges, "101 Experiments in the Philosophy of Everyday Life" by Roger-Pol Droit.[129] I had seen this book on a number of previous visits to the shop but had usually been there in search of something else and so, guided by my motivation, had tended simply to walk straight past it with no further consideration beyond a fleeting curiosity. On this occasion, however, no such alternatives were in my mind and so I picked it up to have a closer look through. It contains 101 experiments for defamiliarising and disrupting the habituation of everyday life, each one headed by three categories relating to the experiment's duration, props, and effects. Each experiment is described in clear language and capped off with a few lines on its conceivably 'philosophical' significance/purpose. I turn to the first one, out of convention rather than anything else; what I see really strikes a chord with me. Titled "Call yourself", the task involves being at home alone and calling out your own name as if you were someone else calling you.[130] This is founded on the premise that while we often hear our name coming from other people's mouths but not our own. This expected effect of calling yourself repeatedly, in a range of different tines and vocal volumes, is a kind of "doubling effect" that comes after an initial period of awkwardness and uneasiness. In order to end the experiment you simply need to answer yourself with "I'm coming", or another such phrase.

This experiment really resonated with all that I had been thinking about throughout the dérives and with my general ambition of nurturing the non-habituated aspect of day to day behaviour. I don't often feel such a strong connection to shop items and so the significance of my feelings were probably over interpreted. Nevertheless, even reading through the experiment, still in the bookshop, my whole body felt strange, locked in myself almost, but outside of it at the same time. I didn't know that commodities could have this

---

[129] R-P Droit, *Astonish Yourself! 101 Experiments in the Philosophy of Everyday Life*, New York, Penguin, 2003).
[130] Ibid., 1-3.

effect on a person. Maybe this is what Julie feels like when she sees a nice pair of shoes, or what a child feels when he stands face to face with the world's greatest cool-drink vending machine, or other such escapist capitalist contraption. And so it was primarily based upon this emotional response that I decided to buy the book—like I was trying to purchase the strange feeling that I had just felt, getting carried away with my desire to possess myself through this little square object. It represented a point of identification with my self-expectations, with my recent Melbourne experiences and, as I left the shop, I felt quite astonished, but for a very different reason than Roger-Pol Droit would likely have anticipated.

[3:00pm]

I am sitting in a tavern, in a quiet corner next to a small window. It is complete with a dark crimson red curtain and I am on a red cushioned chair. The varnish on the wooden arm rests is worn through to bare wood on their inside edges, probably from the friction caused by repeated rubbing against arms and bodies of many a thirsty punter, so that it now has the appearance of an antique. The low lit interior of the pub has the effect of exaggerating the brightness of the day that I see outside. The edges of the wall around my seat at my head level have the appearance of having been lacquered within an inch of their life in what I imagine have been multiple attempts to slow their rate of decay and damage caused by window sill sitters, pickers, and kickers and other such common social breeds. Dark drips of honey tined lacquer set on top of broader lacquer brush strokes mean that the history of the sill has been preserved like some ancient bug in a blob of amber, a history set in stasis behind the windows of its glossy and imprisoning skin. Instances of more recent picking, having once more exposed the whiteness of the plaster underneath which the day's air now reaches, exist in varying degrees of contrast depending on the depth of the lacquer around that has been the focus of an entirely new tactile finger sport—the syrupy source of a fidgeting digital stimulation. The sound of a solitary piano plays a haunting melody through the tavern stereo—it evolves into a series of electronic samples and a basic but strong drum beat that plods slowly along the base line. It now seems darker in here than it was when I first arrived, perhaps due to the fact that I have spent the last few minutes or so staring out of the window into the brightness of the day in what, to the unseen onlooker, might be akin to a posture of contemplation, vague and secluded in the corner of the room. Though this might come across as an image of pretension, this was not my intention. I just wanted a place to makes my notes in peace over a beer, and away from the glare of the ultraviolet light which never needs long to burn my skin.

I had been reading my new book and an experiment that involves telling a stranger that she is beautiful, something that I have occasionally been tempted to do but never had to courage for. Every now and then, I will see a girl who, by her appearance alone, stands alone among the crowd, more than just another person spends maybe an hour everyday trying to look like someone else—someone conceivably more desirable. No. What I am talking about is very different to that. Every now and then, I will see someone whom make-up could not improve through the simple fact that they are already stunning. This is not about sexual desire, nor is it a matter of sheer objectification.

For now, my attention returns to the music in the pub, now growing louder and more intense in its sounds. An orange light enters into the left side of my peripheral vision and I turn in its direction out of reflex. I see five people seated on an old faded sofa. I hadn't even noticed them arrive or sit down, having been too caught up in my own thoughts to know what was happening immediately around me. They are all looking in the same direction, like the smallest of audiences, but attentive. Four metres in front of them is a walkway, perhaps only about a metre wide though it has, curiously enough, been blocked off with sheet of clear plastic wrap, of the kind that you might use for helping to keep food fresh in the fridge. This is not all, for perched up the wall, elevated above ground level and moving around in the style of an experimental dance routine, is a male in his twenties and wearing a while singlet. I gather from the occasional broken attention and low volume banter of the viewers that he is rehearsing and, these people, his co-dancers.

After a couple of minutes of watching him moving up and down and against the wall, I hear a female voice say, "And now it's your turn", at which point he stops what he is doing while an Asian female and a Caucasian male begin a different routine to the right of the couch-critics. They connect, rolling their bodies around each other, uniting, separating, accepting, rejecting. After 2 minutes or so, they stop as the wall toucher once again commences his part-dance part-platonic-frottage. Then, the couple move together again.

"Who's next?" someone asks.

Two women are standing on a table in front of the couch, smiles all around to a series of clicking sounds, go about their contemporary movement—all these scenes taking place under the flicking light of one of the tavern's Christmas decorations. A thick rope of fairy lights has been slung in half loops, like a string of U's between numerous anchor points along the ceiling. I spend a few more minutes watching the dancers engaged in various stages of rehearsal, moving around various objects in the room, the base of the staircase for instance.

It's not so dark in the pub anymore, making for an abrupt shock to my retinas once I get out of my chair, and walk back out onto the pavement, joining the other pedestrians in the mixed pitter-patter of pathway meanderings. I make my way up the road, deciding that it is time to head home.

It is interesting the kinds of assumptions that you may make in the course of the day, as you go about making sense of what is happening around you. For instance, in walking home, I take a detour up a back street and see a girl perhaps fifty metres ahead of me and walking by herself. She prepares to cross the road and stops halfway across it when he notices a car driving closer on her left. Of course, being a road, the driver has right of way but, for some reason, he brings the car to a halt, and waves at her to indicate that he is letting her pass. She was not in his path so there had been no threat of running her over, but this mustn't have made any difference to the driver who was now waiting patiently for her to walk across the road. She seemed somewhat confused at this altruism and made a questioning gesture with her arms, saying "What the fuck are you doing?" in the process, though not loudly, before continuing on to the recommencing pathway, and not looking back at the male who was now driving off.

Being a reasonably fast walker meant that I was, by now, much closer to her than I had been a moment ago. In fact, I was now walking behind her in ear shot. Entertained by what had just happened (and with Roger-Pol Droit's urge for spontaneous interpersonal communication still in mind) I said out loud "It seems as though you can stop traffic". She didn't answer. She didn't even flinch. Perhaps she had had enough of unnecessary human interaction for one day and so I crossed the road and kept going on my way. As I walked ahead, I looked to my right over to the other side of the road where she was walking along. I noticed that she had headphones on and was listening to music. That is why she did not respond to what I had said. She simply had not heard me but, because I had heard her speaking when the driver stopped for some reason I had made the erroneous assumption that she would have been able to hear someone else's voice, therefore mine when I had spoken.

This might not seem like a very interesting or exciting event but it taps into the way that our meaning making, and our assumption building, processes need only overlook the slightest detail and be entirely inaccurate. Because I was walking behind the girl, when I spoke to her, I had not realised that her long hair had kept her headphones hidden from sight. Only once I had walked further along the path, looking back at her from a different location, with an alternative perspective, did that piece of the puzzle fall into place.

# CHAPTER 8
# CONCLUSION

## Exploring a Representation of the City[131]

1. START at the GPO and peruse the handbags at Gorman, the different brands at the Fat store, Belinda, Anabella Ramsey. Then "build your strength" at Gill's Diner for some "old school cool." "Time for a little elegance? Wander Italian mosaic floors, hunting for jewellery and bags." Reach 'The Block Arcade.' "Explore the maze of artist's studios, jewellers, designers and milliners" at Flinders Lane. "Descend to the stylish basement for modern French-Vietnamese at Coda." Hop across the two watercolour flowers and continue along the broken pink line, like a bee on a mission, to another pink arrow. Arrive at Christine and "consult the fashion authority." Move on to Journal for a coffee fix, before "buzzing!" back to the Block Arcade.

2. START at the GPO and peruse the handbags at Gorman, the different brands at the Fat store, Belinda, Anabella Ramsey. Continue "on a roll" to Howey Place to see the bags and dresses. "Go undercover in search of boutiques and accessories..." "Pimms on the rooftop..." Sit on a bench on top a building, much higher than a bench in the park. "...at Madame Brussels." Walk to Degraves for a coffee—"Centre Places"—to drink there or to take-away. Continue to Seamstress and Emerald Peacock for alcoholic beverages. "Dress up or down." Return to Degraves for another coffee.

3. START at the GPO and peruse the handbags at Gorman, the different brands at the Fat store, Belinda, Anabella Ramsey. Continue "on a roll" to Howey Place to see the bags and dresses. "Go undercover in search of boutiques and accessories..." "Pimms on the rooftop..." Sit on a bench on top a building, much higher than a bench in the park. "...at Madame Brussels." Go on to Degraves for a coffee—"Centre Places"—to drink there or to take-away. Continue to Seamstress and Emerald Peacock for alcoholic beverages. "Dress up or down." "Go undercover in search of boutiques and accessories..." at Howey Place. Go back to the rooftop. Have another coffee.

4. START at the GPO and peruse the handbags at Gorman, the different brands at the Fat store, Belinda, Anabella Ramsey. Then "build your

---

[131] Tourism Victoria, "Lose Yourself in Melbourne," in *Vogue living Australia*, ed. David Clark (New South Wales: News Magazines Pty Ltd, Nov/Dec 2010), 12-13.

strength" at Gill's Diner for some "old school cool." "Window shop" along Little Collins Street. "Handbags need heels." Visit the shops at 'The Block Arcade.' "Explore the maze of artist's studios, jewellers, designers and milliners" at Flinders Lane. Need a "coffee fix"? Why not head over to Journal for a coffee fix, before "buzzing!" back to the Block Arcade.

5. START at the GPO and peruse the handbags at Gorman, the different brands at the Fat store, Belinda, Anabella Ramsey. Then "build your strength" at Gill's Diner for some "old school cool." "Window shop" along Little Collins Street. "Handbags need heels." Visit the shops at 'The Block Arcade.' "Explore the maze of artist's studios, jewellers, designers and milliners" at Flinders Lane and then "catch some sunshine" on the rooftop at Madame Brussels. Walk to Degraves for a coffee—"Centre Places"—to drink there or to take-away. Continue to Seamstress and Emerald Peacock for alcoholic beverages. "Dress up or down." "Go undercover in search of boutiques and accessories..." at Howey Place. Go back to the rooftop. Have another coffee.

6. START at the GPO and celebrate "with bubbles and baubles" at Self Preservation. "Pop!" "Flaunt your finery at Emerald Peacock."

7. START at the GPO and peruse the handbags at Gorman, the different brands at the Fat store, Belinda, Anabella Ramsey. Head to Little Collins Street for some window shopping, wander through the Block Arcade, because "handbags need heels," before moving on to "Explore the maze of artist's studios, jewellers, designers and milliners" at Flinders Lane. Make the short walk to Louise MacDonald to see the hats on display, before you "Descend to the stylish basement for modern French-Vietnamese at Coda" to "cool down."

8. START at the GPO and peruse the handbags at Gorman, the different brands at the Fat store, Belinda, Anabella Ramsey. Head to Little Collins Street for some window shopping, wander through the Block Arcade, because "handbags need heels," before moving on to "Explore the maze of artist's studios, jewellers, designers and milliners" at Flinders Lane. Walk ("brrrm") over to Little Cupcakes for a tasty treat. "Still in a girly mood?" Arrive Louise MacDonald to see the hats on display. When you have finished, "Descend to the stylish basement for modern French-Vietnamese at Coda" to "cool down." Pop over to Christine to "consult the fashion authority," walk past Journal, through the Block Arcade and then through Flinders Lane, "brrrm" over to Little Cupcakes, Louise MacDonald, Coda, Christine, Journal, The Block Arcade, Madame Brus-

sels, Degraves, Emerald Peacock and Seamstress, Howey Place. Madame Brussels.

## Final Comments

The two page spread in Vogue Living Australia's November/December 2010 issue leads the human eye on a wander through some of the consumer centres of the city of Melbourne.[132] The wander is not aimless, as the 'bee-line' device might suggest. The aim is to generate business in the designated areas. The 'map' offers a paradigm of activity, constructing the reader not as a citizen but as a consumer and, what is more, a specifically feminine consumer. The map is littered with water-coloured icons: dresses and bags, peacock feathers, an empty white bench on the top of a building during a clear sunny day, empty tables at a coffee stop with white umbrellas, tiny pictures of cupcakes, sunglasses, glasses of wine, flowers, a pair of black boots, a red high heeled show with the symbol a heart surreptitiously incorporated into its side strapping, a white dummy's head sporting a fancy hat, but lacking a face.

There must be a message for the reader in this aspect for advertising costs too much money (a two page spread in a high class magazine has no room for accidents. Time is money; so is page space. And yet I am neither feeling "in a girly mood" nor seeking alternative shopping locations. How I make sense of this representation of Melbourne is going to be impacted upon by my 'otherness' to these circumstances. Nevertheless, this is what I would suggest to someone who would like an alternative approach to negotiating them: While on this bench, perhaps you will survey the built environment, mindful that you are not sitting in a natural world, but rather atop an industrial landscape—the city of Melbourne. Perhaps you will look down at all the people on the streets or the trams driving past and dinging their bells, or hear the hint of a beep from a distant cross-walk. Perhaps you will reflect upon your conduct within this place: What you are doing? How you are doing it? Why you are doing it?

What kind of a map is this? Upon first glance, it reminds me of Guy Debord's *Map of Paris before 1957* (1957), and a comment made by Michèle Bernstein:

> I know Gillie's thing for walking all night, how a café still open late becomes a precious port of call in streets where somnambulists normally don't go. After two, rue Mouffetard is deserted. You have to go up to the Pantheon to find a bar, to rue Cujas. The next stop is by the Senate, then rue du Bac, if you really want to steer clear of what we still call the Quartier. Here, I guess Carole told him the story of her life (if she even

---

[132] Tourism Victoria, "Lose Yourself in Melbourne," in *Vogue living Australia*, ed. David Clark (New South Wales: News Magazines Pty Ltd, Nov/Dec 2010), 12-13.

had one yet). And then the sun starts to rise over Les Halles—it's a ritual.[133]

Although the *Lose Yourself in Melbourne* 'map' can be seen to hold these connections, the historical and socio-political significance of these has been replaced with the faint trace of benign cultural negotiation, much like the advertisement featuring the woman with the ball of red wool. And why use the colour red? Is it an allusion to communism? Surely not, given its use in a context that speaks to the pervasiveness of capitalism—presented here as a game in which immediate gratification and materialistic indulgence compensate for the drudgery of industrialised labour, in the office, behind the counter, handing out 'specials' pamphlets to passers-by on a busy sidewalk in an effort to stimulate trade.

The map may be treated in any way that the reader chooses, but the context of the magazine (the demographics of its readership) have already primed the path with beliefs, values, and ideas, that are also present in this particular field of content. Again, there are distinct ways n which I do not meet the requirements of this readership (as indicated to me by the use of words like "girly mood," the proliferation of shoes and gloves and hats and bags, none of which I am interested in purchasing. I represent an anomaly in the equation. This I snot meant for me, and yet, here I am, spending nothing but precious time trying to explore the suggested detours, the possible pathways of cityscape negotiation as a means to ascertaining just what it is that I am looking at.

The retail map is not as complicated as the design of Georges Perec's exhausting "81 Easy-Cook Recipes for Beginners"—a "mock-cookery exercise" where:

> each recipe consists of four elements (ingredients, first procedure, second procedure, accompaniment). Perec grants himself three alternatives for each of the elements and proceeds to permute all their possible combinations to produce $3^4$ (3 x 3 x 3 x 3 = 81) different recipes.[134]

The map operates under its own limitations—its own constraining circumstances as dictated by advanced capitalism—its reduction to a monetary value. Ironically, sadly, this can be seen to drastically undervalue what Melbourne has to offer, by leaving out (relegating to silence by way of omission) the experience of hearing half a dozen different languages on the tram or train while travelling to a destination. It fails to communicate the creative

---

[133] Mck. Wark, *50 Years of Recuperation of the Situationist International* (New York: FO-RuM Project and Princeton Architectural Press, 2008), image number 14.
[134] Bellos, David, "Introduction," in G. Perec, *Thoughts of Sorts* (Boston: David R. Godine, 2009), x.

grunginess of the suburbs around the city of Melbourne, such as Fitzroy. The fact that Fitzroy is Melbourne's oldest suburb is interesting itself-another indication of the emptying of history that the campaign, in general, is privileging.

"The difficulties of drifting are those of freedom."[135]

Although no-one can force a person to put the retail map's suggested pathways into practice, nevertheless it is designed in line with a range of cultural meanings that many people desire to emulate—with which to identify— because they are taken as signifiers of success, happiness, and freedom. The consumer is 'free' to start at the GPO and free to choose whether to go straight to the seller of champagne, or have a quick look around the stores in housed in the GPO before heading off to Gills Diner, and who knows what next. The multiplicity of options suggests that the consumer is free to exercise personal choice. But the choices on offer all appeal to a limited palette, pertaining to a narrow field of cultural engagement based on the exchange of money for goods and services. Two friends might wander around the shops together, sharing conversation, meanings, ideas about what looks good or not, what is worthy of the price tag that it displays. Such a social, interpersonal dimension, while not conjoined to commodity culture, provides the cradle in which the privileged minority's human relationships rock.

If "there is no outside to culture", then the point is not to escape it, to run from it.[136] The point, that I have pushed, is to find a way of living within its limitations and expectations and to remember that these are not unmovable objects. They are abstractions and they are arbitrary. Our cultural circumstances are not the end products of sprouts from the ground; they have evolved over time and shall continue to do so. Wandering aimlessly around the city streets might seem like a frivolous and pointless exercise, because a destination is not being entertained, because things are open to revision along the way, at any one stage.

But this is far from, maybe even symptomatic of, an 'ahistorical' vantage point—a vantage point that is not separate from history but seemingly unfamiliar with it. We don't carry out our day to day lives in vacuums, but rather exist and operate in ways that are grounded within a particular set of historical circumstances and cultural conditions—an advanced, industrialised cultural environment. The dérive might seem out of place when interpreted as a benign event, but when we start to see it with history in mind, when we start

---

[135] Kevin C. Pyle and McKenzie Wark, *Cataract of Time* (2007) (from "Totality for Kids") in McK, Wark, *50 Years of Recuperation of the Situationist International* (New York: FORuM Project and Princeton Architectural Press, 2008), Image number 33.
[136] N. Mirzoeff, *An Introduction to Visual Culture* (London and New York: Routledge, 1999), 23.

to recognise that it is a creative improvisation that is really quite sensitive to culture, passionate about how it is going, concerned for the journey of one's life in relation to it.

In this sense, the dérive does not waste time any more than it enriches life. It is not out of place in a commodity culture but borne from it, another kind of cultural product, if one that seeks broader critical engagement with its place of birth. While the wandering pedestrian might seem to have taken the tourist advice to its literal conclusion and, somewhere along the meandering line, become lost in Melbourne, the dérive, when historical considered, is all about 'location.' Situations can look very different when a new perspective is introduced.

In the theory of the dérive, and in its practice as defamiliarisation, we may consider less its function as an indulgence. Rather, in view of its historical import, we may understand it as an expression of a vital existential concern—summated well in Perec's words ('Approaches to What?' from *L'Infra-ordinaire*):

What we need to question is bricks, concrete, glass, our table manners, our utensils, our tools, the way we spend our time, our rhythms. To question that which seems to have ceased forever to astonish us. We live, true, we breathe, true; we walk, we open doors, we go down staircases, we sit at a table in order to eat, we lie down on a bed in order to sleep. How? Where? When? Why?[137]

---

[137] G. Perec, *Species of Space and Other Pieces*, J. Sturrock, trans. (London: Penguin Books, 1999), 210.

Adorno, Theodore, and Max Horkheimer, *The Culture Industry: Enlightenment as Mass Deception*, London: Continuum International Publishing Group, 1976.

Adorno, Theodore, and Max Horkheimer, *Dialectic of Enlightenment*, London: Verso, 1979.

Adorno, Theodore, *The Culture Industry: Selected Essays on Mass Culture*, London: Routledge, 1991.

Adorno, Theodore, *Essays on Music*, California: University of California Press, Ed. Richard Leppert, 2002.

American Psychiatric Association, *Diagnostic and Statistical Manual of Mental Disorders DSM-IV-TR Fourth Edition (Text Revision)*, Arlington, Virginia: American Psychiatric Publishing, Inc., 2000.

Appignanesi, Richard, and Chris Garratt, *Introducing Postmodernism*, United Kingdom: Totem Books, 2005.

Aussie Home Loans, http://www.aussie.com.au/

Baudelaire, Charles, *The Flowers of Evil*, "The Voyage," CT: Wesleyan University Press, 1859.

Baudrillard, Jean, "Seduction, or the Superficial Abyss," The Ecstasy of Communication, New York: Semiotext(e), 1987.

Bauman, Zigmund, *Community - Seeking Safety in an Insecure World*, Oxford: Polity Press, 2001.

Bennett, Andrew, and Nicholas Royle, *An Introduction to Literature, Criticism and Theory*, United Kingdom: Pearson Longman, 2004.

Binfield, Kevin, *Writings of the Luddites*. Baltimore; Maryland: The John Hopkins University Press, 2004.

Booth, Martin, *British Poetry 1964 to 1984*, London & New York: Routledge, 1985.

Bottomore, Tom, *The Frankfurt School and its Critics*. Key Sociologists Series, UK: Routledge, 2002.

Bourdieu, Pierre, *Outline of a Theory of Practice* (tr. Richard Nice), Cambridge: Cambridge University Press, 1977.

Braidotti, Rosi, *Nomadic Subjects: Embodiment and Sexual Difference in Contemporary Feminist Theory*, New York: Columbia University Press, 1994.

Brettell, Richard R., *French Impressionists*, Chicago; The Art Institute of Chicago and New York: Harry N. Abrams, 1987.

BBC News [British Broadcasting Corporation], World Edition, *Millions join global anti-war protests*, 2003.

British Council, The, http://www.contemporarywriters.com/authors/?p=auth212#authorstatement

Brooker, Peter, *Glossary of Cultural Theory*, 2nd ed. London: Hodder Arnold, 2003.

Bruns, Gerald L., *Modern Poetry and the Idea of Language: A Critical and Historical Study*, University of Illinois: Dalkey Archive Press, 2001.

Christian Television Association, http://www.christiantelevision.org.au/

*CIA World Fact Book*, 2008.

Clark, Timothy James, *The Painting of Modern Life: Paris in the Art of Manet and his Followers*. Princeton: Princeton University Press, 1984.

Confucius, *Analects*, c. 400 B.C.

Conord, Andre F., "Next Planet," in *Potlatch*, Paris, July 19, 1954, translated into English by Gerardo Denís, Situationist International Online.

Crick, Nathan, "Rhetoric, Philosophy, and the Public Intellectual," *Philosophy and Rhetoric*, Vol. 39, Number 2, (Pennsylvania: Penn State University Press, 2006), 127-139, DOI: 10.1353/par.2006.0012, accessed: January 21, 2010.

Cristin, Renato, *Heidegger and Leibniz: Reason and the Path*, Gerald Parks, trans. Vol. 35, Dordrecht: Kulwer Academic Publishers, 1998.

Crouch, Christopher, ed. *Subjectivity, Creativity and the Institution*, Boca Raton, Florida; BrownWalker Press, 2009.

Cryder, Cynthia E., Jennifer S. Lerner, James J. Gross, and Ronald E. Dahl, "Misery is not Miserly: Sad and Self-Focussed Individuals Spend More," (Research Report) *Psychological Science: A Journal of the Association for Psychological Science*, Vol. 9 No. 6, Sage Journals, 2007, Accessed July 8, 2010, http://www.psychologicalscience.org/journals/ps/19_6_inpress/Cryder.pdf

Dasey, Donald, "How our Greed Costs Millions Every Year," May 8, 2005 *The Sydney Morning Herald*, Accessed Feb 11, 2010, http://www.smh.com.au/news/National/How-our-greed-costs-millions-every-year/2005/05/07/1115422849473.html

Debord, Guy, "Theory of the Dérive" (1958), reprinted in Ken Knabb, ed. *Situationist International Anthology*. Berkley: Bureau of Public Secrets, 1995.

Debord, Guy, "On the Passage of a Few Persons Through a Rather Brief Unity of Time" (1959), in *Complete Cinematic Works*. California: AK Press, 2003.

Derrida, Jacques, *Of Grammatology* (G. C. Spivak, trans.), Baltimore and London: The Johns Hopkins University Press, 1976.

Droit, Roger-Pol, *Astonish Yourself! 101 Experiments in the Philosophy of Everyday Life*, New York, Penguin, 2003.

During, Simon, ed. *The Cultural Studies Reader*, 2nd ed. Oxford: Routledge, 2007.

Eagleton, Terry, *Literary Theory: An Introduction*, MA: Blackwell Publishing, 2008.

Fiske, John, *Understanding Popular Culture*, London: Routledge, 1991.

Giddens, Anthony, *Modernity and Self-Identity: Self and Society in the Late Modern Age*. Stanford, California: Stanford University Press, 1991.

Giles, Steve, *Theorizing Modernism: essays in critical theory*. London and New York: Routledge, 1993.

Gorra, Michael Edward, *The Bells in Their Silence*. Princeton: Princeton University Press, 2004.

Guardian, 'The Observer', Sean O'Hagan, Interview: Scott Walker, 2008, http://www.guardian.co.uk/music/2008/nov/09/scott-walker-interview

Hegarty, Paul, *Noise/Music: A History*. New York, London: Continuum, 2008.

Henson, Jim, *Fraggle Rock*, Nick Abson et. al (dir)., Canadian Broadcasting Corporation (CBC), 1983.

Hibbert, Christopher, *The French Revolution*, London: Penguin Books, 1982.

Hussey, Andrew, *Paris*. London and New York: Penguin Books, 2007.

Inglis, David, *Culture and Everyday Life*. The New Sociology, series, London and New York: Routledge, 2005.

Johnson, Richard, Deborah Chambers, Parvati Raghuram, Estella Tincknell, *The Practice of Cultural Studies*, London: Sage, 2004.

Jones, Colin, *Paris: Biography of a City*. London: Penguin Books, 2004.

Knabb, Ken, ed. *Situationist International Anthology*. Berkley: Bureau of Public Secrets, 2002.

Koshar, Rudy, *Histories of Leisure*. Oxford: Berg Publishers, 2002.

Lacayo, Richard, John Cloud, Emily Mitchell, Wendy Cole, Declan McCullagh, Timothy Roche, and Rochard Woodbury, "The End Of The World As We Know It?" *TIME Magazine* (Jan 18, 1999), Accessed February 11, 2010, http://www.time.com/time/magazine/article/0,9171, 990020-1,00.html

Lewis, Jeff, *Cultural Studies: the Basics*. London: Sage, 2002.

Mirzoeff, Nicholas, *An Introduction to Visual Culture*. London and New York: Routledge, 1999.

Moran, Joe, *Reading the Everyday*. London and New York: Routledge, 2005.

National Walk for Values, http://www.nationalwalkforvalues.org/

Negus, Keith, *Creativity and Culture*, London: Sage, 2004.

Neill, Alex, and Aaron Ridley, *The Philosophy of Art*: Readings Ancient and Modern, 1st ed. New York: McGraw-Hill College, 1994.

Newsom, Joanna, "Sprout and the Bean," from *The Milk-Eyed Mender*, Chicago: Drag City Records, 2004.

Nietzsche, Friedrich, *The Will To Power*, Preface, Nov. 1887-March 1888.

Nietzsche, Friedrich, *Beyond Good and Evil: Prelude to a Philosophy of the Future*, H. Zimmern, Trans. 3rd ed. Vol. 12, London: T. N. Foulis, 1911.

Nietzsche, Friedrich, *The Twilight of the Idols and The Anti-Christ: or How to Philosophize with a Hammer*, London: Penguin Books, 1990.

Oxfam, http://www.oxfam.org.au/act/events/walk-against-want

Perec, Georges, *Species of Space and Other Pieces* (J. Sturrock, trans.), London: Penguin Books, 1999.

Perec, Georges, Thought of Sorts (D. Bellos, trans.), Boston: David R. Godine, 2009.

Pigrum, Derek, *Transitional Practices and Place: "Potential Space," the place of the classroom and the "semiotic chora" in secondary arts education.* Paper presented at the Philosophy of Education Society of Great Britain, Oxford University New College, (2004b, April).

Raine, Craig, *A Martian Sends a Postcard Home*, Oxford: Oxford University Press, 1979.

Rand, Ayn, "The Soul of an Individualist," *For the new Intellectual: The Philosophy of Ayn Rand.* New York: Signet; First Thus edition, 1963.

Rivkin, Julie, and Michael Ryan (eds.) *Literary Theory: An Anthology*, 2nd ed., Malden: Blackwell Publishing Ltd, 1998.

Sampson, Edward, "The Deconstruction of Self," in Kenneth Gergen & John Shotter (Eds.), *Texts of Identity* (Inquiries in Social Construction Series, Vol. 2), Newbury Park, California: Sage, 1989.

Sartre, Jean-Paul, *Nausea*, London: Penguin Books, 1965.

Schultz, Wendy L., Sliding Into Our Futures: provocation as a path to critical futures fluency [excerpted from *Futures Fluency: explorations in leadership, vision, and creativity*], University of Hawaii at Manoa, 1995.

Smith, Mark K., (1996, August 26, 1999). "Praxis: an introduction to the idea plus an annotated booklist," Accessed February 12, 2010, http://www.infed.org/biblio/b-praxis.htm#praxis/

Socrates. *The Dialogues of Plato*, Apology. 38a.

Teich, Mikuláš, and Roy Porter, *Fin de siècle and its Legacy.* Cambridge: Cambridge University Press, 1991.

*The Dialogues of Plato*, Vol. 1, (Benjamin Jowett, trans.), London: Sphere Books Limited, 1970.

Thompson, Edward Palmer, *The Poverty of Theory and Other Essays*, New York: Monthly Review Press, 1980.

Tomlinson, John, *Cultural Imperialism: A Critical Introduction*, London: Pinter, 1997.

Victorian Government, *Tourism Victoria Video Room*, "Lose Yourself in Melbourne," Accessed July 10, 2010, http://www.visitvictoria.com/videostub/4F2E7E78-A361-4753-AE5E130F515F1201.cfm

Tourism Victoria Video Room, "Lose Yourself in Melbourne," Accessed July 10, 2010, http://www.visitvictoria.com/videostub/4F2E7E78-A361-4753-AE5E130F515F1201.cfm

*Trainspotting*, [film] director; Danny Boyle, writer; by Irvin Welsh, screenplay; John Hodge, 1996.

*Vogue Living Australia*, (ed. David Clark), New South Wales: News Magazines Pty Ltd, Nov/Dec 2010.

Wallace, David Foster, *A Supposedly Fun Thing I'll Never Do Again*, London: Abacus, 1998.

Wallace, David Foster, *This is Water: Some Thoughts, Delivered on a Significant Occasion, about Living a Compassionate Life*, 1st ed., New York: Little, Brown and Company, 2009.

Wark, McKenzie, *50 Years of Recuperation of the Situationist International*, New York: FORuM Project and Princeton Architectural Press, 2008.

Waugh, Patricia, *Literary Theory and Criticism: an Oxford Guide*, USA: Oxford University Press, 2007.

Wegscheider-Cruse, Sharon, *Learning to Love Yourself: finding your self-worth*, Florida: Health Communications Inc., 1987.

Western Michigan University (WMU) Theatre, *Mother Courage and Her Children* [promotional video for the production], Western Michigan University, 2009, Accessed July 10, 2010, http://www.youtube.com/watch?v=oeY wFzBNk2k&feature=related

Winnicott, Donald W., *Playing and Reality*. London and New York: Routledge, 2005.

WMU Theatre promotional video for Mother Courage and Her Children, 2009. Youtube, Accessed 10 July, 2010, http://www.youtube.com/watch?v=oeYwFzBNk2k&feature=related

Yalom, Irvin D., *Love's Executioner and other tales of Psychotherapy*, New York: Penguin, 1991.

Zola, Émile, *The Lady's Paradise* (1883), Oxford World Classics, Trans. Brian Nelson, Oxford: Oxford University Press, 2008.